THE BRITISH DOG

Its History from Earliest Times

THE BRITISH DOG

Its History from Earliest Times

Carson I. A. Ritchie

ROBERT HALE · LONDON

© *Carson I. A. Ritchie 1981*
First published in Great Britain 1981

ISBN 0 7091 8589 8

Robert Hale Limited
Clerkenwell House
Clerkenwell Green
London EC1R 0HT

Photoset, printed and bound
in Great Britain by
REDWOOD BURN LIMITED
Trowbridge & Esher

Contents

Acknowledgements

It is a pleasure to acknowledge the numerous kindnesses I have received while writing this book. I should like to thank Miss Pat O'Driscoll, editor of *Coast and Country*, for helpful suggestions. The librarian, deputy librarian and staff of the London Library were, as always a great support, while the A. H. Higginson Collection, now housed in the library, proved a very valuable source. Mrs Belinda M. Killen, the assistant librarian of the Institute of Archaeology, University of London, was extremely helpful. I would like to express my gratitude to Mrs Roundell of Spink and Son Ltd, Anthony Spink also of Spink and Son Ltd, Dr J. Close-Brooks, the assistant keeper of the National Museum of Antiquities of Scotland, Nicholas Wadham of Phillips, Miss A. Jennifer Price, Keeper of Archaeology, Salisbury and South Wiltshire Museum, and the librarians of the R.S.P.C.A. and Imperial War Museum for help with illustrations.

Once again I would like to express my appreciation to my photographer, Mrs Stella Mayes Reed, for the indispensable services she has rendered me and to Mr Jeffreys of the Book Barrow, who sold me the books about dogs that awakened my interest in this subject more than nineteen years ago.

Illustrations

Foreword

Before I leave the reader to read and, I hope, enjoy this book I should like to explain what I have tried to do and how I have tried to do it. My reason for giving an explanation is that this book differs radically, both in style and content, from previous books written about dogs. Sportsmen, breeders and owners have developed a conventional language which is used with reference to these animals, a language which custom has rendered almost sacrosanct. The term 'dog' has been appropriated to those dogs which hunt by sight, so a greyhound is a dog, not a hound. Animals which hunt by scent, on the other hand, are usually called 'hounds', so that a foxhound is a hound, never a dog. Every part of a dog has a special term by which it is known, while the habits of dogs, in and out of the hunting-field, have also given rise to a whole vocabulary of technical terms – terms which are often unintelligible to all save the initiated few who have lived all their lives with dogs.

In an attempt to write this book in plain English, I have avoided as much of this technical jargon as I could and have tried to use the two terms 'dog' and 'hound' indiscriminately, so as to avoid what would otherwise have been an intolerable monotony. I have also tried consistently to refer to dogs in the neuter sex instead of calling them 'he' or 'she' and have carefully labelled dogs' names with inverted commas. This has been done to prevent confusion between the dogs and the humans who constantly intrude on the book. I hope breeders, owners and sportsmen will forgive me for calling a dog a dog and referring to it as 'it'.

As it was impossible to write a book about British dogs without dealing with the British as well, I have tried hard not merely to recount how new breeds emerged and old ones disappeared, but also to assess how dogs helped to change the life of these islands. Even the most ardent dog-lover would admit that dogs are important not for themselves alone, but for the effects that they have on their circle. Some of the conclusions I have drawn from the history of dogs may startle the reader. Did Shakespeare really leave home because, as a butcher's son, he had charge of the family mastiffs? Were the famous 'Laws of Howel the Good' really forgeries which can be demonstrated to be wholly spurious because of their impos-

sibly anachronistic picture of dogs in early Wales? Did the defeat of the
Spanish Armada really stem in large part from the addiction of sixteenth-
century Englishmen to deer-hunting? Did Florence Nightingale really
decide to become a nurse because she had successfully saved a sheepdog's
life by devoted nursing? I cannot pretend to dictate the answers to these
questions, and many others that this book poses. The reader must decide
for himself; I can merely put the evidence, as I see it, before him.

Yet I would strongly suggest that the role of the dog in British history has
been one which, till a generation or so ago, has been greatly undervalued.
It is only in our own day, to take but one example, that archaeologists have
begun to give serious consideration to remains of dogs at archaeological
sites. The archaeology of the dog has now become such a subject for serious
enquiry, and has produced such numerous and startling discoveries that I
felt compelled to enlarge the original draft of my first chapter very considerably.

Though not everyone may agree with my reasons for ending the history
of the dog with the death of Queen Victoria – reasons which I give in the last
chapter – I am sure that everyone would agree that the material available
for the story of the dog since 1901 would require a second volume, at least
as large as this one, to deal with it adequately.

If I had been a medieval writer on animals, I would unhesitatingly have
developed the morality of my theme. Instead, I leave the reader to draw his
own conclusions. He may well decide, as others have done, that the dog is
an unchanging creature, seemingly different every century, yet still the
same, a being whose qualities are eternal, like the colour of the flowers and
the brightness of the sunlight, one over whose head the rolling centuries
pass in vain; and he may even feel that in the long journey between Star
Carr and Queen Victoria's death-bed it has lost fewer virtues and acquired
fewer vices than 'that most savage of all brutes, the human one'.

London   C.R.

A Short Chronology of the British Dog

c. **10,000** BC Domestication of *Canis familiaris*.

c. **7538** BC Oldest European dog remains from Star Carr, Yorkshire. The Senckenberg dog, from Frankfurt-am-Main, West Germany, is supposedly of the same date.

2450–2280 BC Grimes' Grave Dog, a young, healthy dog with a short wide head, standing about 52 centimetres high at the shoulder, dies mysteriously in a horizontal gallery in a flint mine at Grimes' Grave. It may have been a sacrifice to the gods of the underworld; it could never have crawled into the gallery if it had simply fallen down the shaft – as other later dogs did in these 'Dene Holes'.
    Grimes' Grave Dog appears closely to resemble other neolithic dogs, such as those from Easton Down, Windmill Hill and Quanterness, suggesting that there was a single, fairly homogenous population.

63–21 BC Strabo mentions the export of luxury hunting-dogs from Britain. At about the same time, archaeological discoveries suggest the existence of a dog allied to the modern miniature Pinscher and one similar to *Canis matris optimae*, a relative of the sheepdog.

19–9 BC Grattius describes British dogs.

AD *c.* **43** Coin of King Cymbeline (Cunobelin), who dies this year, depicts a gigantic hound ridden by a goddess.

c. **50** The sons of Uisnech flee from Ulster to Scotland taking 150 hounds with them.

c. **80–120** Occupation of Corbridge Roman Station in Northumberland by a garrison whose dogs have been identified as 'bassets' and 'small greyhounds'.

121–180 The column of Marcus Aurelius in Rome depicts dogs fighting in armour.

161–180 Oppian describes a British dog called the *agassaeus* – probably a terrier.

283–284 Nemesianus praises the swiftness of British dogs in his book *Cynegetica*.

727 or 730 The death of St Hubert, Bishop of Liege. A hundred years later his remains are transferred to the Abbey of Andain in the Ardennes, the name of which is changed to St Hubert. The saint is later credited with the development of the hounds bearing his name, the Black St Hubert (possible ancestor of the bloodhound) and the White St Hubert (supposed ancestor of the Southern hound).

c. **800** Pictish huntress with hounds portrayed coursing deer on the Hilton of Cadboll Slab, Scotland.

871 Alfred the Great ascends throne of Wessex and gives instruction to royal kennelmen.

c. **959** King Lud of Cambria pays King Edgar a tax of 300 wolves annually. At the end of four years he reports that wolves are now extinct.

1016 First Forest Laws imposed by Canute in a Witan held at Winchester. Keeping of greyhounds forbidden to anyone under the status of a freeman.

c. **1070** The Bayeux Tapestry depicts only two breeds of dogs, one of which may be a mastiff.

1199–1216 King John said to have ordered the slaughter of all mastiffs and other dogs within the Forest Jurisdiction.

1206 Henry de Neville pays 10 marks a year for having charge of royal wolfhounds.

1213 King John sends 'three of our red and black greyhounds and one sorrel-coloured one' to Warren Fitz-Falcon.

1224 Henry III's Charter of the Forest allows any archbishop, earl or baron coming to court at the sovereign's order, who is passing through the royal forests, the privilege of 'killing one or two of our deer by view of our Forester, if he is present, or else he shall cause one to blow an horn for him, so that he shall not seem to steal our deer.'

1301 Archbishop Winchelsey allows the Abbot of Gloucester to keep twelve hunting dogs.

1304 Edward Prince of Wales offers to send from Wales 'some of our bow-legged harehounds, which can well discover an hare if they find it sleeping, and some of our running dogs which can swiftly chase it.'

c. **1310** The Abbot of Cluny forbids any English monasteries of the Cluniac Order to keep dogs, except those which have the right of hunting.

1323–1404 William of Wykeham writes to the Prioress of Romsey Abbey to reprove her for allowing her nuns to bring dogs to church.

1335 Edward III imports Irish hounds.

1340–1400 Geoffrey Chaucer makes first reference to spaniels in *The Wife of Bath's Prologue*.

1371 Traditional date for combat between Aubrey de Montdidier's Irish hound and its master's murderer, Macaire.

1387 Gaston Phoebus, Count of Foix, begins his work on hunting: *The Chase*.

1389 Complaint to the House of Commons that 'Artificers and labourers, and servants and grooms', keep greyhounds for poaching. They are forbidden to laymen with less than forty shillings a year rent and priests with a living worth less than ten pounds.

1406–1413 Edward, second Duke of York, writes *The Master of Game*, largely based on Gaston Phoebus's work. He implies that wolves are unknown in England.

1485 The Code of Cluny complains that dogs 'defile monasteries and often-times trouble the service of God by their barking, and sometimes tear the church books.'

1486 Dame Juliana Berners describes the ideal greyhound as follows in her *Book of St Albans*: 'Headed like a snake, necked like a drake, footed like a cat, tailed like a rat, sided like a bream, chined like a beam.'

1509–1547 Henry VIII bans dogs from court.

1512 The Percy family own 5,571 deer in twenty-one parks and forests in the counties of Northumberland, Cumberland and York.

1570 Dr John Caius publishes a book about British dogs.

1576 Turberville publishes his *Booke of Hunting*.

1576 Abraham Fleming describes the use of terriers for hunting fox and badger.

1577 Sir Martin Frobisher and his crew are the first Englishmen to see Eskimo dogs.

1579 Seven hundred deer parks in England and twenty-one in Wales are marked on Christopher Saxton's maps.

1584 William Shakespeare leaves home after a poaching affray. The English garrison in Virginia are forced by starvation to boil their mastiffs into soup.

1587 Mary Queen of Scots is accompanied to the block by a pet lap-dog.

1608 Sir John Harington writes to Prince Henry in praise of his dog 'Bungey'.

1617 First use of the word 'collie' in reference to a Scots bishop, Alexander Forbes of Aberdeen, who, like a dog, keeps dropping into dinner, uninvited.

1618 Pugs popular in Holland.

1621 Gervase Markham gives a description of the setting spaniel in *The Art of Fowling*. He also describes the waterdog.

1624 King James dog, 'Jowler', has a letter tied to his collar asking the King to stop hunting and go home before the countryside is ruined.

1625 A bulldog is portrayed on a plaque at Burgos; it is possibly the ancestor of the French bulldog.

1632 First mention of the word 'bulldog'.

1642 End of the office of 'Master of the Royal Game of Bears and Mastiff Dogs', which had been founded by Henry VIII.

1653 Dorothy Osborne writes to Sir William Temple to ask for an Irish hound.

1670 John Evelyn sees a combat between an Irish hound and a mastiff.

1674 Nicholas Cox, in *The Gentleman's Recreations*, says hounds will do better if only used for that game to which they were first entered.

1682 Last wolf in England killed in County Durham.

1683 Wild boar now confined to those kept in captivity in Chartley Park.

1685 The pug is mentioned in the play *Cuckold's Haven*.

*c.*1700 English red deer largely killed off. Only thirty-five head in the Forest of Pickering.

1700 A troop of performing poodles, 'The Ball of Little Dogs', perform before Queen Anne.

c. **1716** Painting of two Dalmatians by Castiglione.

1721 Alan Ramsay mentions use of collie sheepdog for herding sheep.

1728 First carted run at Windsor, an elk.

1730 Sir Robert Walpole tries unsuccessfully to establish the post of Master of the Royal Foxhounds.

c. **1731** A pack of foxhounds, Lord Hertford's, are allowed for the first time to run uncoupled, at Sandiwell Park, Gloucester.

1732 The Newfoundland dog, under the name of 'the Bear Dog', is described as being in use in England as a guard-dog and for turning water-wheels.

1739 'The Great Charlton run' of 24 miles in 11 hours and 5 minutes, that is, at a speed of 2½ miles an hour.

1740 Mention of a pug in a play by David Garrick.

1745 Record hunt with the Grafton, 60 miles in 12 hours or 5 miles an hour.

1765 Major Robert ('Roger's Rangers') describes the use of Newfoundlands for draught purposes in Newfoundland.

c. **1770** Oliver Goldsmith, Irish author of *Animated Nature*, says that Irish hounds are rare and the largest he has seen is 'about four feet high'.

1776 Swaffham Coursing Society begun.

1777 Bloodhounds used to track down offenders in Westmorland and Cumberland.

1780 Ashdown Park Coursing Society begun.

1782 Hugo Meynell forms his pack at Quorndon from Arundel hounds, which soon become so fast that, to his disgust, Mr 'Flying Childe' takes to following them at a gallop, leaping fences in the way.

1786 Hester Piozzi says she can think of only one pug owner in England, Lord Penryn.

1787 Foxhound pedigrees begin.

1790 One of the eight remaining Irish hounds is measured by A. R. Lambert, who records it to be 30 inches from hind toes to hind shoulders and 28½ inches from toe to foreshoulder.

1790 Thomas Bewick draws a Dalmatian accompanying a carriage.

1791–1811 John Corbet hunts in Warwickshire and breeds a famous stud hound, 'Trajan'.

1791 Colonel Thomas Thornton purchases 'Czarina' and 'Jupiter' at the sale of the late Lord Orford at Tattersalls.

1792 First mention of the Pomeranian as a native of Pomerania, by George Vancouver.

1794 A terrier runs a mile in 2 minutes and 6 miles in 32 minutes.

1796 The first duties on dogs in England, five shillings on 'outdoor' dogs and three shillings on 'indoor' dogs. George T. Clark, the introducer of the motion, is sent dozens of dead dogs in hampers, packed as game and there is a massacre of dogs by owners who do not want to pay the duties.

1796 Dog population estimated at one million.

1800 2nd February Two Lincolnshire greyhounds run 4 miles (probably much more when the turns were counted) in 12 minutes. Dogs' speed a mile in 3 minutes or 20 miles an hour.

1800 Edwards describes the Harlequin Great Dane.

1800 24th February the 'Billesden Coplow run', in which Hugo Meynell's hounds cover 28 miles in 2 hours and 15 minutes at a rate of 12 miles an hour.

c. **1800** Foxhunting begins to make an appeal to those outside the area of the hunt.

1800 Edwards depicts the rough- and smooth-coated collie.

c. **1806** Melton Mowbray has become the centre of fashionable foxhunting.

1808 Lord Byron builds a tomb for his dog 'Boatswain', who was born at Newfoundland May **1803**. Byron's plans to be buried alongside his pet are frustrated when he has to sell Newstead.

1800–1877 Edward Laverack, the developer of the English setters called 'Laveracks'.

1802 An unsuccessful attempt to abolish bull-baiting. The bill is defeated by thirteen votes.

1803 Fatal duel over a Newfoundland dog between Colonel Montgomery and Captain Macnamara, R.N.

1803 William Taplin declares the Irish hound probably extinct.

1805 Chase of wild fallow deer in Epping Forest given up by last huntsman, Mr Mellish.

1813 The Royal Harriers are given up.

1815 *Guy Mannering,* is published by Sir Walter Scott, in which Dandie Dinmont terriers are described.

1815 The Revd John ('Jack') Russell begins breeding terriers.

1815 First St Bernard in England kept at Leasowe Castle. It is described as 'an animal of burden'.

1820 The Bedlington terrier supposedly introduced from Holland by a weaver of Longhorsley.

1821 Alken's *National Sports of Great Britain* portrays a recognisable bull terrier.

1824 Foundation of The Society for the Prevention of Cruelty to Animals. It later becomes a Royal Society.

1825 Six bulldogs and bulldog mastiff crosses are pitted against a lion owned by menagerie keeper Wombwell, at Warwick. The lion is defeated.

1827 First record of the St Bernard being used at the hospice in the Alps to save travellers' lives.

1827 Death of the fourth Duke of Gordon, originator of the Gordon setter.

1829 First full account of the life-saving role of the St Bernard is given by William Brockedon in his *Passes of the Alps*. It goes unnoticed by dog historians down to the present year.

1829 A bill to end bull-baiting is defeated by forty-five votes.

1830 Four hundred cases of rabies in dogs 'within a very brief space of time'.

c. **1830** 'Old Lal's' team of four foxhounds passes stage-coaches travelling at 12 miles an hour.

1831 8th February An unsuccessful attempt to pass a bill 'to prevent the spreading of canine madness'.

1835 First act to prevent cruelty to animals.

1835 First successful prosecution for cruelty to dogs.

1835 Bull-baiting and dog-fighting banned but dog-fighting continues to exist clandestinely.

1836 The Waterloo Cup Meet begins at Sefton Altcar, near Liverpool. Silver collars are awarded to the winners till **1803**, when a cup is instituted.

1839 The Metropolitan Police Act (enforceable 1st January, **1840**) forbids the use of dogs to draw 'any cart, carriage, truck or barrow'.

1841 Maltese dogs are brought from Manilla as a present for Queen Victoria.

1843 The Skye terrier is first mentioned.

1844 26th July Report of the House of Commons from the Select Committee on Dog Stealing.

1844 A corps of ten Newfoundland dogs is trained to save life in the Seine in Paris.

c. **1845** Death of the famous St Bernard dog 'Barry' along with two guide companions while attempting to save travellers on the Little St Bernard Pass.

1847 A description of the 'English terrier' suggests that it is a Manchester terrier.

1849 The Greyhound 'Bang' jumps 30 feet.

1850–1891 Captain John Edwardes develops the Sealyham on his estate at Sealyham in Haverfordwest, Pembrokeshire.

1854 Cruelty to Animals Act, **1854** extends the prohibition of dogs for transport to all places in the United Kingdom. It is estimated that this act will affect about 20,000 dogs. The act takes effect on 1st January **1855.**

1858 National Coursing Club formed.

1859 'Stonehenge' says of the dachshund: 'This little hound has been introduced into England within the last few years, a few couple having been presented to the Queen from Saxony.'

1859 First dog show, at Newcastle.

1859 Entry of foxhounds at Cleveland Agricultural Show.

c. **1860** The Hon. Dudley Marjoribanks (later Lord Tweedmouth) starts golden retrievers from a yellow retriever, one yellow pup in a litter of black and wavy-coated pups that he has bought from a Brighton cobbler.

1860 Occupation of Peking by the allied forces. During the seizure of the Imperial Palace, Lord John Hay, General Dunne and a relative of the Duke of Richmond obtain Pekingese from dogs belonging to the Emperor's aunt, who has just committed suicide.

1862 Captain G. A. Graham attempts to revive the great Irish hound, using deerhound blood.

1865 D. F. Rennie sees the Palace eunuchs selling inferior specimens of Imperial Pekingese at a monthly six-day fair held at Peking.

1867 'Stonehenge' comments on the fondness for putting stuffed toy terriers in glass cases.

1870 A Mr W. C. of Halifax, Nova Scotia, mentions the report that the Beothuk Indians had 'a dog, but that it was a small breed. . . . The Labrador dog is in my opinion a distinct breed . . . formerly they were only to be met with on that part of the coast of Labrador which to us is known as the South Shore of the mainland in the Straits of Belle Isle.'

1873 Kennel Club set up.

1877 Foxhound Show at Peterborough founded.

1880 Queen Victoria gives 'Bobby' the Afghan Medal.

1882 Greyhound Stud Book.

1884 Black and Tan Terrier Club established.

1886 First Crufts Show. Terriers only.

1888 Eskimo dog exhibited at Kennel Club show.

1895 Saluki introduced to England.

1896 Pekingese 'Ah Cum', and 'Mimosa' bought from Palace in Peking.

1899 'Ah Cum', dies and is stuffed for Natural History Museum, South Kensington.

1901 Strict quarantine regulations on imported dogs.

1901 22 January Queen Victoria's favourite Pomeranian on her death-bed.

1

From Stone Age to Dark Age

Like a forest with occasional clearings, the early history of Britain now conceals and now reveals the British dog, but only in part. Though, now and again, we are so near to the dogs of antiquity that we can even see the spots on their coats or hear their names called by the hunter, much remains hidden from our view.

The trail of the early dog is such a faint one that the difficulties in following it may be briefly stated before we begin the chase. Broadly speaking, evidence for the existence of dogs in early Britain depends on skeletal remains, pictorial representations and references to dogs in the literature of the time. All these sources of evidence bristle with difficulties and great caution must be exercised in using them. At first sight the skeleton of a dog might appear something positive, evidence that could not be set aside. Skeletons of dogs are rarely complete, however. So far as I have been able to discover, there are only two well-known articulated skeletons of early British dogs in existence. Even when a skeleton is complete and the bones have not been chewed by other dogs, or man, it can tell us nothing about the colour of the dog, its coat or its general appearance. Most skeletons of dogs cannot be identified as belonging to types of dog known today. After examining 1,156 specimens of dogs found in Romano-British sites, R. A. Harcourt remarked, with admirable caution, that one specimen, an incomplete femur and tibia from a Roman villa at Hemel Hempstead, was 'indistinguishable from the bones of a Pomeranian in the writer's collection'.

It might seem from the figure of Romano-British dogs examined by Harcourt (a figure which does not include all those found at sites of this period) that there was an abundance of skeletal material for the British dog. This is by no means the case for every period: as we shall see, there is either a plethora of archaeological evidence, or not as much as one would wish. Dogs have unfortunately been very much undervalued by archaeologists in the past. Many dogs unearthed on archaeological sites have simply been thrown away, without any record being made of them. Harcourt cites a Romano-British site at Asthall in Oxfordshire, excavated as recently as 1955, where five complete dog skeletons were found and subsequently thrown on the rubbish heap, without any details of them being given in the report of the excavations. An ancient Roman would have been more aware of the value of dogs as evidence: Homer had Achilles say it would be easy to discover the remains of Patroclus amongst the ashes of his funeral pyre because they would be in the centre of the pyre, while round about would be the bones of his two favourite dogs.

Great has been the indifference with which archaeologists have treated dogs. Although we know that the Romans kept watch-dogs in their towers on the *limes* or frontier fortifications to give warning of the approach of enemies and also used them to carry messages, with letters attached to their collars, those dog remains reported from the Roman Wall of Hadrian are virtually confined to the finds made at Corbridge (Corstopitum).

It is much easier to identify a dog from its picture than its description. Even so, pictorial material has provided its own crop of difficulties. A picture or a sculpture in Greco-Roman times was an idealised representation of something or somebody of which the reality may have been very different. Few Greek or Roman women could have looked as beautiful as those depicted in sculpture and there is no reason to suppose that painters and sculptors sought for a lower standard of excellence when it came to portraying animals. Most dogs represented in early art are not accompanied by human figures, hence it is impossible even to guess at their size. In 1932 the most famous representation of a Romano-British dog was found at Lydney Park in Gloucestershire. It was one of seven statuettes of dogs, six of which were of relatively mediocre workmanship, but the seventh a beautiful bronze of a dog with a narrow head, rather like that of a greyhound, and very fine, clean lines. Was this the famous Ancient British hunting-hound, or was it a much smaller creature, perhaps a toy, such as the Italian greyhound? When human figures do accompany a dog in art it is often difficult to decide whether they represent real human beings or imaginary mythological creatures. A case in point is the Cymbeline coin of AD 43 which depicts a great hound, ridden by a figure which sits side-saddle on its back. 'That the size of this dog was considerable,' wrote the prolific writer on dogs, Edward C. Ash, 'is obvious by comparing it to the man riding on its back.' The figure on the dog, however, is not a man, but a woman, as can be inferred from the fact that she has breasts. Since a woman associated with a dog in early British art is almost certainly the goddess Epona, Cymbeline's (or Cunobelin's) coin must represent a larger-than-life animal given heroic stature to match its companion, the goddess.

If Ash was wrong in identifying a goddess as a god, he could equally well be wrong in identifying particular types of dogs that are portrayed in art as corresponding to breeds that exist today. Thus he confidently assumes the Cymbeline dog to be a Great Dane, pointing to its size as an additional proof of its identity.

The difficulties of pictorial representation of dogs virtually disappear, however, if the dog shown accompanies a realistically drawn human being. Identification of the type of dog depicted becomes certain if the creature has been given a title by the artist. Thus a dog painted on a Greek vase from Vulci, accompanied by its proud owner and labelled 'Maltese' (*meltaie*) must surely be a portrait of one of the most famous breeds of classical antiquity, a breed that almost certainly reached Roman Britain. If we felt that the Vulci portrait of a Maltese dog looked rather like a Pomeranian, it would be possible to go a step farther and identify the Maltese dog as the breed kept by an owner of a Roman villa at Hemel Hempstead.

The Coventina Terrier

Unfortunately skeletal, pictorial and literary evidence hardly ever come together in this way, but there is another kind of identification which is almost as good: when we see a picture or sculpture of a dog which so resembles an existing breed that we feel it must be one and the same. This is the case with the Roman bronze statuette of a terrier from Coventina's Well in Carrawburgh. It may be a statuette of a toy terrier or of a much larger hunting one; it is possible to argue, at length, about the breed depicted, but there can be no doubt that a terrier of some sort is represented. Yet the presence of a bronze terrier in Northumberland is no guarantee that any such dog existed there in real life. Romano-British art was international. Were the dogs depicted on the beautiful mosaics at Cirencester (which will be discussed in a later chapter) Romano-British dogs, or had they come to Britain solely in the form of a sketch made by a Hellenic artist in Alexandria, or even as a ready-made component of a kit for making a mosaic pavement?

Of all types of evidence, literary references are the most difficult to interpret. Just as everybody at Queen Elizabeth's court knew who Shakespeare's 'Mr W. H.' was, so that nobody bothered to set down his identity on paper, so classical writers rarely bother to describe particular breeds of dogs in any detail. They knew that an acquaintanceship with the kennel was part of every gentleman's education, so there was no need to waste papyrus by describing what was common knowledge already. Consequently our knowledge of the dogs of classical antiquity is often confined to a list of names, a list which it is very difficult to match up with any breeds, present or past. The picture is not quite so black as it seems however: much of our knowledge about dogs of classical times comes from two poems by the Latin poets Nemesianus and Grattius and as poets are compelled to use language for ornament as well as instruction they tell us more about the kind of dogs they knew than any other source.

The history of the dog in Britain starts with one found in the remains of a mesolithic (Middle Stone Age) settlement in Yorkshire, on a locality called Star Carr, a site so remote that it is not mentioned even on large-scale atlases. The carr country of Yorkshire has always been notable for its dogs, because in historic times it was badly infested with wolves. According to William Taplin: 'They used to breed in the carrs below amongst the rushes, furze, and bogs, and in the night time come up from their dens, and unless the sheep had previously been driven into the town, or the shepherds indefatigably valiant, great numbers of them were destroyed.' To counter these attacks by wolves, the shepherds of the Wolds bred special wolf dogs, which much later, in the nineteenth century, were to contribute their special qualities to the greyhound.

The Star Carr dog had lived more than nine thousand years before the Yorkshire shepherds used their dogs to hunt down the wolves and collected 'wolf money' for their heads. It is the oldest dog in Europe, the oldest in the world, in fact, save for the jaw of an American dog found in the postglacial late Wisconsin gravel bed in Illinois, U.S.A. and some remains from the Natufian in Israel. Its age, dated at 7538 ± 350 BC. takes us back almost to the beginnings of the history of man himself, the Old Stone Age.

Old as it was, the Starr Carr dog must have had ancestors in the Old World, for the American dogs which had crossed the land-bridge from Asia to America with their Indian masters must have originated in Asia, probably as long ago as the tenth millennium BC. So far, nobody has found the remains of these, the oldest European dogs. A skeleton of a dog, comparable in age to the Star Carr animal, was however found at Senckenberg, near Frankfurt-am-Main, in Germany. In 1914 a new chemical institute was being built there and a shaft had to be sunk through a bog. Close to rock-bottom was found the skeleton of the dog and that of an extinct wild ox, *Bos primigenius*. It is possible to imagine that the Senckenberg dog was hunting the ox and in the heat of the chase both became trapped in the peat bog. Though the remains of the dog were destroyed, apparently in an air raid, in World War II, a plaster cast of the skull has survived. The examination of this skull has recently proved that the Senckenberg dog was of a quite different breed from the Star Carr one, about the size of a poodle. It was also, apparently, more recent, because it lacked a peculiarity unique to the Yorkshire dog, having quite normally placed teeth.

It was this peculiar feature of the Star Carr dog, a feature absent from all other ancient dog remains (including a dog from the seventh millennium recovered from Jericho) that made it the object of such intense interest. It was a missing link between the dog of today and the ancestor of all breeds of dogs, the wolf. The dog had jaws like a wolf, with overlapping teeth, but smaller teeth and weaker jaws than a real wolf would have had. In any case the size of the skeleton showed that the Star Carr animal was a fairly small dog – smaller than a wolf would have been. It was related to a breed of dog whose remains will be mentioned more than once as belonging to much later times, the *Canis familiaris palustris*, a type which, as *palustris* meaning 'swampy' suggests, is associated with the lake dwellings of neolithic times.

Why did the Star Carr dog have overlapping premolar teeth, a condition hardly ever found in adult dogs nowadays? Magnus Degerbøl, who described the remains of the dog in 1961, argued that this was one of the changes produced by turning a wolf into a domesticated dog. An investigator named Wolfgramm had experimented with domesticating the wolf as far back as 1894. He had discovered that when a wild animal was taken out of its natural environment or 'biotype', and kept under more or less unnatural conditions, it began to change. If the animal had been born in captivity or captured while young, these changes might even affect its skeleton.

One change that was readily visible was that the animal was smaller than its wildlife counterpart would have been. In wolves, the jaw and muzzle shortened in relation to the size of the head. The teeth, particularly the carnassial teeth, did not shorten so much and might overlap the jaw. These were the sort of changes which had created the Star Carr dog. It was the descendant of a domesticated wolf, had probably never been given enough to eat in adolescence and had probably been kept fairly closely confined in the settlement, perhaps penned in an enclosure or even tied up.

Had the primeval British dog originated from the savage wolves of the East Riding? It is much more likely that it was a far-off descendant of an

Eastern Asiatic wolf because the further east one travels, the smaller the wolves become, and the smaller a wolf is, the more likely a subject it is for the domestication experiment, if only because it is less likely to tear the experimenter apart if the experiment fails.

It seems, therefore, at least likely that the domesticated dog was bred out of the captive wolf in some agricultural settlement of the tenth millennium, such as Jericho, from an eastern specimen of the wolf, such as *Canis lupus arabs* or *Canis lupus pallipes*, wolves which are so dog-like that their carnassial teeth are no larger than those of very large Eskimo dogs. As dogs are undoubtedly more useful to the hunter than the farmer, because they often begin their hunting career by attacking the farm livestock, the domestication of the dog may have begun before people started to farm. The Star Carr dog is not the first stage of domestication. If that stage is ever found it may well be possible to prove that the dog was one of the very earliest tools of man in Asia.

How had the Star Carr dog got from Asia to Yorkshire and what was it doing in the settlement? It seems quite possible that some domesticated dogs became 'feral' (went wild) again. Some of them may have made the trip from Palestine (in Jericho at least two kinds of dogs were known, one the size of wolves, the other the size of fox terriers) and simply wandered in search of game across Europe, following the migrations of animals such as the wild oxen. Going feral would not have obliterated the characteristics that the Star Carr dog had already acquired and, from time to time, individuals of these feral packs would have been tempted into the homes of men and returned to full domesticity.

The purpose of the dog at Star Carr is more obscure. Its small size does not preclude that it was used for hunting purposes. It is the heart that makes the hunter and Jim Corbett has described in his account of his hunts for the man-eating tigers of Kumaon in India how he was always accompanied by his diminutive fox terrier. Nor would the dog's small size (22 inches) have precluded its use as an efficient watch-dog.

Whatever its primary function, the Star Carr dog undoubtedly had the secondary one of being a source of food. Its bones had been well chewed, whether by other dogs or humans is not apparent. The fact that the dog did not live out its full adult life may indicate that it was a food animal, kept for a time of want. Dogs have been eaten throughout many parts of the world and still are today. They are a source of protein. Amundsen's success in racing Scott to the South Pole has been attributed to his policy of eating his sledge dogs as he went along. Each husky, it has been calculated, produced fifty pounds of edible meat. Whereas to Scott it would have seemed a piece of unspeakable cruelty to eat his dogs, it would not have seemed so to Stone Age folk, who had broad ideas about diet and occasionally indulged in cannibalism.

One of the reasons why only two mesolithic dogs have been discovered may be the fact that they were eaten and so produced little in the way of recognisable remains. In the following period, the neolithic, the paucity of dog skeletons is due to an entirely different reason. Hardly any domestic sites, such as houses or farms, have been discovered. Consequently the only place where dog remains are to be looked for are those sites that have been excavated: causewayed camps, long barrows, Dene holes, flint mines and henge monuments. The finds from these very restricted areas have been few: only thirty-seven long bones and six skulls.

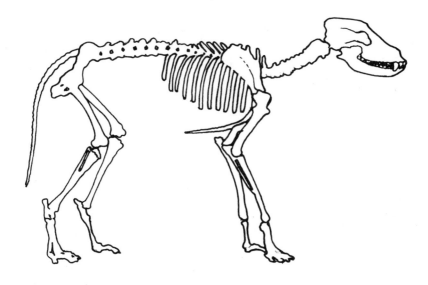

The Easton Down Dog

The finds make up in quality what they lack in quantity because they include the earliest complete skeletons of dogs, complete down to the small bones of the feet and the tail, those found in the neolithic fort of Windmill Hill and in a flint mine at Easton Down. The Windmill Hill dog is of a breed already mentioned, *Canis familiaris palustris*. It was discovered in 1928 by Mr Arthur Keiller, an archaeologist who had put his family fortune (derived from a famous brand of marmalade) to good use in purchasing and excavating the greatest stone circle in Britain, Avebury. Nearby he found the remains of six domesticated dogs, of which one set yielded a complete skeleton. Keiller felt that the dog bore a marked resemblance to the dogs found among Swiss lake dwellings; it was long-legged, short-backed and small-headed, with a skull shorter than that of a greyhound or harrier. It was not a specialised dog, not intended for either hunting or herding, but an all-purpose one and possibly a scavenger as well, a sort of Ancient British pariah in fact.

Keiller's conclusions have been abundantly borne out by much more recent investigations into Ancient British dogs, notably that undertaken by R. A. Harcourt in 1974. Though it is obviously difficult to reach definite conclusions from such scanty material, Harcourt, arguing from four neolithic dogs that stood about 23½ inches high, said that there was only a single type of dog and that it varied little in appearance even though at the end of the neolithic period it had risen somewhat in size.

The owners of the Windmill Hill dog, the Beaker Folk, Iberian cultivators and pastoralists who had invaded Britain from the Continent, probably did not feel the need for specialised dogs. There is no evidence that they were great hunters, there seems every evidence that they were peaceful folk with a simple way of life. They were not likely to require war-dogs for battle, nor hunting-dogs, either gazehounds, which hunt by sight, or scenting-hounds, which trail a quarry by scent.

The Celts, who began to arrive in Britain around 400 BC, were a very different folk from the Iberians who had preceded them. They were very warlike, as their innumerable hill forts testify even today. They were international in outlook, great mercenaries and traders who were to be found all over the known world. They liked imported luxuries and did not care what they spent to get them. Dogs were connected with many aspects of their life and they introduced into Britain not merely different types of dogs, with different functions from those known hitherto, but probably also the love of dogs and love of animals generally that came to be so characteristic of the British in later times. Love brings its reward, and the Celts were undoubtedly great dog-trainers. A dog is very much what you make it: much may be done with even such unpromising material as a pariah dog. In the end the wealth that British dogs constituted and their fame throughout the civilised world were to prove irresistible attractions to Ancient Britain's most powerful neighbour, the Roman Republic.

Having said that the Celts were dog-lovers, it may seem paradoxical to add that they ate dogs. The greatest of all heroes of Celtic poetry, Cú Chulainn, had a taboo laid on him that he was not to eat dog's flesh, a taboo that would have been meaningless unless dog meat figured fairly regularly on the menu. The dog from which Cú Chulainn took his name ('Hound of Culann') was a very specialised breed indeed, a watchman dog trained as a man-killer. It was owned by a non-noble freeman, Culann, who was a smith and therefore probably a man of great respect and some substance. In the story Culann is dispensing lavish hospitality to his king, Conchobar, who is Cú Chulainn's uncle. He has ordered fresh rushes to be strewn on the floor of his house and drink to be served to the king and his attendants. The party is getting under way and realising that the claims on him as host may be so overwhelming that he may not be sufficiently attentive to guarding his property, he gets his dog to do it for him. He looses this great hound from its chain and it immediately sets about its task of guarding the settlement. After running round and round the enclosure filled with the houses of Culann and his dependents it retires: 'to the mound where it was wont to be while guarding the dwelling and it lay there with his head on its paws.' This was a very dog-like thing for the hound to do, a realistic touch which seems to confirm the authenticity of the description of the hound at its work and indicate that the author was recording contemporary practice.

It is at this point that realism gives place to fantasy. Before loosing the hound, Culann has asked the king whether all his followers are now inside the house, for fear the dog catches them out of doors and takes them for intruders. Conchobar replies that they are, forgetting that his nephew, Cú Chulainn, has lingered behind to play with some young friends. When the sound of the beast's frenzied barking reaches him as he sits at table he rises in anguish, convinced his nephew has been killed by the dog. Instantly his bodyguards leave the feasting hall and scale the palisade so as to arrive more swiftly at the scene of slaughter. Great is their surprise and the king's when they discover that it is Cú Chulainn that has killed the hound. The boy has given his first proof of being cast in an heroic mould. The rejoicing is great – except in the heart of the smith, Culann, who complains that now he has lost his faithful servant which used to watch over his flocks and herds. It is at this point that Cú Chulainn steps forward and offers to be a human watch-dog for the smith, receiving his name and the taboo that went with it, in consequence.

Archaeology has nothing to tell us about what kind of dog Culann's was. Few remains have been found from this period. Those dogs whose remains were unearthed show a slight increase in size over those of neolithic times, with larger dogs being either more common or better represented in archaeological discoveries. The dogs found ranged between 11½ and 23 inches in height, down somewhat from those of the previous period.

Either Culann's dog was a complete invention by the bardic poet, which seems unlikely, or it was a portrait of some contemporary animal whose type has not been recovered by the archaeologists. Artistic finds from the Iron Age in Britain, however, portray two types of dogs, either of which might well have sat as a model for the watch-dog hound. One, of unknown provenance, is a bronze of a leaping dog, wearing a broad collar and apparently a muzzle as well. The other is the famous Cymbeline coin of AD 43, showing the goddess Epona riding on an animal which might well be a mastiff. Mastiffs were known to the Assyrians and are thought to have been imported to England by the Phoenicians who came here to trade for tin. They could equally well have been brought by the Celts when they invaded Britain, because Celtic armies took everything with them, cattle and women and children, on the march. Literary evidence of much later date, but which, like the story of Cú Chulainn, probably incorporates authentic details, describes the migration of the children of Uisnech, who fled from Northern Ireland to Scotland in the first century AD. They brought with them a shipload of greyhounds, 150 dogs or more.

The dog was all the more essential to the Celts in that it figured largely in

The Cymbeline Coin

their religion and had connections not merely with the goddess Epona, portrayed on the Cymbeline coin, but also the god Nodons, who was worshipped at Lydney, in Gloucestershire. It has been suggested that Nodons may have been a were-dog, capable of taking the form of a dog as well as of other of his cult animals. This is all the more interesting in that were-dogs or spirit-dogs play a large part in the British images of the supernatural.

Whichever way the mastiff arrived in Britain, it seems to have been a breed that was suited for more than one role. One of these was the boar hunt, which played a very important part in Celtic life. Mastiffs are not fast-moving dogs and might be at a disadvantage in pursuing a fast-moving animal such as a deer. But it could face a boar, the only British animal which will turn at bay when it has not been cornered first. (Strabo, a Greco-Roman writer about Britain (63 BC–AD 21) mentions how fiercely the British boar will attack those who approach it.)

The mastiff seemed also well-suited for another primary use of the dog by the Celts: warfare. Fighting-dogs were stationed in the front rank of Gaulish armies, dogs so savage that the most ferocious of all the hounds of Greece and Rome, the Molossian dogs from Epirus in Thessaly, quailed before them. These dogs were exported from Britain and had no doubt been brought to Gaul by the Britons who sailed across the Channel to help their countrymen there against the invasion of Julius Caesar.

The help given by the Britons to the Gauls was one of the pretexts that

Julius Caesar put forward in his *Commentaries*, for his decision to invade Britain. His real reason for crossing the Channel was to gain possession of the riches of the island. These included tin, copper, slaves, iron, lead, corn, cattle, pearls and amber. He admits that one of his purposes in beginning the invasion was 'to get gold, horses, hounds and skins'. Though the value of the other products of Britain was open to question (the pearls were mis-shapen and discoloured, the slaves surly and the gold apparently non-existent) there could be no doubt about the value of the dogs. If displayed in the Roman arena they would prove an unsurpassable attraction, a show which as yet no other politician had been able to put on. Julius Caesar's whole career was directed towards achieving his ultimate aim – to become sole ruler of Rome – and the acquisition of British fighting-dogs would un-doubtedly have added very much to his popularity as a politician. There were also other British dogs that it was important for him to secure – hunting-hounds, about which more will be said later. Gifts of these dogs would obviously have been very welcome to his political backers.

Caesar's two unsuccessful invasions of 55 and 54 BC constituted his grea-test failure. Yet though Roman military force had been compelled to fall back, the influence of Rome became stronger yearly in Britain. The Cym-beline coin, struck probably shortly before Cymbeline or Cunobelin's death in AD 43, is entirely classical both in the legend on the coin, the form of the lettering and the representation of the goddess and her dog. In the same year as Cymbeline died, Claudius sent Aulus Plautius with four legions and many auxiliaries to invade Britain. By AD 85 or 86, when the Roman general Agricola was withdrawn from Britain by the Emperor Domitian, the conquest may be said to have been established. Rome imported to Britain her whole way of life, including her dogs. The archaeo-logical picture, fairly clear hitherto, now becomes rather complex.

The dogs of Roman Britain included the native stock and importations not merely from Italy but probably from all over the Roman world. It is small wonder that instead of there being a single population of dogs – very similar to one another and determined by deliberate selection or, more likely, by the fact that there was only one interbreeding stock of dogs – there is now a wide variety of breeds. Dogs were undoubtedly much more evident in Roman Britain than they had been in previous times. R. A. Har-court included 1,156 specimens in his survey and there were many more that could have been drawn on. The dog finds varied in size between 9 and 28 inches. For the first time house-dogs or lap-dogs appear, dogs too small to have had any useful function either for food or as a scavenger and which were too delicate to have lived unassociated with men and women. At least three distinct breeds could be observed.

Harcourt's study was immensely valuable for two reasons: he demon-strated that for the first time we can recognise a particular breed of dog, known to exist today, as having been present in Roman Britain – the Pomeranian, known to the Romans as 'the Maltese dog'; and because he could find no evidence of what we might expect, from literary sources, to have been the most important breed, the greyhound. Before abandoning the solid bedrock of archaeological discovery for the much less secure ground of conjecture based on literary sources, let us glance at a few archaeological finds.

In the neighbouring island of Ireland, certain breeds of dog continued to flourish during and after the Roman occupation and these dogs presumably have some relationship with those found in Britain. Dog finds included one made on the artificial island or 'crannog' of Loch Gur, County Limerick, of a skull identified as that of a sheep dog, *Canis familiaris intermedius*. Crannogs near Dunshaughlin in County Meath yielded examples of *Canis familiaris palustris* – the lake dwellers' dog. This, curiously enough, is described as looking very much like that relative of the Pomeranian, the Swiss Turfdog or *torhund*, a Spitz-like creature with a pointed nose and bushy tail. The most interesting find, however, were undoubtedly remains, from the same site, which were confidently identified as *Canis familiaris leineri*, an example or close relative of the great Irish hound.

More will be said later about the Irish hound, but first we must glance at the Lydney dog, a greyhound if there ever was one, and a bronze terrier from Coventina's Well in Carrawburgh, Northumberland. The problems relating to these dogs have already been raised – were they votive animals made in Britain, from British models, or were they imported from Gaul or even farther afield?

I feel myself that this problem can be resolved by assuming that the model dogs were at least recognisable as dogs by the worshippers who left them with Nodons and Coventina. If they were animals which were completely unfamiliar to the worshipper he would probably have refused to buy them, or sacrifice them, on the grounds that the god might fail to recognise them either and thus not grant his prayer.

We could take a somewhat similar approach towards other portrayals of the dog in Romano-British art. In those days customers had to have what they wanted and the patron who ordered a very life-like and recognisable hare for the middle of his mosaic pavement at Cirencester probably had his counterpart in other purchasers who stipulated that they wanted dogs that they and their friends could recognise. The fierce, mastiff-like dog that appears on a Roman pavement from Withington, Gloucestershire, attacking a wild boar, would, then, be either a local dog or sufficiently like one to be readily recognised.

The same principle holds good for the exquisite Castor Ware potted at Durobrivae (near Castor) in Northamptonshire. The pottery of these drinking goblets and bowls shows a good deal of late Celtic influence. The beautifully lively hare, deer and coursing greyhounds are applied by 'barbotine' – wet clay squeezed through a funnel like icing for a cake. A potter decorating his pots in this way would, I think, be much more likely to model from memory a dog that he knew than take a sculptured model from farther afield.

There are one or two other archaeological finds of art objects from Roman Britain depicting dogs almost certainly derived from particular breeds popular in Britannia. Mention has already been made of the Cirencester mosaics. One tessellated pavement found in Dyer Street and depicting the Seasons shows two kinds of dog: one I shall nickname 'the prick-eared hound', resembling the dog of the Gaulish bronze; the other a dog which is possibly meant for a greyhound. Another find at Corinium (ancient Cirencester) was the bronze handle of an instrument, now probably lost, but published in 1850, which shows what can only be a Pomeranian. This last find is particularly interesting in that it proves my point that Romano-British patrons liked representations of dogs actually kept in Britannia. In antiquity the Pomeranian was known as 'the Maltese dog' (not to be confused with the Maltese dog which became very popular in the nineteenth century). It was a pet dog likely to be popular in this civilian and holiday centre.

It is then possible to demonstrate from the archaeological evidence that there was a varied dog population in Roman times, more than at any previous period. The dogs in fashion ranged from very big ones, capable of tackling a boar or a deer – dogs so big that their bones may have been confused with those of the wolf in some archaeological investigations – to very small lap-dogs. There must have been many intermediaries between the pampered pet dog and the equally pampered hunting-hounds: dogs which undertook work such as the sheepdog and guard-dog, or which simply hung around the villages living on scraps, just as pariah dogs do in Africa today. Such pariah packs must have existed in England from Roman times, if not before, at least down to the days of Elizabeth I. While working on ecclesiastical court records for that period I discovered the case of a girl who had been thrown from her horse after it had been hunted by the dogs of the village. Such packs, then, constituted a danger to travellers at every epoch but were tolerated because they would give warning of the approach of cattle-thieves or other raiders.

It was on just such a raid that the Roman guard-dogs had signally disgraced themselves by failing to give the alarm. The Gauls, besieging Rome in 364 BC, stealthily escaladed the Capitol. They were almost in the citadel itself and no warning had been given to the garrison by the dogs – not a pariah pack but specially kept for this purpose – when the geese began to cackle. For centuries after, on the anniversary of the unsuccessful attack, the Romans led some unfortunate dogs round the city and then killed them, probably by crucifixion.

The failure of their guard-dogs to bark a warning may have given the Romans a distaste for their own breed of dogs. At any rate we hear no more of Roman breeds. Instead, the Romans became the first collectors of dogs on an international scale. Nemesianus, who wrote a poem called *Cynegetica*, was a native of Carthage who must have put pen to papyrus some time between AD 283 and 284. His readers knew what to expect from the title of his work, 'About Dogs', and he did not disappoint them. He mentions Spartan, Pannonian, Umbrian, Spanish, Molossian and Lybian hounds. Grattius, an earlier writer, who wrote between 19 BC and AD 8, adds to our list of Roman dogs (which are all sporting breeds). He mentions Parthian, Celtic, Gelonian, Mede, Arcadian, Hyrcanian, Thessalian, Azoran and Acamian. Grattius' poem (called *Cynegetican*) was praised by Julius Caesar, a fact which makes it seem even more suspicious that Caesar should have made no mention of British dogs in his account of his invasion of Britain. I think that this can only indicate his pique at having failed to obtain any British dogs – with his usual skill he glossed over his own failures.

There was no reason why a Roman sportsman resident in Britain should not have imported at least some of the breeds mentioned in the previous paragraphs. They were all regarded as having good qualities and breeding between them would cancel out the defects and emphasise the qualities. An Umbrian dam, says Grattius, will give hunting flair to a slower-witted Gaulish dog. Hyrcanian hounds will impart pugnacity to a Gelonian dog, while a Calydonian crossed with a Molossian will lose its tendency to be constantly giving tongue.

The continuous supply of wild creatures to the Colosseum for the combats shows how well the Romans had organised the transit of animals. They must have had a great flair for animal handling or could employ assistants who had. Nor did they spare any trouble when it came to collecting. So very likely numbers of these exotic breeds did reach England. Dogs which would almost certainly have been brought to Britannia – though we have no direct evidence that they arrived here – were the Roman guard-dog, featured in the famous mosaic at Pompeii, and the Molossian, probably the best known Roman sporting-dog.

Yet the Romano-British sportsman who could not import his hounds would have little to complain of as the native British dogs and their counterparts (the dogs introduced by the Gauls into Britain) are spoken of as being the best in the world.

Grattius says that whoever possesses a British hound will have made an investment much more valuable than the money he has spent obtaining it. The fact that he says British dogs are not good-looking and that he mentions crossing to Britain from the territories of the *Morini* (a Gaulish nation helped by the Britons in their fight against Caesar suggests he had mastiff war-dogs in mind). Strabo remarks 'Britain produces corn, cattle, gold, silver, and iron, together with skins, slaves, and dogs of a superior breed for the chase. The Gauls use these dogs in war, as well as others of their own breed.' In the passage already quoted, Grattius mentions that it is in vain for the Molossian dog to compete with British hounds. Evidently both authors are thinking of a very large and combative beast, probably the British mastiff which was pictured on mosaic pavements, hunting boar.

Later Romans were able to make financial and political capital out of the wonderful qualities of the mastiff. Pliny the Younger (AD 23–74) refers to the training of war-dogs and mentions that they were formed into platoons and fought in the front of battle 'with wonderful boldness', never retreating except when ordered to do so. Claudian, a Roman poet of the fourth and fifth century AD, tells his readers that in the arena British dogs can break a bull's neck with a single bite. Symmachus, a consul of the fourth century, thanks his brother 'for the present you have made me of seven Scottish dogs. They were shown at the games in the Circus to the great astonishment of the people, who could not believe that dogs of such ferocity could have been brought to Rome, except in iron cages, like lions and tigers.' Before the end of the Roman Empire a special official, the *procurator cynegii*, was stationed at Winchester to supervise the collection and export of British hounds to Rome, possibly as hunting hounds for the emperor's use, more likely for the wild-beast shows in the arena.

The big dogs matched against wild beasts and men and women in the arena might have been mastiffs from Britain. They might equally well have been the *Canis familiaris leineri* or great Irish hound. The great Irish hound is now extinct. Attempts were made to revive it during the nineteenth century but with too few of the original stock to be entirely successful.

Irish legend teems with stories of large and ferocious dogs which might be great hounds or mastiffs. Besides the legend of Culann the smith's dog, already quoted, there is an account of King Mesroda of Leinster who owned a great hound named Allbé. It was so savage and ferocious that it was an army in itself and the kings of Connaught and Ulster wished to possess it. Fabulous sums, lands, slaves, weapons and 6,000 head of cattle are quoted as prices offered for the hound, in vain.

Dogs for the arena were only part of the traffic in hounds from Britain. The great favourites of the Roman were the sporting breeds. It was these that were referred to in an oft-quoted Roman proverb, that the best things about the Britons were their dogs.

One of these breeds has already been mentioned, the great Irish hound, a beast which would course (pull down unaided by the hunter) deer, wolves, boar or hare. The other, and much the favourite British dog, was the greyhound. The greyhound was easily the most famous of all dogs of the time and it was called *vertragus* in Latin. Philologists puzzled their heads as to what this name could mean. Turnebus suggested that the name should really be *vertrahus*, meaning a dog which dragged or pulled wild animals, but Vossius, and everybody else after him, agreed that this was a Gallic word that had nothing to do with Latin etymology. We know that *vertragus* was a greyhound because of a verse of Martial which describes it as hunting the hare and bringing it back unharmed in its mouth to its master. It is also one of the few Latin names for dogs to be explained by commentators. Other writers help to build up our general picture of the dog: it was, says Grattius, 'coloured with yellow spots'. It may thus be a

remote ancestor of the lemon pye hounds of later England. The same
writer praises its marvellous swiftness: 'swifter than thought or a winged
bird it runs, pressing hard on the beasts it has found, though less likely to
find them when they lie hidden'. In other words, it was a proper gaze
hound and hunted not by scent but by sight.

The first importation of *vertragi* into the world of antiquity had been one
of the features that helped to revolutionise hunting in Greece and Rome.
Until 372 BC, the time of the Celtic invasions into the Greco-Roman world
(when incidentally the Roman guard-dogs let their masters down), there
were no dogs capable of following and catching a hare. Hares, like other
game, had been driven towards a net by dogs trained to flush them. Once
entangled in the meshes of the net they would then be taken by hand. As
we have already noticed, the Celts travelled with their dogs on warlike expeditions as in peacetime and although the Celtic aggressors recoiled from
Greece and Rome, some of the *vertragi* remained. Now with better dogs,
Greek and Roman sportsmen could hunt hares on horseback, just as the
Gauls did. The Gaulish coursers set off after the hare on horseback and
slipped their hounds on the trail. The *vertragi* were natural coursers, travelling after the hare at great speed and demanding equal dash on the part of
the courser. It was no accident that the better-to-do Gauls, who hunted on
horseback (poorer people had to be content to follow on foot), produced
the best cavalry in the world.

There are several mysteries connected with the *vertragus*. One is that it is
difficult to see why the Gauls should have bred dogs to course hares when
the hare was taboo to them and could not be eaten. Obviously they enjoyed
the chase, but it is strange that they did not concentrate on coursing deer.
Perhaps they had got their *vertragi* from some foreign source, possibly
from the Middle East where the Saluki, a dog greatly resembling the greyhound, must have been well known to the Phoenician traders who visited
the shores of Gaul and Britain. Another and much more puzzling mystery
is the apparent absence of the greyhound/*vertragus* from Britannia.
Archaeologists came up with nothing as R. A. Harcourt recorded:
'Although nearly 100 skulls of dogs from the Roman period have been examined in this course of this study, not one has been found that bore the
slightest resemblance to that of a greyhound.'

There are possible explanations for this absence of greyhound material.
One is that greyhound skeletons found on archaeological excavations
have simply been thrown away. Another is that it was a Gallic custom for
the favourite dog to be slaughtered and burned with his master on the
funeral pyre. The Britons, who bore much the same relationship to the
Gauls that the Americans do to us, may well have followed this custom,
even if they were Romanised.

That the greyhound was the favourite animal of many cannot be
doubted by anyone who has read Arrian, a Greek sportsman who took
Roman citizenship in AD 124 and who died in the reign of Marcus Aurelius.

Like most sportsmen, Arrian was fond of all animals and wanted no unnecessary killing. He refers his readers to the custom of the Gauls who
'course for sport, rather than for what they get'. In an admirable book on
coursing, Arrian urges his readers to give the hare a good start and never to
let more than two greyhounds off the leash to chase it at one time. Arrian
makes it clear that his greyhounds were allowed the run of his house. His
favourite dog sat beside him and when he got up, the dog got up too and
followed him through the city to the gymnasium, where it kept an eye on
his clothes. It then walked back home with him, watching him carefully to
make sure that he did not give it the slip by going off down a side street. If
he sat down to dinner without feeding the greyhound first, it would
mumble his foot gently with its jaw – just as it did a hare that had to be
brought back alive – as a reminder that it, too, wanted food. When Arrian
got into bed at the end of the day, it followed and enjoyed the warmth of the
bed as much as its master.

Arrian's glowing account of his greyhound – working dog and pet as
well – reminds us that dogs were much less trouble to keep in antiquity
than they are now. If you were poor you lived in a hut with a mud floor and
there was no damage the dog could do to it. If you were rich, you lived in a
house with a mosaic pavement, which was indestructible and was swept
several times a day by a large staff of slaves. The furniture, which in Britain
was often made of materials such as bronze or Kimmeridge shale, also set
attacks by dogs at bay.

Beside, the *vertragus*, a Gallic hound resident in Britain, there were two
other hounds very associated with Britannia. It is difficult even to guess
what they were because the classical philologists, who are usually prepared to explain any Latin word, give no equivalent for their names. One of
the breeds was the *segusius*. Arrian says it is an ugly, shaggy dog, compared by the Gauls to beggars who solicit alms by the side of the road. It has
a melancholy bark and a slow gait and if it catches a single hare during a
season it will do very well. Is this a scientific observation on Arrian's part or
does it show the prejudice of the dog-lover for whom there can never be a
second breed? Nemesianus says that British dogs are swift and well suited
to the chase in our country'. It is tempting to identify the *segusius* with the
animal so often portrayed in Romano-British art, the dog I have nicknamed: 'the prick-eared hound'. This identification seems all the more
likely in that the other most notable British dog, the *agassaeus*, was obviously small, too small to tackle a deer, as the prick-eared hound is shown
doing in the mosaics. It is well described by Oppian, a Roman author of the
century:

But there is a certain strong breed of hunting-dogs, small, but worthy of a
sublime song, which the wild tribes of painted Britons maintain, and they call
them by the name of *assageii* and use them for tracking purposes. This dog is
round in shape, very skinny, with shaggy hair and a dull eye, and provided in its

feet with deadly claws and rows of sharp, close-set teeth. In its power of scent it is easily superior to all other hounds and the very best in the world for hunting, since it is very clever at finding the trail of these creatures that walk the earth, but it is also able to indicate with accuracy a scent that it is only just lingering in the air.

It is difficult not to identify this dog with the bronze terrier from Coventina's Well, a dog spare, shaggy and well-teethed. One is actually depicted with a Briton and the other was offered to a British deity; in a word both are real tribesmen's dogs. The discovery of the Coventina terrier shows how archaeological finds can help literary sources over the style. As late as 1948 the historian Josephine Creasey argued, with great plausibility, that the terrier breed could not have emerged in Ancient Britain because there was no work for them to do. The conditions of life and of hunting were diametrically opposed to those of the time for which we have literary evidence of its existence, the eleventh century.

The re-emergence in the Middle Ages of the supposedly extinct British terrier suggests that other breeds may have appeared to have died out, but really have survived. The possession of specialised breeds of dogs is just as good a proof of cultural superiority as any other. There were other survivors. Mastiffs, which had possibly been brought to England by the Phoenician tin traders, survived to become the great dog of the Middle Ages. The greyhound also stayed behind as the last galleys put out from Lyme Regis or Dover. Other breeds may have survived, for a time, in Ireland. Yet almost all the many breeds that made up the dog population of Roman Britain disappeared, to be replaced by a dog population of just two breeds in Anglo-Saxon England, breeds with a range of shoulder height of between 9 and 28 inches. Some few of the Romano-British breeds must have travelled with fleeing Britons to Britanny, Wales and Cornwall; the others simply disappeared, eaten by their owners in time of famine or by the ever-present native wolves.

And so the last Pomeranian scampered from the burning villa to the deceptive refuge of the forest as its terrified barking drowned the jingling of the amulets of red Maltese coral that its prudent owner had attached to its badger-skin collar. What effect did it and the fellow-canines have on Britain during the first five thousand years of their stay here?

Britain, a comparatively unknown, almost a mythical island before the Roman invasions, had now become firmly placed on the maps of Europe. The storms of barbarism now swept over it, but once their worst impetus had passed rescue expeditions would be sent out to retrieve it for Christendom and civilisation. British dogs had revolutionised the Roman hunt and the changes they effected were to influence the whole of the history of hunting in Western Europe. As the hunt was the principal amusement of the wealthy and important people of the Dark and Middle Ages and had

very significant effects on culture and art, it is worthwhile enquir[
these changes were. Old style Roman hunting had been a very slo
Game was driven by beaters and dogs into a trammel net and all
other elaborate snares were used. The object of the hunt was not s
to enjoy a cracking gallop after the game as to fill the larder. The younger
Pliny, who was admittedly not a typical Roman sportsman, found the long
wait at the nets so monotonous that he read and even wrote while waiting
for the boar to be netted. The arrival of the Celtic *segusii* and the British
agassaeus revolutionised the hunt for big game – boar and deer – as much as
the introduction of the *vertragi* had hare-hunting. By the end of the first
century AD the hunt had become a wild scurry in which fast horses and
good riders were needed to keep up with the fast-running British and
Gaulish hounds. The change of method is recorded by Hadrian, emperor
between AD 117 and 138, who wrote an epitaph on the horse which had
carried him so fleetly through the forests of Etruria in search of deer and
boar:

Perfect in his youth and still unimpaired in strength, but cut off on his appointed
day, Borysthenes, the Emperor's light hunting horse, an Alan steed from
Scythia, lies buried here in this field. He was accustomed to fly across plain and
marsh, and the mounds where the Etruscans lie buried. When he rode in chase
of the boars of Pannonia in Greece none of them dared to harm him with their
foaming tushes, as often happens, or even so much as sprinkle the tip of his tail
with the froth from their jaws.

The demand for fast British hounds survived the fall of the Roman
Empire in Britain and it was to have important effects on the revival of Christianity and learning after the storms of the barbarian invasions had begun
to abate. Around AD 405 a teenage British Christian called Sucat, baptised
in the name of Patricius, was carried off from his home by Irish raiders.
Patricius had been born in Alban in Scotland and was probably a Pict. As
will be seen later, the Picts were passionately devoted to hunting and had
splendid hounds. Patricius spent six years as a slave in Ireland and was
given the job of shepherd, a task which allowed him plenty of time for
meditation about religion. Finding it impossible to live a Christian life in a
pagan world, Patricius decided to escape back to Christendom and then
return to Christianise the country that he had so unwillingly adopted. The
only problem was how to escape from Ireland. It was easy enough to get to
the coast but the only craft likely to be in Irish waters were the *curraghs* of
raiders such as those who had carried him off. Then, in a dream, Patricius
learned that there would be a ship waiting to take him off. He hurried to the
shore after, we may be sure, saying a tearful farewell to the shepherd's dog
that had been his only friend during his long years of exile. Sure enough,
there was a ship, from Gaul. The master had put into the dangerous waters

of Ireland in the hope of getting a cargo of hunting-hounds. It shows how much these beasts – almost certainly the great Irish hounds – were fetching on the European markets at this time that he was prepared to risk his life and his ship to get them. Possibly he had been waiting a long time to make up his cargo, for, as will be seen, the ship was badly under-provisioned. No Roman captain of a ship supplying animals for the wild animal hunts of the arena would have been so improvident as this Gaulish captain.

Patricius had some difficulty in getting the captain to take him aboard – he had nothing with which to pay his passage. A factor which may have finally persuaded him was Patricius' obvious knowledge of dogs. Someone brought up in a good family in Pictland who had then been a shepherd for six years ought certainly to have known how to tend dogs. Perhaps Patricius was taken aboard to feed and clean out the hounds.

The ship duly left port and at the end of a three-days' voyage made Gaul, not at a frequented port but a spot which was either a desert island or a completely isolated and deserted stretch of coast. There were many areas of the Roman Empire, even in Italy, which had become completely deserted in this way, owing to the ceaseless activities of the barbarian sea-raiders. Stores were running out and there was nothing on which to feed the dogs. The ship's complement now set off on foot, away from the coast, to try to find the dwellings of men. No act could have spoken more about the value of a British hunting-dog. The famished beasts, trudging along at the end of leashes held by the crew, were actually worth more than the ship. Even so many of them had to be left behind, as they were too weak from lack of food to move. Patricius prayed to God for food and a miracle occurred, one of those miracles which, like many of them, seems afterwards the most natural thing that could have happened. A herd of wild swine appeared on the trackless wilderness. Instead of bolting straight away, they stayed within reach long enough for the starving men to kill enough of them to feed the dogs and themselves.

It would be an understatement to say that Patricius' stock went up with his companions from that moment. They abandoned any intentions of selling him as a slave in the first town they reached (why else should they have given him a free passage?) and henceforth treated him as one of themselves, offering him combs of wild honey found in the trees. During the course of his long and adventurous life Patricius was to be made a slave twice more, on the second occasion being sold to his fellow countrymen, the Picts, who released him. It was not until 432, after his mother and father – his last ties with Scotland – had died, that he was able to achieve his life's ambition and return to the island where he had been held prisoner. His thoughts had often gone out to Ireland and after its first apostle, Palladius, had died he was able to complete the work of evangelisation begun by him.

Patricius, or to give him the name by which he is known in the calendar, St Patrick, founded the Celtic Church which was to become a fruitful mother of saints and scholars. It was to Ireland and Scotland that the ravaged countries of barbarian Europe were to apply for teachers and church leaders. In monasteries founded by the Celtic monks the language and learning of the Roman Empire were preserved until the dark ages of barbarism were over. But for the dog-boat that brought St Patrick from Ireland to Gaul we should know almost nothing either about the dogs of classical antiquity or the civilisation of Greece and Rome.

Patrick had not merely helped to save Europe for Christianity and civilisation, he had also imbued the British with the love of animals which was henceforth to be one of their principal characteristics. The lives of the Celtic saints who were trained on his model breathe the fondness for animate life which he himself possessed in such a large measure.

St Patrick's people, the Picts, had stood outside the Roman Empire, though not beyond the reach of Roman evangelists. They had retained their native system of government and warfare, so that they were able to go on much as before when the Empire collapsed. During the barbarian invasions they gave a good account of themselves and by the eighth century, under the leadership of a mighty king, Angus (Oengus) son of Fergus, they had become the most powerful people in North Britain.

The Picts are a mysterious folk but one conclusion that can be formed about them was that they were great artists. Much of their artistic effort was concentrated in a series of great stone monoliths and crosses, influenced by Christian ideas but still full of national themes. The secular monuments may be described as a paean in stone to the joys of the hunt. Many of the hunting monoliths are sited near strongholds of the southern Pictish dynasties of Angus and Gowrie. Hunting scenes are characteristic of the whole group and appear on at least twenty of the stones. The game hunted is invariably a stag or a hind and it is always being pursued à force, that is, out in the open at full speed and not in an enclosure such as a circle of nets. Hounds follow the quarry and seize it by the flank or try to turn it. The dogs themselves look like smooth-coated Irish hounds or short-haired greyhounds. It is impossible to tell which breed they belong to because they are depicted according to the conventions of Pictish art. In Pictland the sculptor enjoyed giving a smooth, slick, silhouette-like outline to his figures. Even the huntsmen, galloping at full tilt, look as though they had had their long hair waved and set before they got into the saddle.

On the Hilton of Cadboll slab is the first portrait of a British huntress, a lady riding side-saddle. The speed and craft of the hounds is well suggested in this monolith, in which one dog turns the hind and another seizes it by the flank. Huntsmen on foot, blowing long, straight horns, accompany the hunt. Perhaps, as in the Roman hunt, they are starting the game, or perhaps the blasts they blow direct the movement of the hounds. Superbly modelled hounds and horses appear on an eighth-century slab from Eassie and on the monument of Ferat Mac Batot (846–9), one of the last kings of Gowrie, at St Vigeans in Angus. These Pictish monuments are of particular interest to dog-lovers because they are the oldest representations of British dogs that can be seen, standing in the open in the places where they were first set up. Even as a child I used to marvel at the wonderful preservation of these monuments and wonder what their purpose might be. Francis Klingender suggests that 'the prominent display of hunting-scenes on tombs of warriors or kings, their ceremonial character and the restriction to a single species of game, all suggest that hunting the stag had a special meaning for the ruling Pictish clans' (*Animals in Art and Thought to the End of the Middle Ages*).

As the pictures on the monoliths are usually accompanied by the strange and undeciphered Pictish sign language – symbols such as mirrors, combs, crescents and spirals – it may be assumed that the stones carried a message intelligible to the Picts, probably to their neighbours the Scots and to the English of Northumbria. What that message was can only be a matter for conjecture, but one of the few traditions about the Picts that their supplanters, the Scots, have bothered to preserve is that they were passionately fond of good dogs. Hector Boece, a Scottish chronicler writes:

Several young Pictish gentlemen visited King Crathlint [a Scots king] to hunt and make merry with him, but when they were ready to depart homewards, perceiving that the Scottish dogs did far excell theirs in beauty, speed, and strength, and also in endurance and wind, they got some of the Scots lords to present them with some dogs and bitches of the best breeds, and not content with that, they stole a hound from its keeper which belonged to the king, the best of all he had. When the Master of the Leash was told about this, he set off in pursuit of the thieves who had stolen the dog, intending to get it back from them. They refused, a quarrel broke out, they struck the Master with their boar spears and he died immediately. His servants raised a hue and cry, and some Scots who were coming back from hunting, attacked the Picts.

In view of the known fondness of the Picts for dogs, it may well be that some at least of these monuments record the exploits of some of their most notable hounds. Of course there are other possible explanations. The sculptured slabs may be records of famous hunts. This was an idea as old as the Pharaohs, who had scarabs carved to commemorate hunting exploits, and it was to have a long history in Scotland. When, for example, in the thirteenth century King John Baliol of Scotland visited his master Edward I of England and went hunting, he had the antlers of the stags he had killed nailed to trees in the forest, where they remained until vandals broke them off four centuries later. There may be another and a much simpler explanation of the monoliths: they may simply be 'No Trespassers' signs in and around the royal Pictish forests.

One thing at any rate is certain, the Pictish stones are unique in Europe in that they mingle dogs with Christian symbols in a way that was prohibited in the rest of Christendom. Here we can see the influence of the Celtic church, because artistic representations of dogs were taboo elsewhere in Church, because artistic representations of dogs were taboo elsewhere in work for churches or of an ecclesiastical nature was carried out, would have quoted the verse in Apocalypse 22:15, almost the last words in the Bible: 'Outside [the Heavenly Jerusalem] are the dogs and sorcerers and fornicators and murderers and idolaters, and everyone who loves and practises falsehood.' It is quite obvious that the word 'dog' is used symbolically here, as the dog cannot be accused of any of the sins mentioned in this passage – unless you count its fondness for its master as idolatry.

The love of dogs was characteristic of the whole Celtic world at this time. In Dark-Age Ireland, epic songs of the Fenian Cycle poetry, which reflects the spirit of the time, describe the dog as sharing the same bed as his master (not a difficult matter when bed and floor were one) and fighting alongside him in battle. 'Hounds, horses, and men lay alike slain in heaps on the field,' says one song. As usual in Irish poetry, hyperbole keeps breaking in, as when we are told of a fighting dog which grasped the axle tree of a chariot in its teeth and refused to let go its grip, even though its head had been cut off. Hounds went out to battle gorgeously clad in greaves of bronze and chains of silver ornamented with apples of gold. In Wales, where Irish hounds were cherished possessions worth a king's ransom, they were dressed in coats of purple, ornamented with gold and wore collars of rubies round their necks.

It seems evident from these tales that one of the parts of the dog's training took the form of schooling him to stand over the body of a dead or wounded master to defend it against all comers – war-dogs, wolves and human warriors.

Irish heroes often became identified with dogs in a mysterious and symbolic way. We have already mentioned Cú Chulainn and the mystic tie which unites him with dogs, so that he cannot eat their flesh. When he breaks this taboo, his luck runs out and he dies. Taureann, the aunt of Finn, is also mysteriously re-embodied as a hound, in whom everyone recognises the lady. Finn's son, Oisin, is tempted to leave Ireland and go to fairyland with the bribe of a white hound with tawny ears. While he is away from home time goes on more quickly than he thinks, as is often the case, and when he returns from fairyland he finds that all his friends have died. The old gods have disappeared and the day of the heroes has gone and that of the saints begun. Oisin is converted by Patrick and asks as a favour that he may take his hounds with him to Paradise. I think we can guess what the saint replied.

Scotland, an Irish colony on British soil, could not be unaffected by the Irish love of dogs. 'A thousand dogs fly off at once,' wrote Ossian, 'grey bounding through the heath. A deer fell by every dog, three by the white breasted Bran. He brought them in their flight to Fingal that the joy of the king might be great.'. . . 'Call,' said Fingal, 'call my dogs, the long bounding sons of the chase. Call whitebreasted Bran, and the surly strength of Luath. . . . Fillan and Fergus, blow the horn that the joy of the chase may arise, that the deer of Cromla may hear, and start at the lake of the roes!' Ossian, as transmitted by Macpherson may be inaccurate as to detail, but he certainly transmits the spirit of a people whose hearts were with their hounds.

Now we descend from the fantasies of poetry to the deceptions of forgery. I refer to the so-called 'Laws of Howell the Good'. For a century and more these institutes, a law code supposedly enacted by a king of South Wales at the beginning of the tenth century, have been referred to reverently by dog-lovers. Howell, penning his enactments at his hunting lodge in Carmarthenshire before transmitting them to the Pope for confirmation, found time to make a surprising number of references to dogs, considering how many other matters the Code contains.

Amongst the dogs he mentions are the *gellgi*, translated confidently as being 'large dun or bay-coloured buckhounds', *milgi* or 'greyhounds', *olrhëad* or 'sleuth hounds', *bytheuad* or 'harriers', *cholwyn* or 'spaniels', *bugeilgi* or 'shepherds' dogs', *ki-taeog* or 'peasants' dogs' and *callawet* or 'watch-dogs'. In passing it may be said that these Welsh names translated by Edward Ash, have been translated quite differently by other writers on the subject.

The harrier is only mentioned in connection with Howell's Code because 'There is no legal amount of money assigned for the loss of a harrier. There was no dog of that kind in the days of Howell the God, therefore the damages will have to go to arbitration.'

On the face of it Howell's code appears to present the reader with an enormous amount of information about the development of the dog in Britain. Much may be gathered from it directly, much more inferred. Dog historians have conjecturally traced the development of British dogs from the 'original' animals described by Howell. Thus the *ki-taeog* might well be the origin of our word 'cur', a word which has now acquired a pejorative meaning but which originally meant a shepherd's dog. *Corgi*, a dog's name not present in the Code, is another candidate for the origin of 'cur'. Historians have also tried to work out the value of particular dogs at this time according to the legal damages allocated to the loss or destruction of each kind of dog in the Code. Thus a royal buckhound was worth twenty shillings when trained, but only ten shillings before training, five shillings when a year old, two shillings and sixpence when a whelp in the kennel, and 'fifteen pence from its birth until it shall open its eyes'. As a stallion was quoted at twenty shillings, historians have assumed that the buckhound was particularly prized. The value of dogs in the Code descends rather quickly. A cur, even belonging to a king, was worth only fourpence. What was more, for a woman to call her husband a cur was such an insult that 'she was to pay him three cows or, if she preferred, receive three blows with a stick, the length of his forearm and the thickness of his middle finger, on any part of her person her husband pleases, except her head'.

The Code is concerned with many other subjects besides dogs: hunting is one of them. There is mention of a royal hunting establishment with a chief huntsman with hunters under him. One of the duties of the hunts-man was to care for wounded dogs and this care seems to have been fairly rudimentary as the only surgical instrument mentioned is a needle. The chief huntsman was engaged in regular hunting duties throughout most of the year. From Christmas to February he and his hounds were hunting the hinds. At Midsummer he began the chase of the harts and as winter set in he turned to the pursuit of the wild boar. The royal hunt did not pre-empt all the hunting there was to be had. Nobles might slip their hounds in pursuit of game after the royal hounds had been sent after it three times. Any traveller wounding a wild animal while travelling on the road through the royal forest might pursue it so long as it remained in view. Another hunting enactment the mildness of which compared with the Anglo-Saxon and Norman Forest Laws has often been commented on is that 'No man is to lose his life for a dog stolen, a bird, or a wild animal.' If stags entered corn, anyone might hunt them. Foxhunting and other hunting were free to anyone, even on private land belonging to another person: 'For the fox and the otter are always on the move, they have no haunts.'

We are only concerned with the Howell Code so far as it relates to dogs and what is said about them cannot possibly date from 930 – one of the dates suggested for its composition – but must have been framed in much later times. There are no manuscripts of the Welsh version of the code older than the twelfth century, so it is impossible to prove that the laws really originated in the way they were supposed to have done, from a meeting between the king, the Archbishop of Menevia, other bishops and clergy, the nobles of Wales and four laymen and two clerks from each 'comot' as-sembling in 'the white house on the river Tav'.

What grounds are there for regarding the provisions about dogs in the law code which, so far as I know, have never been questioned before, as a forgery? There are two notable omissions. Nothing is said about wolf-hounds, though we know that in 959 King Edgar of England demanded a tax in wolfsheads from his Welsh neighbours. No doubt Welsh wolves, like Welshmen, were fond of slipping over the border into England and creating mischief there. If there were wolves in Wales there must have been some kind of dog for hunting them, but it is not mentioned in the Code.

Then again, there appears to be no mention of the one dog we know to have been present in Wales in historic times, the great Irish hound. What makes it really impossible to accept Howell's Code at its face value, however, is the number of dogs involved – eight. How could a poor and troubled country such as Wales possibly have had eight different kinds of dogs when there is archaeological evidence for only *two* varieties in the much more settled and prosperous neighbouring English kingdom?

As usual for this period it is impossible to say exactly which breeds are represented by the two dogs known to have made up the Anglo-Saxon dog population. They were larger than those the remains of which had been found in previous periods.

It may well be asked why anyone should want to forge a code of laws and write into it bogus enactments relating to dogs? There are two other Welsh law codes and, unlike Howell's, both are admitted to be spurious. They are the Laws of Prince Dymal Moel Mud and the Laws of Marsia, to both of which a great antiquity was originally assigned. They were supposed to date from before the Roman invasion, or even from 400 BC. A forged law code could be the work of a misguided patriotic sentiment. Howell's Code, drawn up in its latest surviving form when the Parliamentary movement in England was very much in the air, might have been intended to prove that the Welsh were every bit as much concerned with forming democratic institutions as their English neighbours. Where someone goes to the trouble of forging a whole document, or in this case a whole series of documents, however, the assumption is that he hopes to profit from it in some way. Acceptance of Howell's Code, as it stood, meant that the Welsh would have been exempted from those very irksome regulations, the Norman Forest Laws, laws so draconian that not merely the Welsh but the English as well were constantly trying to evade them.

The Forest Code had begun with the last Anglo-Saxon kings and it was a reflection of the growing interest that the kings of England showed in their favourite pursuit. Hitherto, it might be assumed, they had been too busy fighting to have any time for hunting, but with Alfred the Great the royal house began a close connection with hunting which they were not to lose till the seventeenth century. Young Alfred had been a keen hunter since the age of twelve. He was an expert at the sport, able to instruct his kennel-men, huntsmen and other servants in their duties. No doubt his frequent journeys abroad had introduced him to continental hunting techniques. The royal kennels had always been well stocked. After King Athelstane defeated the Welsh king Constantine at the Battle of Brunanburgh in 937, he imposed on him a tribute of 'keen-scented hounds for hunting wild beasts'. Alfred travelled as far as Cornwall in search of sport, no doubt hunting with the methods we know to have been followed by his successors. These included driving boars up to the huntsman with hounds. One Anglo-Saxon grammatical dialogue describes how this was done and how the huntsman then killed them with a spear. A contemporary manuscript illustrates a hunter armed with a boar spear, which was furnished with a cross-piece to prevent the infuriated animal thrusting itself right up the spear shaft and tusking the hunter.

Another animal driven into nets was the deer. When St Edward the Confessor rode out to hunt, as he always did every day after he had heard divine service, and found that a peasant had broken down his deer nets, his wrath was terrible. 'By God and His mother,' he shouted at the churl who had allowed a herd of stags to escape, 'I would punish thee severely if I could trust myself to do it!' Deer were also hunted *à force* by being chased with a pack of hounds. Once King Edmund, Alfred's grandson, was pursuing a stag near Ceoddri at such a cracking pace that the stag bounded over a precipice, followed by the whole of the pack. Edmund was only able to rein in his horse on the very verge of the abyss. In the few seconds it took to do this he thought about his sins and decided to recall St Dunstan, whom he had exiled from the court.

Other quarries included the wild cattle of the forest, now confined to just one herd in Chillingham Castle, and the wolf. The wolf was evidently not a popular beast of the chase, possibly because a wolf-hunt took so long. The wolf is the most completely developed type of the trotting dog; no dog can outstay him when he trots.

In order to ensure that wolves were hunted, Anglo-Saxon kings sentenced criminals to hunt them as a punishment and also, as has been seen, enjoined the hunting of wolves as a tax upon the Welsh. One Welsh king reported to his English overlord that he had killed all the wolves in Wales, but this was merely an attempt to evade the tax.

The royal hunt was administered in a fairly modest way. Four thanes supervised it, and took charge of the royal forests. Deer-hunting was expressly reserved for the king or for those whom he graciously invited to share his sport. By the end of the Anglo-Saxon period the scope of the hunt's activities had risen considerably. St Edward the Confessor's hounds consumed an incredible quantity of bread. One reason for the increase in the numbers of royal hounds was the imposition of the Forest Laws by the Viking conqueror of England, Canute. These laws made it impossible for ordinary folk to hunt at all because they were forbidden hunting-dogs. Canute forbade the keeping of greyhounds by anyone except 'freemen' – people who were quite elevated on the social scale. Dogs kept within the area of the royal forests had to be mutilated, either by having a sinew split, or cut, or having the claws of the fore foot cut off. Exception was made in the case of *velteres*, dogs which were evidently a pet breed possibly small greyhounds. Just at the end of the Anglo-Saxon period there is a hint that there may have been more breeds in England than the two suspected by archaeologists. Another pet dog is mentioned in legend. Lodebroch, a Danish prince, is said to have visited Edmund, king of the East Angles, accompanied by his pet dog, a spaniel. This legend is probably as apocryphal as Howell's laws concerning dogs, as spaniels are usually assumed to have been unknown in England before the fourteenth century.

Edward the Confessor made no attempt to repeal the Forest Laws that Canute had imposed on his conquered kingdom. Like that other well-known English saint, Thomas à Becket, Edward was obviously able to renounce all the pleasures of life, except those which concerned the stable and the kennel. He enjoyed cheering on his fast hounds with his own voice and he probably had no intention of spoiling his own sport by liberating his subjects from Canute's oppressive laws. Moreover he may have been afraid that a more liberal policy towards the Forest Laws might lose him the support of his court nobles, who were allowed to join in the royal chase.

The Forest Laws, inaugurated during the Anglo-Saxon period and which were to become more and more oppressive during the reigns of the Norman and Angevin kings, are, like the Game Laws, one of the ways in which the existence of English dogs profoundly modified the lives of Englishmen. Most of the other privileges of the mediaeval kings of England could be justified somehow, but it always appeared to their subjects supremely unjust that they should have the monopoly of the best hunting. The so-called Laws of Howell the Good are examples of one kind of protest against the Forest Jurisdiction and there were to be plenty of others. Indeed protests against the Forest Laws were not to end until the laws themselves finally fell into disuse after 1688.

It was in the heat generated by the injustice of these laws that many of the liberties of England were to be won.

Opposite: 'Prick-eared cur' depicted on the mosaic floor of a private house in Pompeii, and now in the Naples Museum. Such mosaic pictures bear the legend '*Cave Canem*' or 'Beware of the dog'.

Below left: Representation of the 'prick-eared cur' on the left, with another Roman dog, in the mosaic from Corinium (Cirencester). This mosaic, now in the Cirencester Museum, is illustrated here from a nineteenth-century antiquary's drawing. The subject of the whole mosaic is 'The Seasons'. *Below right:* A Romano-British Castor Ware goblet, showing a greyhound. Castor Ware was produced in a number of localities in Britain, notably Gloucestershire.

Below: This Castor Ware design shows a greyhound pursuing a stag.

Shepherd's Dog

Below: Mastiff

Bottom: Bull Dog
All from
illustrations to
*The Sportsman's
Cabinet* by
William Taplin,
London, 1803,
painted by Philip
Reinagle (1749-
1833) and
engraved by John
Scott (1774-1827).

Top: Scotch Deer
Hound.

Above: Irish Wolf Hound.
Both the above drawn and engraved
by W. R. Smith for Edward Jesse's
Anecdotes of Dogs, London, 1846.

Opposite: The 'Irish Greyhound',
or as it is called throughout
this book, The Great Irish Hound,
from *The Sportsman's Cabinet*.

Rough- and smooth-haired greyhounds as shown in the *Livre de la Chasse* of Gaston Phoebus, 1387, now in the Bibliotheque Nationale, Paris (ms ffr 616).

Manuscript illustration from the *Livre de la Chasse*, showing the proper way of arranging a kennel.

Raches or running hounds are shown in this manuscript illustration to the same book.

Bloodhound, from an illustration to *The Sportsman's Cabinet*.

The Southern Hound, from the same source.

Above: 'Otter terrier, drawn and engraved by W. R. Smith for Edward Jesse's *Anecdotes of Dogs*, London, 1846.

Opposite: Poodle, drawn by H. Weir and engraved by Dalzeil for J. G. Wood's *The Illustrated Natural History*, London (no date).

Below: Water Spaniel, from the same source.

Maltese Dog.

Spaniel.

Pomeranian.
All these drawings by H.
Weir and engraved by Dalzeil
for J. G. Wood's *The
Illustrated Natural History*,
London (no date).

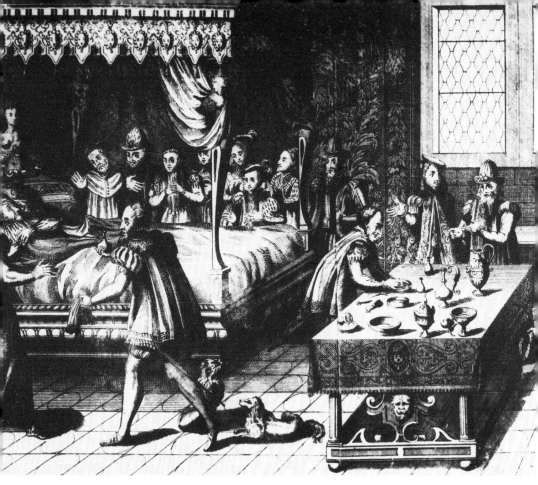

Above: The only contemporary portrait to show Mary Queen of Scots associated with a dog. This engraving of Henri II on his death-bed with Mary at his side, also shows two French griffons on the floor. It is from Perrissin and Tortorels *Guerres, massacres et troubles advenus en France*, Lyons, 1569-70.

Spaniels, from Edward Jesse's *Anecdotes of Dogs*, London, 1846.

2

The Middle Ages

By comparison with the tangled undergrowth of classical antiquity, the Middle Ages seem like a forest where broad rides have been cut and where attractive open clearings open on every side. At the same time it is a forest of vast extent, which it is difficult to compass adequately, while the clearings offer so many attractive vistas that it is tempting to stray down some of them. Yet, disregarding such distracting side issues, it is possible to sum up the role of the dog in the mediaeval period under just a few headings: it was a warrior which fought on the battlefield beside its master and guarded his castle in times of peace; it was the unwitting protagonist of the long struggle over the Forest Laws; it was the faithful ally of man in the hunting-field and his companion out of it.

The place of the war-dog, or bodyguard-dog in mediaeval England is symbolised by the presence, under Guy's Tower in Warwick Castle, of a miniature castle between the tower and the curtain wall. Its sloping walls, built from the same stone as the castle itself, are pierced not by a doorway or a sentry box, but by an opening only large enough to admit one of the giant war-dogs of the Middle Ages. This feudal dog kennel stood at the doorway of the Master Tower, the headquarters of the castle and the home of its owner. Here couched the savage Alaunt, the deep-fanged Talbot and, grimmest of all, the great Irish hound; retainers whom no treachery could seduce or allurement bribe and who would relinquish their loyalty to their master only with life itself. The war-dogs of England were adversaries that anyone might dread to meet in open battle. 'They seized the bold bull and slew the ferocious boar, neither did the majestic lion them intimidate.' Yet what made them dreaded was not so much their physical strength and wild ferocity, as they dashed into battle, clad in complete suits of armour, or with no other defence than a wide gilded collar with their master's name and arms to protect the jugular veins, so much as the intuitive powers with which the breeds were credited and which some specimens really did possess. So the secret assassin, the man whom Chaucer describes as 'the smiler with the knife under the cloak', might well think twice before he passed the fortified kennel at the foot of the Master Tower at Warwick and saw the four-legged sentinel looking at him attentively out of its brown eyes.

Not merely did the war-dog protect its master during his lifetime. It would straddle his wounded or dead body and defy all attempts to carry it off from the battlefield until it too lay dead.

'Of all animals,' wrote the Welsh Gerald de Barri in the twelfth century, 'the dog is most attached to man, and recognises him most readily. Sometimes, when deprived of his master, he pines and dies, and he will brave even death for his master's sake, ready to die with him or for him.' Gerald gave an example from his own personal experience to show what he meant. A certain Welshman called Cadwalladon, 'through inveterate malice', murdered his brother Owen, but not before Owen's greyhound had hurled itself at the assassins and wounded several of them, being pierced with seven different wounds by arrows and lances. Miraculously, the dog, which was probably a great Irish hound, survived. William Earl of Gloucester ordered it to be nursed back to health and then forwarded it to King Henry II, who was so fond of hounds and hunting that he was reproached with spending more time in the hunting-field than the Lord's anointed ought to do.

Another example of Gerald's is also taken from Wales. The Welsh had inflicted a sharp defeat on Henry II's army in a wooded defile called Coleshill, in Flintshire. Among the dead left on the field was a young Welshman who had been killed trying to force his way through the king's army. His greyhound faithfully stood guard over the body for eight days without food or water, driving off attacks made on its master's body by birds of prey, wolves and other dogs 'with a wonderful attachment'. 'Would a son have done this for his father?' asks Gerald and adds that 'as a mark of favour to the dog, which was almost starved to death, the English, although bitter enemies to the Welsh, ordered the body, now nearly decomposed, to be buried with all the usual rites.'

There are other examples of men being protected by their dogs on the battlefield, in time for their lives to be saved. Sir Piers Legh, who fought at Agincourt, was struck down and badly wounded. His mastiff bitch, which he had brought with him to the field, stood over him till he could be carried away. He was brought back to England and died there of his wounds, his bitch attending the funeral. The strain of Legh Hall mastiffs which had originated with the puppies of this bitch was kept up till as late as the nineteenth century.

Well might Shakespeare exclaim in *Henry V*: 'That island of England breeds very valiant creatures; their mastiffs are of unmatchable courage.' Yet the mastiff, as has been already noticed, was only one of the breeds of English war-dogs, all of which were, if not native to the country, at least residents of very long standing.

The greatest of all war-dog breeds, the dog round which most legends have clustered, was the gigantic Irish hound, an animal which its admirers referred to in the same breath as being either a greyhound or a wolfhound.

The name 'grey hound' did not necessarily denote the colour of the beast. The hound presented by William Earl of Gloucester to King Henry II had a splendid parti-coloured coat. Originally the 'grey' of 'greyhound' had been spelt 'grae' or 'gre', meaning quality, as in our own word 'degree'. 'Grae', a corruption of the Latin word *gradus*, denoted that the beast was of ancient lineage, as indeed it was. Its coat could be sandy-coloured, red, pale yellow or even white. Traditionally the hounds which accompany the Queen of Faery in Celtic legend have white coats, a belief which may be a reminiscence of Celtic history.

It was not the colour of its coat but the speed of its attack and the impetus of its charge that made the great hound formidable. It was the size of a calf, as one ancient wolfhound's skull, recovered from a bog in Ireland, indicates. The skull is 17 inches long, just over a quarter longer than the skull of any modern specimen of the 'restored' modern breed. Modern specimens may stand as tall as 38 inches, so the wolfhound in its palmy days must have been about four feet high. It is necessary to emphasise that the great Irish hound is very much a breed of the past. A specimen figured by William Taplin in 1803 stood a mere 30 inches high. Taplin added that the dog looked like a cross between a greyhound and a mastiff, had a long muzzle and short ears, with a deep flank, straight, long legs, and sandy-red or pale-yellow coat. Modern specimens tend to be a dark iron-grey – another indication that the true breed has not been recovered.

Formidable in appearance, the hound was winning in its disposition. Though ferocious as a lion in combat, it was as quiet as a lamb in the family circle. It was thus an ideal bodyguard-dog, especially for a child, who would have needed protection from the other war-dogs of the day, the mastiff and Alaunt. The Irish hound had the knack of knowing real friends from pretended ones, no doubt because it could detect the smell emitted by the nervous or guilty individuals whom it encountered. In the mediaeval Icelandic saga of Burnt Njal, a character named Olaf offers his friend an Irish hound as a present. 'He is big,' he says, 'and no less useful than a brave warrior; besides it is part of his nature that he has man's wit, and he will bay at every man whom he knows to be your foe, but never at your friends. He can see, too, in any man's face whether he means well or ill towards you, and he will lay down his life to be true to you.'

The sagas and romances have more than one instance of a bodyguard-hound intervening at the last moment to save its charge. If the hand of an assassin appears round the jamb of the door, grasping a knife or reaching for the cradle where the baby charge of the dog is sleeping, the Irish hound leaps for the hand, grasps it in his jaw, and severs it at the wrist. There is nothing improbable in an Irish hound being able to perform just such a feat. At the end of the nineteenth century, when it had dwindled very much in size and spirit, supposedly after being proscribed in the rebellion of '98, a hound put through its paces ran down and killed a deer single-handed. This happened in England, as Irish deer were already extinct, like

Irish wolves. The extinction of the hound was due much more to the fact that its function as a deer and a wolf killer were over than to any political cause.

The most famous Irish hound bodyguard is, of course, the dog Gelert. In 1205 King John sent an Irish hound as a present to his son-in-law, Llewelyn the Great. It was characteristic of John's meanness that he sent a single dog, not a leash of them, as was normal. (John Dundon noted in 1698, 'I saw in this house . . . wolf-dogs, or the long Irish greyhounds, a pair of which kind has often been a present for a king.') Gelert became a great favourite of Llewelyn, who was fond of hunting and had a hunting-box at the foot of Snowdon. One day Llewelyn set out for the chase. Gelert refused to follow him and stayed at home instead. With Gelert absent, his master could find no enjoyment in his hunting, he returned home and, to his horror, Gelert met him at the door, its muzzle a mask of blood, its fangs dripping gore. Aghast, Llewelyn sprang past his dog to the room where he had left his infant son in the cradle. The cradle was overturned, the clothes and walls spattered with blood and there was no sign of the baby anywhere. Distraught with passion, Llewelyn drew his sword and plunged it through the Irish hound's heart. As Gelert uttered its death howl a baby's wail echoed from beneath the cradle. Llewelyn lifted it and found beneath it his baby, unharmed. Nearby lay the body of a grim wolf, still bearing the marks of Gelert's teeth in its throat. It was the wolf's blood which had bespattered the nursery and the faithful guardian.

Overcome with grief, Llewelyn picked up the body of Gelert, carried it outside the walls of his hunting-seat and buried it by the side of the road, adding a cairn of stones. To this day the place is known as Beddgelert and thousands of pilgrims visit it, the only dog's grave to be a place of regular resort anywhere in the world.

Though the legendary Gelert probably had a real-life counterpart, the modern version of its story is just as much a forgery as the laws of Howell the Good. In 1793 a man called David Pritchard took over the landlordship of the Royal Goat Inn in Beddgelert, which at that time was called Beth Kellarth or Kelert, after the name of a Welsh saint. Pritchard had heard the story of the dog which saved its master's son's life at the expense of its own and invented the name 'Gelert' for the dog. He introduced Llewelyn as the hero of the story because he was connected with a nearby abbey. With the help of the parish clerk Pritchard built up a cairn near to his inn. Apparently he went to the trouble of actually burying a dog under the cairn, because when it was excavated the remains were found under it, remains too small to have been those of an Irish wolfhound. The 'grave of Gelert' became a tourist attraction and brought a lot of custom to the inn.

Although the modern version of the myth originates with Pritchard, the story was a very old one in his time. It was already well-known before the twelfth century, when Llewelyn lived, and it occurs among the fables of a fifth-century Welsh saint, Cadog the Wise, or Catwg Ddoeth. There is even a Welsh proverb which says: 'I am as sorry as the man who killed the greyhound.' Though Sir George Dasent has pointed out that the story of the dog which protects a child, only to be slain for its trouble, is a common one in mediaeval legend, his observations do not really invalidate the existence of an historical Gelert. In a moment or two I will mention the second best-known story in connection with an Irish hound, the dog of Montargis. The story of this dog, which detects its master's murderer, has also been dismissed as a fable because many versions of the same story occur over a long period of time. Yet there is no reason to suppose that such an incident occurred only once in history. Indeed we know it did not, because in the nineteenth century Sir Astley Cooper, the great anatomist, gives a very precise and scientific account of how a dog did detect a murderer in circumstances not very different from those which surrounded the dog of Montargis. Yet Cooper had never heard of the mediaeval dog, and even if he had was too objective an historian to have let himself be influenced by the story. In defending their charge, in avenging their murdered master, dogs merely conform to the instincts imposed on them by centuries of breeding and training.

Unlike the story of Gelert, which is placed vaguely somewhere in the thirteenth century, the tale of the Dog of Montargis is supposed to have occurred in the year 1371, in the France of Charles VI. The setting was French, but the dog was decidedly British, being a great Irish hound. A certain French noble, Aubri de Montdidier, was murdered while hunting in the Forest of Bondi by a hunting companion, Macaire, and buried under a tree. His wolfhound was not present at the murder – it had probably bounded off in chase of a deer – but it returned to the scene of the crime and remained couched on its master's grave till, driven by the pangs of hunger, it made its way to Paris. There it made a clamorous howling at the door of a house belonging to a close friend of Montdidier and when the friend opened the door it seized him by the sleeve and led him to the grave in the forest. A search revealed Aubri's body and his friend adopted the hound as his own.

Then, while accompanying its new master to court, the dog accidentally encountered Macaire. It instantly leapt at his throat and was only dragged from him with the greatest of difficulty. This incident attracted a good deal of attention because an unprovoked attack on an innocent stranger was not one of the characteristics of Irish wolfhounds. (When John Dundon visited the house of Sir Murragh na Mart O'Flahertie, in Ireland, he noticed that the eighteen great Irish hounds owned by his host 'were as quiet among us as lambs without any noise or disturbance.')

As the hound showed the same hatred for Macaire whenever they met in future, curious folk recalled that there had been rumours of a quarrel between Macaire and Aubri. Charles VI ordered both parties to be brought before him. The hound scented Macaire in a room full of twenty courtiers and leapt at his throat. The king decided that the circumstantial evidence of

Macaire being the murderer of Aubri was now so strong that he should be given the chance of clearing himself if he could.

As it was impossible for the hound to appear as a witness against him in a court of law, the trial should be by Ordeal of Battle. By this process a judicial combat took place in which it was believed that the innocent would always win. All sorts of questions were referred to trial by combat in the Middle Ages, even such unusual questions as whether the Spanish Church should drop the Mozarabic liturgy from its service books. A combat between a man and an animal was absolutely unique, however. One of the features of a trial by combat was that both sides had to swear on the sacrament that they believed in the rightness of their cause. The dog could not do this, so one of the royal princes stepped in and took the oath on his behalf.

The fight was arranged to take place between Macaire and the dog on the *ísle de la cité*. Dense crowds, or the swiftly flowing Seine, hemmed in the two combatants. There was no possible way of escape, it would be a duel to the death – and God defend the right! As a counterbalance to the natural superiority of the hound, Macaire was armed with a club, the usual weapon in combat trials, while the dog was given a large barrel into which it could retreat to draw breath if it felt hard pressed.

When the hound was slipped off the leash it made an instant dart at its adversary, running round him, avoiding his blows and darting in to snap at him whenever occasion occurred. It was in vain that Macaire tried to keep up with his adversary, twisting round and round to beat it off as it continually altered its direction of attack. Gradually the constant exertion and the weight of the leather armour allowed to combat ordealists, not to speak of the weight of a bad conscience, began to tell on him. Macaire dropped his cudgel end just enough for the Irish hound to jump in past his guard. It bounded forward and seized its adversary by the throat. Lying on the ground with his jugular veins between the hound's great fangs, Macaire was just able to shout out that he really was guilty and would someone pull this fiendish creature away from him so that he could go and be hanged?

If the Irish wolfhound was the image of the perfect, gentle knight, a lion on the battlefield and a lamb out of it, the Alaunt was just the opposite. It was the type of those mediaeval knights, such as William Wallace and the Black Prince, who seem to be overcome by a frenzy for destruction. The Alaunt is spoken of in the Middle Ages as being a completely individual breed of dog, a breed now extinct unless some of its blood continues in the English mastiff, a dog to which the Alaunt was apparently closely allied. It has been pointed out that the mediaeval mastiff did not look like one of the modern breed and may even have been a different type of dog altogether; well, the Alaunt certainly looked a little like a modern mastiff.

The best Alaunts came from Spain, where they were used for bull-baiting, and even nowadays bull- and bear-baiting dogs are called *alanos* there. The dreadful pastime of animal-baitings had already taken root in

England by mediaeval times, but it was not nearly so widely practised as it was later to be.

The chronicler Fitzstephen, writing in 1174, a time when stags, bucks, boar and wild cattle abounded in the forest north of London, tells us . . .

many citizens take delight in birds, as sparrow hawks, goss hawks and such like, and in dogs, to hunt in the woody ground. The citizens have the right of hunting in Middlesex, Hertfordshire, the whole of the Chilterns, and in Kent as far as the water of Cray. . . . In winter almost every holiday, before dinner, foaming boars fight for their heads, and boar pigs armed with murderous tusks, must be added to the bacon, or gigantic bears have violent combats with their opponents, the dogs.

It is quite possible that some Alaunts were imported to take part in the London animal-baitings. They were to be found in France as well as Spain, where they were described by Gaston de Foix, about whom more will be said later. A very doubtful tradition ascribed the origin of the Alaunts, and their name, to people called the *Alani*, who invaded Gaul and later overran Spain, bringing these dogs with them. In Foix's account of the Alaunt it will be seen that there were really *two* dogs which passed under this name, if not more:

An Alaunt is of the manner and nature of hounds. And the good Alaunts are those which men call 'Alaunts gentle' (that is, well-bred Alaunts). There are others which men call 'Alaunts veutereres', and others again are Alaunts of the butchery. Gentle Alaunts should be made and shaped as a greyhound, in all things except for the head, which should be great and short. And although there are Alaunts of all colours, the true colour of a good Alaunt, and that which is most common, is white with black spots about the ears, small eyes, and white ears standing up with sharp points.

More attention should be paid to the training of an Alaunt than to any other dog, because its shape and strength make it capable of wreaking greater destruction than any other creature. What is more, usually Alaunts are hare-brained by nature and they do not have as much good sense as many other dogs have. An Alaunt seeing a man running to catch a horse has been known to attack the horse. They also attack oxen, sheep, and swine, any other beasts, other hounds and men. For it has been known for Alaunts to kill their masters.

In every way Alaunts are treacherous and malicious, and more foolish and hare-brained than any other kind of dog. And no man ever saw three Alaunts which were well conditioned and good in a row. For the good Alaunt should run as fast as a greyhound, and any beast that he can catch he should hold with his jaws and not leave it. For an Alaunt by his very nature holds faster when he bites than can three greyhounds of the best sort that any man can find. And therefore it is the best hound to hold and to seize all manner of beasts and keep them fast.

When an Alaunt is well-conditioned and perfect, men hold that he is the best of all hounds. But men find few that are perfect.

A good Alaunt should love his master and follow him and help him in all eventualities and do whatever his master commands. A good Alaunt should go fast and be hardy to take all kinds of beasts without swerving, and hold fast and not leave the quarry. He should be well-conditioned and completely obedient to his master, and when he is such a dog, men hold, as I have said that he is the best hound there can possibly be to take all kinds of beasts.

The other kind of Alaunt is called 'veuterere'. They are shaped almost like a greyhound, they have a great head, great lips and great ears, and with such dogs, men aid themselves in baiting the bull, and at hunting the wild boar, for it is their nature to hold fast, but they are heavy and ugly, and if they are killed by the wild boar or the bull it is not a great loss. And when they can overtake a beast they bite it and hold it fast, but by themselves they could never take a beast unless greyhounds were with them to make the beast slow down.

The other kind of Alaunt is the Alaunt of the butchery, such that you may see in large towns. They are called great butchers' hounds, and the butchers keep them to help them bring in their beasts that they buy in the country, for if an ox escape from the butchers that lead him, his hounds would go and take and hold until his master had come, and should help him to bring it to the town again. These Alaunts cost little to feed as they eat the offal found in the butcher's row. Also they keep their master's house. They are good for bull-baiting and for hunting wild boar, whether it be with greyhounds at the tryst, [A drive or *battue* which took place in a part of a wood enclosed with fences.] or with running-hounds at bay within the covert.

For when a wild boar is within a strong thicket of wood perhaps the running-hounds may not be able to flush him out although they try all day. And when men let such mastiffs run at the boar they take him in the thick wood so that any man can slay him, or they make him come out of his lair, so that he shall not remain long at bay.

Gaston de Foix's words, as translated by Edward Duke of York, show that there was a strong connection between the Alaunt and bull-baiting. York has actually added the words 'bull-baiting', twice to the text where they did not occur in the French original. What is more Alaunt seems, in the light of the quotation just given, to be a very imprecise descriptive term – like so many terms used in historic times to describe dogs. It covers a large, mastiff-like dog, which is even described as a mastiff at one point in the text. It refers to another, quite different type of dog, which was a large greyhound, perhaps a great Irish hound. Other kinds of Alaunts are mentioned, which are presumably not so full-bred; these are the butcher's dogs.

The connection between Alaunts and butchers' bulls shows how bull-baiting could have evolved in England, if it were not imported from the Continent. The butchers' Alaunts would be despatched to bring back a bull which had turned round and bolted back towards its pasture. Often the bull would be unwilling to come. Occasionally it would fly into a fury, become a 'mad bull', and a great combat would ensue. One mediaeval magnate was so diverted with this spectacle that he left a legacy to provide an annual bull-baiting.

As well as bull-baitings, which had become an institution in Stamford as early as 1209, there were bull-runnings, rather like those seen in Spain today. 'Old John of Gaunt, time-honoured Lancaster', founded just such an annual running at Tutbury, in Staffordshire.

On the day appointed for the event, the people of the town proceeded in a body to church, then dined, and afterwards went to the Priory Gate in Tutbury. There everyone had to stand back save the minstrels, in whose honour the running had been founded. Led by the King of Music, the minstrels assailed the bull and tried to cut off an ear or a piece of hide. If they succeeded the bull belonged to them and it was claimed by the King of Music. If they failed and the bull escaped into Derbyshire, it belonged to the Lord Prior.

Though this was a bull-running, not a bull-baiting, it only needed the intervention of the butcher's dogs, those fast-holding Alaunts, which would have helped to escort the bull to the Priory Gate, to turn it into a bull-baiting. It is not difficult to see in the Alaunt the ancestor of the bull-baiting mastiffs of the Renaissance, as well as of the much more modern bulldog.

Everything that York has to say about the Alaunt's ferocity and irritability is borne out by other writers. When in Chaucer's poem, *The Knight's Tale*, King Lycurgus is brought upon the scene, twenty white Alaunts, as large as steers, precede his chariot. These dogs are trained to catch the deer or the lion, but to prevent them seizing anything except their legitimate prey, the mouths of the animals which escort Lycurgus are closed with studded gold muzzles.

Several origins have been suggested for the Alaunt. The country of the *Alani* in the Caucasus, Sclavonia, Spain, Albania and Gaul have all been indicated as their country of origin. It seems much more probable that the Alaunt was a native British breed, descended from the fighting-dogs of the ancient Britons. Oppian describes these fighting-dogs as having light brown eyes, truncated muzzle, like a monkey, loose folded skin above the brows and a broad back, poised on tall, muscular legs. This description tallies with pictures of Alaunts which have survived from the Middle Ages, as do the habits of the dog itself. It was so ferocious that it could not be coupled with other dogs in the chase but on the battlefield it came into its own. The period that elapsed between the end of the Middle Ages proper and the development of accurate firearms, capable of picking off fighting-dogs at a distance, saw a considerable use of Alaunts. Henry VIII took 400 of them on his expedition to fight with Charles V against the king of France. Each dog was equipped with 'good iron collars, after the fashion of that country', and was led by a soldier. At the siege of Valencia English war-dogs took heavy toll not merely of their human foes, but of the war-dogs opposed to them. Alaunts were employed as sentries to keep guard at night, they could also be released on the enemy foot or cavalry to throw them into confusion.

Alaunts were not bred only in England; they were employed in several European countries and breeding kennels existed in Milan and probably Spain as well. Though these soldier-dogs had been continuously employed in battle since the time of the Assyrians, the arrival of accurate firearms brought about their disappearance from warfare. As is so often the case, once the purpose for which the breed had been evolved had disappeared, the dog itself followed shortly afterwards. Nowadays the Alaunt is extinct, like many other fine breeds, it survives only in heraldic art, where two Alaunts form the supporters of the shield of Lord Dacre of Hurstmonceaux, the Fiennes coat-of-arms.

Curiously enough, the next war-dog to be considered, the Talbot, has also a place in heraldry. Two Talbots support the coat-of-arms of the Shrewsbury family, whose family name is Talbot. Were the supporters assumed because of a punning allusion to the name, or did the family have something to do with popularising the breed? It is certain that dogs often become associated with people who had no responsibility for them. The hounds of St Hubert, about which much will be said later, had no connection with the saint.

The Talbot is the modern bloodhound, or a dog sufficiently like it to be recognisable as such. It was called a 'bloodhound', 'limer', 'limehound', 'liam' and 'Talbot' at various stages in its history, but there is no doubt that all these names refer to the same animal. The Talbot, or bloodhound, was a dog which had been brought from the hunting-field on to the battlefield to carry out a very specialised task, tracking a fleeing enemy. The suitability of the Talbot for this purpose had been discovered through observation of its tenacity in following a blood trail left by a stricken deer (hence its name of 'bloodhound'). A trail of blood leaves a much stronger scent than the mere lingering scent of human sweat and other bodily smells. A deer struck by an arrow would bleed, even if it were only slightly. The limer or Talbot could follow up this trail, even though the drops of blood were far apart. Once on a blood trail the tenacity of the dog was remarkable: it would never leave a trail, no matter how cold and unpromising, until it was called off. This fixity of purpose on the part of dogs has often been admired by humans, who are themselves all too prone to be distracted from their main aim by trifles. When the Dominican friars, one of the new religious orders founded in the High Middle Ages, adopted the punning nickname of Domini canes, 'hounds of God', they probably had the unswerving pursuit of the Talbot in mind.

The man who fled from a battlefield in the Middle Ages would probably have a much stronger blood scent about him than a stricken deer. Even if he were not himself wounded he might have 'waded in red blood to the knee', as the Border ballads put it. During mediaeval times, and for long after, it was essential to pick up the trail of fugitives. Their trail would show where the main body of the defeated army had retreated to. The fugitives might include men of rank and importance such as Robert the Bruce and Wallace, both trailed by English Talbots. The fugitives might well be carrying valuable spoil and this applied especially to the cattle-raids which were the commonplace of the English and Scottish border.

The Talbot is an extraordinarily interesting dog because it has such a long history and such a wide geographical distribution. When the last moss-trooper had abandoned cattle raiding, the Talbot continued to be used to track down sheep-stealers. Even a harrier with Talbot blood could be pressed into service to deal with these big-game poachers. One harrier called 'Trueman' which hunted in the west country during the nineteenth century led its fellow harriers in pursuit of a hare and then came to a patch of ground sprinkled with blood. This was enough for the hound to begin a chase which led the pack to the secret cave headquarters of a gang of sheep-stealers and poachers.

It was on the American continent that the bloodhound was to find its greatest scope. Imported by Philip II of Spain from England to the New World, it was to be used to track Indian and Spanish fugitives and, later, escaped negro slaves. In this chapter, however, we are only concerned with the activities of the 'sleuth hound', yet another name for the Talbot during the Middle Ages.

The two most important Talbot man-hunts of mediaeval times have been already mentioned, the search for Wallace and Bruce. On one occasion during the Scots war of resistance to Edward I 700 men set off to find Wallace in his hiding-place in the wilderness. In their midst, according to the Scot who retails the legend, 'Blind Harry the Minstrel', there marched a sleuth-hound bred in Gisland in Cumberland. It had been so well trained 'on Esk and Ledaill' that once it had scent of a blood trail it would follow it to the end. The party of English trackers caught up with Wallace and there was a bitter fight in which the giant with the two-handed sword took a heavy toll of his pursuers. In the end the disparity of numbers forced him to flee once more, with only sixteen companions. Once again the Talbot showed its capacity to follow a single quarry through a very mixed and crossed trail, whether that quarry were a wounded deer or a blood-marked man. The hound refused to be shaken off and the pursuers hurried on relentlessly. One of Wallace's party, an Irishman called Fawdon, a big, burly man who had been wounded during the skirmish, found himself unable to keep up with the rest of the party. Wallace cut Fawdon down. The fugitives ran on; the pursuers followed hotly behind them. Then the hound came up to where Fawdon lay and refused to go any farther. Wallace's ruthless act had saved the rest of the party. No doubt his trail had been mingled with Fawdon's, perhaps he had been helping him to walk, with an arm round him.

Wallace's successor as the leader of Scottish resistance, Robert the

Bruce, managed to escape from not just one, but two bloodhound man-hunts. On the first occasion, pursued by the men of Carrick in Galloway, he turned at bay and drove off his pursuers in a narrow pass. His second chase was a much more serious affair, as it was led by one of his own dogs. Bruce had raised this Talbot himself, giving it its food with his own hands (a usual proceeding in those days with this kind of hound), so no dog could have been better acquainted with his scent. Somehow his great enemy, John of Lorn, got possession of the hound and with Sir Aymer de Valence and a great company of men of Lothian and Englishmen, 800 or more, set off in pursuit of Bruce. The Talbot hurried along at the head of its new owners; for once the supposed intuitive power that the great mediaeval hounds possessed – the power of sensing the thoughts of those who intended to harm their masters – was in abeyance. There was nothing the Talbot wanted more than to be reunited with the hunted king.

Bruce hurried deeper and even deeper into the forest and there divided his party into three groups, telling them to scatter in different directions. Then with the pursuers hard on his heels, he plunged off at a tangent, only to find that the Talbot was still following his party and no other. Bruce split his little band once more. Now he was left with only his foster brother. Once more, inexorably, the hound chose the right trail. By this time the king had probably begun to suspect that he was being followed by his own favourite dog; he may even have recognised its voice if it gave tongue during the chase. Nor could there be any doubt in the mind of John of Lorn that it was Robert whom he was pursuing. He hastily handed over the dog to five of his best men-at-arms and ordered them to follow swiftly in the Bruce's footsteps while he and the rest of the party came up as quickly as they could.

The whole of history now rested on the collar of a dog, tugging at the leash as it bounded forward on the well-loved and well-remembered scent of its master. If the hunt had succeeded then the whole world we know would have been immeasurably changed. The Stuarts would never have come to the English throne, bringing with them the fatal dynastic curse of the 'royal disease' porphyria which was to paralyse the energies of George III during his most formative years. There might have been no American Revolution; there almost certainly would never have been an English Revolution: England might have been re-absorbed into the Continent of Europe, as she had been by the Romans.

It was at this juncture that the Talbot played a decisive part. Bruce decided to turn at bay and fight the five picked men-at-arms while he and his foster brother still had breath enough. In a desperate encounter the brother killed one of Lorn's men, and Bruce the other four. I do not think Bruce fought unaided: odds of four to one are a little too long even for such a hero. Probably the hound, reunited with its master at last, realised where its true loyalty lay and attacked Lorn's men.

Bruce and his foster brother now plunged into a stream that lay in their path, waded down it for a bow-shot and emerged on the farther side, confident that they had thrown their pursuers off the scent.

Of the three English war-dogs, none was more characteristic of the Middle Ages than the mastiff. During the Hundred Years War numerous mastiffs accompanied the English army to France and the role played by one of them, the dog belonging to Sir Piers Legh of Lyme Hall, in Cheshire, has already been mentioned. The Lyme Hall strain of mastiff breed was kept up almost to our own day, a Lyme Hall mastiff being exhibited at the Crystal Palace Exhibition in 1872.

Mastiff dogs were a familiar sight in the Middle Ages and two are sculptured on the tomb of the Beauchamps in Worcester Cathedral. William Harrison describes the breed in 1586. 'The mastiff,' he says, 'is a huge, stubborn, ugly and impetuous hound, with a large frame that renders it slow of movement. Its natural savagery is increased by the course of training to which it is submitted, being pitted against bears, bulls, or lions, if the latter could be found.' The great dogs were taught to fight either with a collar to defend their throats, or unarmoured. Many collars that must have belonged to mastiffs have survived. Some are garnished with protruding spikes, others more ornamental. Most of the collars which have survived, such as those to be found in Warwick and the superb collection preserved at Leeds Castle, in Kent, are of post-mediaeval date. They are practical, made of hammered iron, or ornamental. The ornamental collars are often superbly embossed, gilded and bear the owner's names or coat-of-arms. There is abundant evidence for the employment of collars in mediaeval tapestries and illuminations.

Though the mastiff was occasionally employed to drive wild cattle and boars or tackle that hard-biting opponent, the badger, it was essentially a dog trained to face human opponents, either on the battlefield or while protecting its master's home. Mastiffs were trained with a man who wore an armoured coat or who defended himself with a pike-staff, club or sword. When not in training the mastiff seems to have spent a good deal of its time chained up at the gate, hence one of its names, 'tie dog'. It was also called a 'ban dog'.

The mastiff was so much of a security-dog that many legends have clustered around its ability to detect evil intentions on the part of seemingly innocent visitors. A story about this intuitive ability is related of a dog which belonged to Sir Henry Lee. Sir Henry, who lived at Ditchley long after the Middle Ages, had a mastiff who guarded the house and yard but who had never been paid any particular attention by its master. Though really an outdoor dog, the mastiff one night followed Sir Henry upstairs and Lee allowed it to lie down in his bedchamber. At midnight the bedroom door opened and his Italian valet entered very quietly. The mastiff immediately pinned him to the floor and he admitted he had come to murder his master. The mastiff was so devoted to its owner's family that when William Harrison, author of the preface to Holinshed, tried to beat his children it would seize the rod with which he was whipping them in its teeth or try to drag down the clothes that he had pulled up to lay the rod across the children's bare bottoms. Harrison's mastiff knew perfectly well what a weapon was and it would not allow any visitor to bring in his sword farther than the gate. It would allow visitors to walk about the house but the moment they touched anything it would seize them.

Though these incidents occurred many years after the mediaeval period ended, they show that the mastiff was essentially a dog belonging to a time when security was valued above comfort. Once conditions became more settled, mastiffs were bound to be considered as unnecessary and a hindrance to the coming and going of visitors to the house. Secure conditions were markedly absent from the Middle Ages and the mastiff was in universal use for all who could afford to buy and keep one. It occupied such a special position as a security-dog that it became one of the causes of friction between king and subject in connection with the Forest Laws. The resentment over the Forest Jurisdiction did not arise from deer-poachers but from dog-owners, particularly the owners of two kinds of dogs, mastiffs and greyhounds. As the ill-feeling caused by the restrictions laid on these dogs by the Forest Laws was to have such wide repercussions throughout the whole of English history, it is necessary to say something about them.

The Laws of the Forest had come into being because the mediaeval kings, like their subjects, were extremely fond of dogs and hunting. 'William the Conqueror,' wrote the mediaeval chronicler, Walter Mapes, 'took away much land from God and men, converting its use to wild beasts and the sport of dogs, demolishing thirty-six mother churches, and driving away the inhabitants of many villages and towns, measuring together fifty miles in circumference.' There has been much controversy about the accuracy of Mapes' figures, but his words certainly express the resentment felt by Englishmen that one man should monopolise all the best sport in the country. There were sixty-nine Royal Forests, thirteen chases and 800 parks in England. A subject could not own a forest, though, as will be seen, other people besides the king and his friends were allowed hunting rights. A forest was not an unbroken extent of trees standing branch to branch with thick undergrowth beneath. Such country would have ensured that all hunting took place on foot and the mediaeval kings loved a gallop. The forests contained woodland but in addition great stretches of heath and moor, with baronial lands, manors and villages. It was the humans found within the stretch of the forest that produced the trouble that was continually breaking out over the laws that governed them.

Many, if not all, the inhabitants of the forest were dog-owners and right from the beginning of the Forest Jurisdiction savage enactments had been passed regarding mastiffs, and greyhounds, which were either forbidden within the boundaries of the royal hunting-grounds or ordered to be cruelly maimed. Canute had set up the jurisdiction over the forests, codifying existing Anglo-Saxon laws and, incidentally, making them much more severe.

Canute had forbidden everyone except a free person (not a numerous class in England) to keep greyhounds. Those free owners of greyhounds had to have their dogs 'expeditated', that is, rendered incapable of hunting. Expeditation took different forms at different times. To begin with the greyhound's knees were cut, presumably by hamstringing, by the verderers of the forest (officials employed to ensure the laws were kept). Yet even a hamstrung greyhound found within the royal forest could be confiscated and its owner fined severely. Needless to say a hamstrung hound would be useless to its owner, who would also have to suffer the anguish of seeing his pet mutilated before his eyes.

The punishment inflicted on dogs and their owners was obviously felt to be too severe and later a new method of expeditation was devised. The ball of the foot was cut out. This equally drastic form of mutilation would hardly find favour with dog-owners, so the law was changed once again. It was decreed that it was enough if three claws of the mastiff were struck off at a blow, with a chisel held against the claws as they rested on a block of wood and hit by a mallet.

The Parker Dog Gauge

Dogs other than mastiffs or greyhounds would be allowed inside the forests, provided they were small. Special dog-measures were kept to measure the animals and determine whether they were big enough to run loose without attacking the beasts of the chase. For a long time one of these gauges was preserved at Browsholme in Bowland Forest, in Lancashire, by the Parkers, hereditary Master Foresters to the Crown. It was an iron ring, oval in shape and looking like a stirrup, having an interior diameter of seven inches by five, with a swivel attached to it by which it could be hung from a girdle. A dog small enough to pass through this ring could be nothing but a lap-dog. Its very existence is interesting in showing that toy dogs did exist in the Middle Ages alongside the working breeds.

Another, much larger, dog-measure is preserved at the King's House at Lyndhurst in the New Forest, where verderers' meetings are still held. It is a stirrup said to have belonged to William Rufus and its greater size is perhaps indicative that a relaxation had taken place in what could be allowed as a small dog. So long as these restrictions existed, however, they were a constant cause of friction between dog-lovers and the Crown. Long after the Forest Jurisdiction fell into disuse, the Browsholme gauge was still being used. In 1770 the Duke of Montague, Lord of the Forest, proceeded to work off the spite he had acquired towards his neighbours because of an election quarrel by seizing their beagles, testing them with the measure and shooting them if they exceeded it.

Apart from the expeditation of dogs, massacres are said to have occurred from time to time, though this is a little doubtful. It is true that Henry de Knyghton, a Canon of Leicester, told his readers that King John had ordered the destruction 'of all the dogs and mastiffs in every forest in the kingdom'. Probably Knyghton only makes this statement because he was trying to heap odium on the head of an unpopular king. Much later in the Middle Ages, Henry VII is said to have ordered another massacre of mastiffs, ostensibly because they had committed treason by daring to fight with that king of animals, the lion. If Henry VII did ever issue such an order, it must have been in an attempt to squeeze money from the mastiff owners of England, who would have hastened to buy exemptions.

Everything about the Forest Laws' treatment of dogs seems to have been calculated to drive the dog-lovers of England to the brink of rebellion. Even a toy dog or a sheepdog which ran after a deer could bring down a savage mulct on the head of its owner. In the Middle Ages the possession of a dog was a real necessity. Even a spaniel could give the alarm if suspicious characters approached its owner's house. Yet the most treasured dog could be wrested from its owner if it were coveted by a Forest Ranger. He would simply withdraw the grant which licensed it. The possession of a dog could also be made the grounds for an accusation of poaching. Until the reign of Richard I, the penalty for poaching was castration, blinding and the cutting off of both hands and feet.

In fact most of the penalties imposed on offenders against the forest laws were fines and there can be little doubt that, from the earliest times, they were used by the law-makers as a device for extracting money. It was only too easy to frame some kind of accusation against a dweller in the forest – provided he had a dog. Thus if the king did not succeed in killing a hunted stag, but chased it out of the forest boundaries, anyone who killed it was a proscribed person. In 1194 Richard I hunted a hart from Sherwood Forest to Barnesdale in Yorkshire and lost it. He had the stag proclaimed at Barnsdale, Tunhill and other places nearby, warning everyone that nobody was to hunt this particular beast, it must be allowed to return to its lair in the forest. If such a royal hart were disturbed, even by the barking of a dog, the direst penalties would follow.

There was no escaping the vigilance of the king, for he virtually ruled England from his royal forests. These areas went on expanding until the twelfth century and during the thirteenth century their boundaries were still very extensive. Apart from the New Forest and Sherwood Forest there was Essex, covered almost entirely by Waltham Forest, the beloved hunting-ground of the last native English king, Harold. Just about the whole country between Lincolnshire and the Thames was subject to forest law, while more forests were to be found in Yorkshire, Cumberland and the West Country.

If you wanted to find an English king you would have to look for him in the forest. He would be transacting business in the intervals between hunting, summoning his Great Council to meetings at places which, apart from his hunting palace, were virtually wilderness and issuing historic enactments dated from places which were often just clearings in the trees, places like Clarendon, near Salisbury, Rockingham and Geddington, where there is a beautiful cross to Queen Eleanor, wife of Edward I.

To the liberty-loving and legalistic English mind the Forest Laws were particularly obnoxious because they were not real laws made by king and Council, or king and Parliament, but simply the expression of the royal will.

Anyone who kept a greyhound, unless he was worth ten pounds a year in land or inheritance or 300 pounds a year in freehold, was liable to be summoned to the Forest Court which met every three years to determine whether greyhounds had been found running in the forest. Anyone who wore Lincoln green was regarded as a poacher. Anyone who cut down some of the undergrowth which formed the 'vert' of the forest under which deer might shelter, who let his sheepdog pursue a hind or fawn which formed the 'venison' of the forest, allowed his little field to encroach on the edges of a forest ride, was slow to turn out to be a beater in the hunt, or let his dog wander loose amongst the haunts of deer would find that he had incurred the heavy displeasure of the king.

The more intelligent and able monarchs of the land soon realised that it was better to have the love of their subjects than the delights of saddling up and calling to their hounds to pursue the hart, the hind, the boar and the wolf, 'the beasts of venery', as they were called. Richard I made the first major concessions on the forest laws in order to ensure the loyalty of his subjects while he was absent on crusade. He abandoned the most severe penalties for poaching – blinding and castration. John, an intelligent even if hardly an able king, embodied further concessions about his control of the forests in Magna Carta, but only after he had driven the whole of England to rebellion. Henry III, though neither intelligent nor able, was prepared to follow where others had led by extending the existing 'Forest Charter'. In return for his condescension, his grateful subjects granted him one-fifteenth of the country's revenues. Edward I abandoned all forests which had been enclosed since the time of Henry I and also allowed the keeping of small dogs within forest limits, thus giving rise to the dog-measures which have been already described. He became the most popular monarch of his century.

Dislike for what they regarded, rightly, as an extra-territorial sovereignty within the kingdom of England blinded contemporaries to the very real virtues of the Royal Forests, these sanctuaries for 'the sport of dogs'. The forests were enormous nature reserves where the wild creatures of the countryside could retreat to safety. They were the nurseries for the mighty oaks which were to build so many of our monastic and cathedral churches. They were the timber reserves from which the Royal Navy was to be built in later years and they were the proving-grounds for the dogs owned by those fortunate few, other than the king and his favourites, who were allowed hunting rights within them.

Other than royal favourites, the most privileged hunters in England – men exempt from many of the onerous burdens of Forest Jurisdiction – were the clergy. Their privileges included exemption from the hated expeditation. Thus the canons of Bridlington Priory, in Yorkshire, a house founded during Henry I's reign, were allowed to keep four watchdogs 'with entire feet' in their cowsheds, though the dogs had to be tied up during the day. Hugh, Bishop of Durham, who as a Marcher Lord enjoyed royal power in his see, allowed the Kypier Hospital near Durham (founded by Ralph Flambard in 1112) to keep shepherds' dogs with unlopped feet. 'The shepherds may lead them with a string,' says the grant, 'on account of the game, in order to preserve their sheep from the wolves.'

Like many other aspects of the Forest Jurisdiction, the enactments concerning clerical hunting privileges seem to have been affected by several changes of policy during the Middle Ages. Canute had allowed the higher clergy, the bishops and abbots, to hunt in the royal forests. Later kings did not abrogate these prerogatives, but Henry II, very jealous of his hunting rights, tried to get the bishops to enforce the canon law on all the clergy. The canons of the church strictly forbade clerical participation in hunting, hawking and other field sports, whether allowed by a royal grant or not.

Sometimes a royal grant allowed clerics to keep dogs for protection – such as the exemption for shepherds' dogs quoted above. Sometimes it was a grant to keep hunting-hounds, within the Forest Jurisdiction. Occasionally the grant specifically limited the kind of game that could be caught with these hounds. Thus grants from several English kings permitted the abbot and monks of Chertsey Abbey to keep dogs for hunting hares, foxes and pheasants. Presumably the pheasants were first pinned down by pointers and then had the net drawn over them and the dogs.

More favoured clerics were given ampler hunting rights. They were, for example, allowed to kill a deer or two as they passed through the forest on their way to Council or Parliament, though they had to notify the Forest Ranger of their intent. Abbots whose monastery lay right in a royal forest, like the abbot of Waltham Holy Cross in Essex, were allowed to keep a huntsman, but many clerics liked to take the field in person.

Walter, Archdeacon of Canterbury, who was promoted to the see of Rochester in 1147, spent the whole of his time in hunting and in his eight-ieth year he was as keen a sportsman as ever. Reginald Brian, who was made Bishop of Worcester in 1352, was another enthusiastic hunter and like some enthusiasts he made no bones about asking for what he felt he needed to carry on his chosen vocation. In a letter to the Bishop of St Davids, Reginald reminded that prelate of a promise he had made him to send six couple of excellent hunting-dogs, the best he had ever seen. Ever since he heard those words he had been waiting anxiously from day to day to receive the bishop's present, his heart languishing for the arrival of the dogs. 'Let them come, then,' he wrote 'oh reverend father, without delay! Let my woods re-echo with the music of their cry, and the cheerful notes of the horn, and let the walls of my palace be decorated with the trophies of the chase!'

With no fighting to do and no family to provide for, clerics who were keen hunters were able to devote their revenue to the sport. One abbot became the acknowledged expert on hare-hunting throughout England. William de Clowne, Abbot of St Mary's in Leicestershire, was paid an annual pension from the king, first by Henry III and later by his son, Prince Edward, as well as by most of the great nobles of the realm, to instruct them on how to hunt the hare in due form. When Clowne petitioned the king to grant him a market or fair for the sole purpose of buying and selling har-riers and other sorts of dogs, so that his kennels might be always well sup-plied, the king replied that, seeing he passionately desired it, he would comply with the abbot's request.

Not everyone approved of this passionate desire for hunting on the part of clerics. Even some of their colleagues felt that the upkeep and company of dogs was an intolerable burden. Around 1200 the canons of Bridlington presented a formal complaint to Pope Innocent III against the Archdeacon of Richmond because when he made his visitations he brought with him so many horses, hawks and attendants that he consumed more provisions in an hour than would have lasted the whole community for a considerable spell. Obviously it was the hounds that were the real offenders here because hounds were fed on a special kind of loaf, made from coarse flour, the kind of bread, in fact, that monks would eat. In answer to the complain-ant's petition, Pope Innocent despatched a bull, directed to the arch-bishop, bishops, archdeacons and officials of the diocese of York, forbidding 'such shameful and oppressive visits in future'.

Yet though some bishops took a severe view of clerical hunters and keepers of hounds, most diocesans would approve of such dog-lovers, albeit tacitly, because, as will be seen, they were an asset to the monastic community. The real critics of monastic dog-owners and kennel-keepers were not the higher clergy, but the laity. In *The Canterbury Tales* Chaucer poked fun at the monk in the *Prologue*. This religious was a manly man, a hard rider to hounds, one that loved hunting and the owner of greyhounds which were 'as swift as birds in flight'. Like William Clowne, his only desire was to hunt the hare and he did not mind what he spent on his amusement. In fact, concludes Chaucer maliciously, he was just the kind of man who would become an abbot. He did not care a jot about the text that says that hunters are not holy men (which is hardly surprising, as it does not exist).

From the legalistic point of view, Chaucer was right. Canon law forbade hunting and hawking by the clergy, while the rules that governed monastic life stated tersely that no other love (not even the love of a man for his dog) must intrude between the religious and his love for God. This rule made good sense, practically as well as spiritually. England's best known saint, Thomas à Becket, changed from being a worldly layman into a saintly monk and cleric in all respects save one. Becket, the son of a well-to-do London citizen, had no doubt been a sportsman in his youth and had ridden out to enjoy the chase in the London hunting-preserve that stretched from the city walls to the water of Cray, in Kent. Yet as a citizen's son he could never have afforded the superior kind of horses and dogs that it was suitable for an archbishop of Canterbury to keep. When he had to represent Henry II in France as his ambassador, according to the chronicler Fitz Stephen, he travelled like a prince, 'and took with him hawks and dogs of various sorts, such as were then used by kings and princes'. A magnificent sporting establishment was, in fact, the one weakness of this austere ascetic who wore a hair shirt covered with lice. It was not merely a weakness, it was a weak point as well. Becket, a genuine animal-lover, hated to see pointless cruelty inflicted on his beasts. When his enemies at court, such as Ranulf de Broc, deliberately mutilated his horses, rode over his land and, worst of all, stole his hounds, Becket was driven into such a fury that he excommunicated them, an act which started the train of events that led to his murder in Canterbury Cathedral on 29th December 1170.

Anyone who broke the canon law, however, was merely breaking a rule, not committing a sin, and he may have felt he had good reasons for doing so. Much later in history, the monks of St Bernard's Hospice on the Great St Bernard Pass in Switzerland were also to break the monastic rules by keeping dogs, not to hunt, but to rescue travellers trapped in the snowdrifts. Chaucer's monk would probably have told us, if we questioned him about his greyhounds and hunting, that he was merely following the injunction given to St Peter, 'Slay, and eat' (Acts 10:13). His fellow monks did not eat a lot of meat, except perhaps on feast days, but there were always the sick in the infirmary, who would benefit from a nourishing game soup. Then there were the guests staying at the monastery guest-house. They could not be expected to relish the coarse vegetarian fare of the religious. They would expect meat dishes too and if they were wealthy and important people they must be given sumptuous fare – such as 'humble pie', made from the 'umbles' or offal of the deer. There was no harm in a monk hunting, so long as he was not a poacher like one Abbot of Whitby who was indicted for killing a hart in the River Derwent, part of the Forest of Pickering; or so long as he did not spend *all* his time in the hunting-field, as did Walter, Bishop of Rochester. Monks needed exercise, like other men, and what better exercise could he find than in cheering on his hounds?

Where lay and clerical reformers agreed was that there was no need for nuns to have dogs. They did not go hunting or accompany men hunters to the chase, but they still seemed to keep dogs, in surprisingly large numbers. The fictitious Madame Eglentyne, who appears, with her dogs, in *The Canterbury Tales*, was representative of many of her religious sisters. She had brought several of these little dogs with her and it is obvious that these would have had no difficulty in passing through William Rufus' stirrup. Her pets were given the finest food: roast meat, milk and cake-bread. Whenever one of the dogs got in the way of the other pilgrims and someone hit it with a stick, Prioress Eglentyne wept, for she had a tender heart. She also cried when she saw a mouse caught in a trap, because, like most dog-lovers, she loved all animals.

The bishops of the Middle Ages could not understand why their Madame Eglentynes should want to keep dogs, even if they themselves kept a kennel. It was strictly against the rules. One archbishop had to forbid an abbess whose nunnery he visited from keeping a number of dogs – and monkeys – in her chamber. Sometimes it was nuns not abbesses who were at fault. William of Wykeham wrote to the Abbess of Romsey Abbey in 1387,

Whereas we have convinced ourselves by clear proofs that some of the nuns of your house bring with them to church birds, rabbits, hounds, and such like fri-volous creatures, to which they give more heed than to the offices of the church, with frequent hindrance to their own psalmody and to that of their fellow nuns, and to the grievous peril of their souls, therefore we strictly forbid you, jointly and singly, in virtue of the obedience due to us, that from henceforth you do not presume to bring to church any birds, hounds, rabbits or other frivolous crea-tures that are harmful to good discipline.

. . . What is more, because through hunting-hounds, and other dogs living within the confines of your nunnery, the alms that should be given to the poor are devoured and the church and cloister . . . are foully defiled . . . and because through their inordinate noise, divine service is frequently disturbed, we therefore strictly order and charge you, Lady Abbess, that you remove the dogs altogether, and that, henceforth, you never suffer them, or any other such hounds to live within the precincts of your nunnery.

Invectives such as these continued to rain down on the heads of religious ladies, without any noticeable effect. If the nuns themselves did not keep dogs, then some of their lady pensioners would. 'Lady Audley, who boards here,' wrote the distracted nuns of a convent, 'has a great abundance of dogs, insomuch that whenever she comes to church, there follow her twelve dogs, who make a great uproar in the church, hindering the nuns in their psalmody, and terrifying them.'

If some of the sisterhood did not like dogs in church, most people were prepared to put up with them. The knight brought his greyhound, the cooks of the abbey their turnspit dogs. William Warburton, Bishop of Gloucester, was in the Abbey Church at Bath one Sunday when the lesson was taken from the first chapter of Ezekiel. It is a chapter in which the word 'wheel' occurs many times and as the turnspit dogs heard this familiar word 'they all clapped their tails between their legs and ran out of the church', back to their wheels in the kitchen.

The attempt to keep clerics out of the hunting-field was coupled with a move to exclude everyone who did not belong to the feudal aristocracy. The Parliament of Richard II, in its thirteenth year, passed an act prohibiting any priest or clerk not possessed of a benefice to the yearly amount of ten pounds from keeping a greyhound, or any other dog, for the purposes of hunting. The same Parliament also complained that, like the clergy, common folk were aspiring to hunt. 'Artificers and labourers, and servants and grooms keep greyhounds and other dogs, and on the holy days, when good Christian people are at church, hearing divine service, they go hunting in parks, warrens and coneyeries [rabbit warrens] belonging to lords and others, to the great destruction of the same.'

There were not wanting some stern mediaeval moralists who went so far as to say that it was the whole country that was, all too literally, going to the dogs. It was not just clerical hunters, but all hunters, including the nobility and gentry, who were at fault.

In these days our nobility esteem the sports of hunting and hawking as the most honourable employments, the most exalted virtues, and to be continually engaged in these amusements is, in their opinion, the summit of human happiness. They prepare for a hunt with more trouble, anxiety, and cost than they would for a battle, and follow the beasts of the forests with greater fury than they do their enemies. By being constantly engaged in this savage sport, they contract habits of barbarity, lose in a great measure, their feeling and humanity, and become nearly as ferocious as the beasts which they pursue.

The husbandman, together with his innocent flocks and herds, is driven from his fertile fields, his meadows and pastures, that beasts may roam there in his stead. Should one of these powerful and merciless sportsmen pass your door, place before him, in a moment, all the refreshment your habitation affords, or that can be purchased, or borrowed in your neighbourhood, that you may not be utterly ruined, or perchaunce accused of treason.

No English gentleman could possibly have agreed with this severe dictum. Every man of breeding was convinced that, next to the service of God, his lady and his king, it was his devotion to hunting that had moulded him and made him the man he was. The love of dogs and hunting was already beginning to make England a country quite different from others on the Continent. An Italian observer of Edward III's reign noted with astonishment that 'The nobles of England think themselves above residing in cities. They live in retirement on their country estates amid woods and pastures.' We cannot have a better guide to introduce us to the English gentlemen and his dogs than the authority on hunting who has already been quoted, Edward, second Duke of York, grandson of Edward III, nephew of the Duke of Gloucester and Master of Game to King Henry IV.

Writing some time between 1406 and 1413, York tried to give a picture of the hunting-dog, and the other aspects of hunting as understood in England. Like his contemporary, Chaucer, York felt that he must base his general thesis on an approved authority, which he would feel free to adapt when it seemed necessary. Whereas Chaucer drew most of his inspiration from Boccaccio, York's work is based very largely on the acknowledged authority on hunting on the Continent, *Le Livre de Chasse*. The author of 'The Book of the Chase' was Gaston III de Foix et de Béarn, a relative of the Plantagenets and therefore of York, who must have met him in Aquitaine during his prolonged residence there.

Gaston was famous for his good looks and fine blond hair, which earned him the nickname of 'Gaston Phoebus', or Gaston the Sun God. He was also renowned for his encyclopaedic knowledge of hunting. Though his two tiny principalities were not very important politically, geographically they were convenient: Béarn was almost at the western end of the Pyrenees and Foix at the eastern. Consequently Gaston merely had to travel from one of his states to another to find plenty of good hunting in the wild mountain country. He owned 600 dogs of various breeds, fierce Alaunts, obtained from neighbouring Spain, which was famous for Alaunts at this time, Gascon hounds, Brittany hounds, those raised at the Abbey of St Hubert in the Ardennes, mastiffs (which may well have been gifts from York) and little greyhounds. The ruler of Béarn had also travelled widely in Europe, even in Scandinavia. He knew all there was to be known about European hunting (except, of course, for England and York's translation had to fill in this gap). Gaston began to put down his knowledge on paper on 1st May 1387, when he began his great book. It was his swan-song: just four years later he was killed by a bear while hunting. For a mediaeval writer, the Count is remarkably objective and scientific. He also writes in a clear and attractive style. This combination of the man of action and the man of intellect have endeared Gaston to many, including the first translator of York's book into modern English, William Baillie Grohman. Baillie Grohman was a big-game hunter and he asked another devotee of big game who also admired Gaston and York, Theodore Roosevelt, to write the foreword.

It is, then, with Edward Duke of York as our guide that we make the first stop in our tour of the mediaeval English dog, a stop which is inevitably the kennels. On the way York explains to us that hunting is in his blood. His father, Edmund de Langley, was as famous for his fondness for hunting as for his disinterest in politics. York quotes the chronicler John Harding's description of his father:

> That Edmund, called 'of Langley' of good cheer,
> Glad and merry and of his own folk always loved.
> Who never did wrong, as chronicles have related.
> When all the lords went to council and parliament,
> He would go hunting and hawking.
> He loved every gentleman's pastime, as becoming a lord,
> He helped the poor, wherever he was staying.
> He never suppressed or extorted money from poor folk.

York shakes his head and wishes he had followed his father's example and kept out of politics altogether. As it is, he says, his political career has been a chequered one. He has been accused of taking part in the murder of his uncle, Thomas of Woodstock, Duke of Gloucester, and even of having carried his severed head on a pole. He has been imprisoned in Pevensey Castle on the charge of trying to kidnap the Mortimers. But, adds York, brightening, his time in prison gave him the opportunity to begin his translation of the *Livre de Chasse*. As we approach the kennel, he quotes from memory his opening passage about the joys of a hunter's life.

> Now shall I prove how hunters live in this world more joyfully than any other men. For when the hunter riseth in the morning, and he sees a sweet and fair morn and clear weather and bright, and he heareth the song of the small birds, the which sing so sweetly with great melody and full of love, each in its own language in the best wise that it can according that it learneth of its own kind. And when the sun is arisen, he shall see fresh dew upon the small twigs and grasses, and the sun by his virtue shall make them shine. And that is great joy and liking to the hunter's heart.

There can be no doubt, adds the Duke, that the greatest delight of the hunter is the joy he finds in his dogs, for the noble nature of hounds is such that only a skilful hunter knows it, and even then only one who has hunted for a long time with the same pack. 'For a hound is a most reasonable beast, and best knowing of any beast that ever God made.'

By this time we have arrived at the Ducal kennel, a wooden building 60 feet long by 25 feet broad. The whole kennel, and the grassy plot on which the hounds can scamper about, is enclosed by a stockade, a palisade of pales, more than the height of a man, sharpened at the point to deter dog-thieves. A latticed door, like a portcullis, lets us into this enclosure and we hurry past a fierce mastiff chained to the palisade just inside the door. The kennel has one door in front and another behind, always kept open, so that there is nothing to prevent the dogs from going out if they want fresh air and sunlight. Everything that can be thought of to promote the health of the dogs has been carried out in designing the kennel. A deep drain runs along the centre, draining off the straw litter on which the dogs sleep. Outside the kennel is a green grassy plot, so contrived that it gets the sun from morning to night.

The kennel proper is a long, low room, which can be heated by a fireplace and chimney to warm the place up and enable the hounds to dry out their coats after a wet day's hunting. With a smile the Master of Game reminds us that fireplaces in human dwellings are rather unusual, unless you count cooking fires, and in bedrooms they are virtually unknown. Above the kennel there is a lofty upper storey which keeps the kennel cool in summer and warm in winter. It is also the home of the kennel boy, who looks after the hounds and sleeps in the kennel at night to prevent hounds fighting. As he lives continually with the dogs, he soon knows whether any of them are showing signs of illness, particularly the dreaded hydrophobia. When not employed in feeding the hounds or cleaning out the kennel he would take them off for their twice daily exercise walk, when they would ease themselves and then be rubbed down with straw. The loft has barred windows and shutters that open to allow a free passage of air. The kennel boy would use it as a workshop as well as a home, filling in leisure hours by spinning dog leashes to couple up the hounds when they were led out to hunt.

Having shown us the general arrangements, the Master of Game now explains that he will introduce us to the principal breeds he keeps there. Those will not include the Alaunts or the mastiffs because 'they be of a churlish nature'. He will begin by showing us the greyhounds. These are the most popular English dog, so popular that of late the upstart common-ers have been beginning to keep them. As recently as 1389 a Member of Par-liament felt compelled to complain in the House of Commons that the fancy for greyhounds was spreading from gentlefolk to 'craftsmen, and

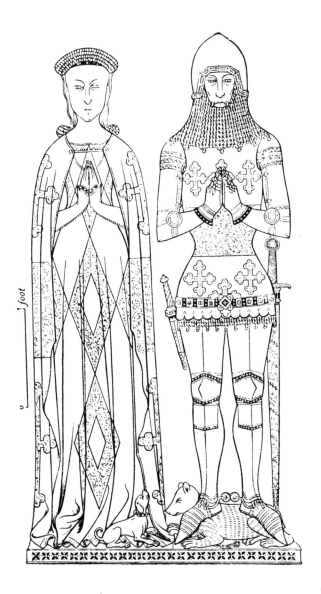

Mediaeval tomb brass with hound and bear foot supporters

labourers and servants and grooms'. York shakes his head over this additional symptom of the revolutionary feelings of the common folk. A greyhound, he says, is a beast fit only for a knight or his lady. This beautiful, highly bred creature is every bit as much an attribute of noble birth as a pair of gilt spurs or a jewelled belt. He quotes a Welsh proverb which says that a gentleman may be known 'by his hawk, his horse, and his greyhound'. His own favourite greyhounds go with him everywhere. When he is at table they sit beside his chair, on the rushes strewing the floor, and eat the bones from his meal, or sometimes the plate of bread on which he has eaten it. They have their place beside the fire and range at will in hall and bedchamber. They accompany him to church, where they behave at least as decorously as some other members of the congregation, and he has trained them to be clean wherever they are.

At a sign from the Master, his huntsmen walk on the greyhounds in couples. Some wear collars of white and green silk tissue, ornamented with letters spelling their master's name and little castles worked in massy silver. Others have round their necks collars made from silk chequered green and black and ornamented with silver letters and bells.

A glance at the ducal greyhounds show that several breeds are represented, large and small, rough-haired and smooth-haired, but all called 'greyhounds'. There are powerful dogs, used to chase the stag, the wolf and the wild boar, and smaller and more delicate animals used for hunting hares. There are great Irish hounds with rough coats and Scottish deerhounds from the Highlands – which bear a close resemblance to the Irish hounds because apparently the Scots keep up the breed by imports of the original Irish stock. There are also smooth-coated, elegant Italian greyhounds.

In response to our admiring glances, York says proudly that Britain can beat any other country in the world when it comes to greyhounds. The historian Froissart took two couples of greyhounds which he had collected in England and Scotland with him as a present for Gaston Phoebus. Their names were 'Tristan', 'Hector', 'Brun' and 'Roland'. The fact that such hounds were a suitable gift for the greatest hunter of the age proved their worth.

A good greyhound, says York, should be middle-sized so that it can be slipped at any quarry. As greyhounds hunt by sight, it is essential that they should be joined with scenting-hounds or 'limers' which will find the game and start it for them. Greyhounds can be slipped as relays to a pack of running or scenting-hounds, or sent out by themselves to course game in open country. They may be placed at passes where the game is likely to run and instructed either to pull down a wounded deer or turn it back so that it can be shot by the hunter. The greyhound is the ideal hunting-hound. It will run with a pack of any other kind of dog and it will tackle red, fallow, or roe deer, wolf, boar, fox, hare, even badger. Because it is such a complete hunting-dog, anyone who walks in company with a greyhound through a forest is assumed to be out hunting, as much as if he were wearing green. To take just one instance, from years back, one Ralph of Eyneston spent some time as a prisoner in Northampton Castle just because he had allowed his greyhounds to walk through the royal forest unleashed.

Though there are many breeds of greyhounds, the ideal dog – which probably only exists in the imagination of Gaston Phoebus – is fallow-red (not white, a common and favoured colour in Britain as elsewhere in the mediaeval world) with a long head, a good large mouth and good teeth, red or black eyes, a black muzzle, small ears, a long, arched neck, a great open chest, shoulders like a roebuck, great and straight legs with cat-shaped feet and large claws.

'A greyhound,' concludes York, 'should be courteous and not too fierce, following well his master and doing whatever he commands it. It should be good kindly, and clean, glad and joyful and playful, showing good will to all manner of creatures save to the wild beasts, against which it should be eager, spiteful, and fierce.'

The Master of Game now shows us another breed from his kennel, the spaniels. York explains that of course spaniels get their name from the word *espagnol*, meaning 'Spanish', but that though originally found only in Spain they are now kept all over Europe. They are only used in hunting birds. Either they accompany the falconer in the field and put up his game, or they act as setters, indicating the presence of game birds such as partridges so that the hunter can draw a net over the area, covering birds and spaniels alike. As waterdogs, spaniels are invaluable for jumping into the water to seize waterfowl which have dived.

Nonetheless, in spite of its virtues, this is a breed which any hunter – as opposed to hawker – may well dispense with. Like the English working-classes, they do not know their proper place, but run across the front of the pack during a hunt, quarrelling, biting and distracting the 'raches' or running hounds with false leads. They will chase cows, horses, geese and chickens and communicate their bad habits to the rest of the pack. Nevertheless, says York, as he bends to scratch one of his spaniels behind the ear, they have got their merits. A spaniel is an affectionate animal that will follow its master everywhere, never leaving him, even in the thickest crowds. A good spaniel has a big head to match its big body and a good, feathery tail. The best are coloured white or tawny.

Now the Master orders up the 'raches', scenting hounds which run in a pack, and a large number are walked past us. A good hound, he tells us, has a large body, big open nostrils, a long snout, great hanging lips and big eyes in a large forehead, a broad breast, with great legs and feet, as well as an emphatic tail to signal its progress through the undergrowth.

Broadly speaking, no breed of hounds was perfect when it came to hunting, though they were the finest animals in existence and there was no music like running-hounds questing after their quarry. Each breed had some defect. Thus the Biscayan or Spanish hounds could manage the short run necessary to bring a boar to bay, but they tired in the long pursuit of a hart.

At a snap from York's fingers a single dog is now brought out, a favourite 'limer' or sleuth-hound. The limer is so called because it is held on the lead or 'liam' while it tracks game. This leash should be 21 feet long, explains York, a length which will prevent unpleasantly abrupt encounters with the quarry in thick undergrowth. The liam, he says, should be made from horse hide, well tawed, and he points out that the liam that this particular limer is attached by is merely the beast's parade uniform, not worn on hunting day. This liam is of white silk, with a collar of white velvet embroidered with pearls and with a solid silver swivel.

A limer is not a particular kind of dog, York tells us; any breed could be trained to act as a limer, but naturally some breeds, such as the Talbots, give better results than others. It is a very special dog which does not rough it in the kennel with the rest of the pack but is the inseparable companion of its master. It sleeps in his room and is fed only by his hand, just like the limer that tracked Robert the Bruce. Every time the master goes out, he takes the dog with him and encourages it to follow up the scent of stags and other beasts of the chase. If the dog picks up the wrong scent, that of an animal that it is not hunting, then it is punished. Limers are expensive companions. Whereas at current prices a rache costs halfpence a day to feed and a greyhound three farthings, a limer costs a whole penny.' Most of a dog's diet is bread, special kinds of bread such as 'manchet' which is made from wheaten flour of the second quality coarsely sifted, or 'brom' bread, made from oats. Some dog bread is also made from bran. Whenever they kill the dogs are given some of the entrails of the quarry during a special ceremony called the *curée*. Game is also killed for the hounds to eat if they have had a bad season and have not killed themselves.

We must now take our leave of Edward Duke of York and take a backward glance, not just at mediaeval dogs, but at the hunting-field as a whole. Mediaeval hunting was not just a pastime or a way of keeping the larder stocked with fresh meat throughout the lean season of the year, though both these factors were important in the institution of the hunt. Rather was hunting an extraordinarily sophisticated and formal code of etiquette which was used as a sort of dividing-line to separate the rich from the poor, the socially privileged from those less so. Strict ceremonial governed the hunting of all the accepted quarries. At different stages throughout the hunt, for example, the hunter had to blow quite complicated blasts on his hunting-horn and utter fairly long sentences in Norman French to his dogs. His relations with the human members of the hunt were even more elaborately ceremonial. The *curée*, the ceremony of breaking up the deer and allocating different parts of it to different members of the hunt, had to be performed with hieratic, ritual gestures which were individually and collectively as important as those that accompany the Tea Ceremony of Japan today. Not to say the right word, not to perform the

right gesture in exactly the right way, damned a man in the eyes of his contemporaries as a clown whose education had been neglected or whose stu-
pidity had prevented him from benefiting from it. The hunt had also
become charged with a deep symbolic meaning – according to some authorities at least. It had become a kind of lay mass, imbued with an importance to which no mere pastime could aspire. If we can believe Francis
Klingender, the annual hunt of the wren was a symbolic murder of the
Lord of the Castle or Manor, undertaken by the young men of the lord's en-
tourage, who were all in love with the Lord's Lady, the most desirable of all
the few women in their restricted military society but one forbidden to
them alike by the ties of feudal loyalty and religious belief.

One of the results of the increased importance of dogs and hunting in
English society was to produce more books of the type written by Edward
Duke of York. One of the most notable amongst them was the first mediaeval best-seller written by a woman, Juliana Berners, *The Book of St Albans*.
Dame Juliana, the Prioress of Sopwell, may have been a Madame
Eglentyne but she certainly lacked the fondness for animals which charac-
terised Chaucer's heroine. Her instructions to her readers sound like those
of a very practical kennelwoman. On the subject of rearing greyhounds
she concludes by telling dog-owners that once their hounds have turned
nine they should be sent to the tanner: 'for the best hound that ever bitch
had, at the ninth year he is full bad.'

The other result of the increasing formalisation of the hunt was that
noble and royal hunters began to concentrate on that technique which
most lent itself to courtly formality, the *battue*. This process was to become
even more popular at the end of the Middle Ages with the advent of the
Tudors. The *battue* got round the difficulty posed by the slow-running
qualities of the mediaeval hound, whether tawny-red Breton, grey Royal
French, blue-mottled Gascon or black and white St Hubert. There was no
need for an elaborate positioning of relays (which might prove useless if
the quarry started in the unexpected direction). The chase took place
within the confines of a deer park or part of a wood enclosed with fences,
where the quarry could never get a lead. As the deer scampered past a
grassy knoll or artificial mound, on which the hunters were gathered, they
were shot down with bows and arrows, while greyhounds stationed by
the exits of the enclosure pulled down wounded quarry or stragglers. Al-
ternatively, deer might be coursed within the park by couples of the larger
greyhounds, and pulled down. A drive of this sort was particularly
popular with Middle Age folk because it allowed the ladies, without whose
participation no pleasure could ever be complete, to attend the feast that
took place after the *curée*, and even to witness the prowess of the hunters.
To protect themselves from the sun and wind they watched from bowers of
green boughs woven by the hunt-servants on the orders of the Master of
the Game.

One further consequence of the increased formalisation of the hunting of the deer must be mentioned; hunters who wanted sport and excitement, rather than formality, now began to be interested in other quarries. The choice of a quarry other than the deer was very much reduced in England. The Duke of York implies that most of his English readers will never have seen a wolf – though there were plenty of them in some parts of the country, such as the Yorkshire wolds. The boar was very sensibly reduced in numbers, wild cattle confined to a few emparked areas and the bear extinct, probably for hundreds of years. 'No good hunter,' says York, 'goes to the woods with his hounds intending to hunt martens and pole cats, nor for the wild cat either. . . . Of rabbits I do not speak, for no man hunteth them unless it be fur trappers.'

That left the otter, the fox and the hare. York speaks in moderately respectful terms about otters but is content to refer his readers to the king's otter-hunter, William Melbourne, who had presumably written a treatise on the otter-hunt, now lost. What York is really interested in is hare-hunting. He writes a complete chapter on this sport because it had not been dealt with sufficiently fully by Gaston Phoebus. Hare-hunting, as described by York, is still a very formal affair but, because of the simpler nature of the sport as compared with deer-hunting, it could not be quite so complex. There was no need for beaters, there was so little of the hare that the elaborate ceremony of the *curée* was not required, the hare was not a 'royal beast of the chase' like the red deer so it could be hunted anywhere. It took a shorter time to find and catch the hare than the deer, yet the sport could be just as exciting, indeed more exciting, because of the way in which deer-hunting had become surrounded with etiquette.

'It is to be known,' wrote York enthusiastically, 'that the hare is king of all venery, for all blowing and the fair terms of hunting cometh of the seeking and finding of the hare. For certain it is the most marvellous beast that is.' Not the least virtue of the hare was its inability to turn and rend its pursuers, as could the wolf, boar and deer. Though there were now few wolves or boars in England, the three kinds of deer, red, fallow and even the roebuck, could be formidable opponents if they turned at bay. A medi-aeval proverb ran: 'If a boar wounds a man, put a leech on the spot. If a hart wounds him, put him on his bier, for he will not recover.'

As hare-hunting offered as much excitement as deer-hunting, at about twenty-five per cent of the expense and none of the danger, it is not surprising that it became a favourite with the quieter and less adventurous sportsman, like Abbot William Clowne.

There was another sport that was rising in popularity as the Middle Ages drew to their close, the foxhunt. Shortly before Edward Duke of York died on the field of Agincourt, he must have seen his royal kinsman, Henry V, place a fox's brush on his helmet. This gesture was full of the symbolism that the Middle Ages loved and York knew what it signified. Henry's strange plume was worn to remind his men that they could expect no mercy from the French and that they must sell their lives as dearly as they could. York must have quoted his own words to his companions: 'The fox does not complain when men slay him, but he defends himself with all his power while he is alive.' Curiously enough, Henry's unspoken message to his men, which was as significant for their morale as Nelson's signal at Trafalgar, has never previously been commented on.

Already by 1415 the fox and the English had begun to develop a special relationship that was to be fraught with historical consequences. Where the fox came from and how it arrived in England is not known, but it may have been a tame animal in Roman Britain, possibly an introduction from the Continent, like the pheasant and the Burgundian snail. At any rate in the famous Orpheus mosaics which appear in Britain and all over the Roman world, Orpheus is shown surrounded by all the animals as he plays, but with two creatures closer to him than any others, the peacock and the fox. I have always assumed that this meant that these two animals were tame already and therefore would be the first to be attracted by the music. The peacock certainly was a domesticated bird in Ancient Rome and was probably imported to Britain.

The Anglo-Saxon successors to the Romans did not see the fox in the light of a charming pet: to them it was merely noxious vermin. No one bothered to hunt it regularly until the time of the Angevin kings when it became a preoccupation with royal hunters and especially John. On 2nd January 1206 the King wrote from his hunting-lodge in Clarendon to tell Hugh de Neville that he had made a grant to Peter Bordeaux, letting him keep six or seven dogs for hunting the hare and the fox, as well as three greyhounds. On 28th December 1213 he wrote to Roger de Neville, informing him that William de Ireby, who had land in Liddledale and Ulvesdale, had leave to keep running-hounds and greyhounds to hunt the fox and hare in Carlisle Forest. On 2nd November of the same year he wrote to Peter de Cancella, the Constable of Bristol, telling him: 'We send you forty of our foxhounds and twelve greyhounds, with two horsemen, two varlets and eight dog leaders, commanding you to make them hunt the fox in your shire and to provide necessaries for them till we send for them, and any cost you may incur through them shall be paid.'

In the same year, on 1st December, William Malet, the king's huntsman, was sent with six greyhounds, forty foxhounds, six varlets and one horse 'to hunt the fox in our forest of Treville' (in Herefordshire).

After John the royal foxhounds are rather lost from view until the time of Edward I when the Master of the Foxhounds, William de Blatherwyke, or William de Foxhunte, is continually receiving sums of money from the king. The foxhunt was an expensive royal pleasure; it was already costing halfpence a day to feed each hound, while Blatherwyke's wages were tuppence a day. He and his grooms received quite a lavish allowance for boots, a fact that reminds us that hunting took place on foot. When Blatherwyke went to the royal forest at Clarendon, accompanied by his two helpers, his dog-keepers and a pack of thirty hounds, there was only one horse for the

Beagle, from *The Illustrated Natural History*.

Below: Bloodhound, from the same source.

Staghound, from *The Sportsman's Cabinet*.

Beagles, also from *The Sportsman's Cabinet*.

Otter Hounds by Henry Alken, an illustration for John William
Carleton's *The Sporting Sketch Book*, London, Howe Parsons, 1842.

English Setter, from *The Sportsman's Cabinet*.

Above: 'Rosa and Cribb', Bulldogs, 1813, by Abraham Cooper (1787-1868). Formerly with Spink and Son.

Pugs, from *The Sportsman's Cabinet.*

'Waiting', Highland deer-hound, foxhound, blood-hound and greyhound, by Sir Edwin Landseer, (1802-1873). Formerly with Spink and Son.

Below: 'Return from Coursing', *c* 1800, English School.

Above: 'Groom with horses and hounds', Samuel Allson (1750-1825). Formerly with Spink and Son

Opposite: 'Pluto' and 'Juno', pointers belonging to Colonel William Thomson, from an illustration to the Rev. W. B. Daniel's *Rural Sports*, London, 1801, painted by S. Gilfin and engraved by John Scott.

Below: 'Death of the Fox', by John Most Sartorius (1755-1828). Formerly with Spink and Son.

'Preparing for the Meet', by John Ferneley Senior (1781-1860).
Formerly with Spink and Son.

'Hunting Scene', by John Ferneley Senior (1781-1860). Formerly
with Spink and Son.

Greyhound, from *The Sportsman's Cabinet.*

Italian Greyhounds, also from an illustration to *The Sportsman's Cabinet.*

whole party and that was to carry the nets used to snare the fox.

Foxhunting was certainly a very different affair in the Middle Ages from what it is today. There was some doubt whether it really was a sport at all and not just the quickest way of exterminating a noxious pest. Gaston Phoebus even has a chapter 'How the fox ought to be chased and taken', in which he gives directions for earth-stopping, taking the animal in purse nets and smoking him out with 'orpiment and sulphur and nitre, or salt-petre'. There can be no doubt that some English huntsmen did pursue the fox in this way, as well as in the other fashion which Gaston recommends, hunting him in January, February and March, with the pack divided into relays of a third of the hounds.

Yet it is evident that many Englishmen were now coming to regard the foxhunt as a sport and not merely a routine extermination of vermin. It is significant that when Edward Duke of York comes to this chapter of Gaston's he runs his pen through it and refuses to translate it. No poison gas for him, let the French do what they like. He does however translate Gaston's chapter 'Of the fox and of his nature', with evident approval, adding little touches of his own.

There was really no reason to hunt the fox unless you wanted to do it for sport. If you wanted to get rid of vermin, such as a polecat or marten, then you would, like the hero of Chaucer's *Pardoner's Tale*, walk into the nearest apothecary's shop and buy as much poison as you needed for this very purpose. A poisoned fox would produce a much better skin 'which is won-derfully warm to make cuffs and furs, but which stink for ever if not well tawed', than would a fox which had been dug out of its earth and torn to bits by twelve couples of Blatherwyke's hounds. The point made by Gaston, that the fox is the greatest destroyer of poultry and must be kept down, is a good one, but I can hardly see King John spending a lot of money on exterminating foxes to protect other folks' chickens.

One of the great benefits of foxhunting from the sportsman's point of view was that it filled in a part of the year that was otherwise dead ground, from 8th September till 25th March. Another reason for the increasing popularity of the sport was that huntsmen had gradually woken up to the virtues of the fox. Closer acquaintance with the fox could not fail to produce admiration. Instead of simply turning at bay, like the stupid boar, it exhausted all its cleverness to escape from the hounds, often with success.

This admiration for the cleverness and determination of the fox found expression in mediaeval Europe's most popular epic poem, *The Romance of Reynard*. Written by various clerks (presumably hunting parsons, like William Clowne) this epic describes the adventures of a hero called Reynard. Although the old French for fox is *goupil*, Reynard became such a popular hero that *renard* is now the modern French word for fox. Sur-rounded by enemies, such as Bruin the bear, or Noble the lion, Reynard never fails to emerge unscathed and victorious from his various trials.

As in every other epoch, during mediaeval times men's attitudes towards dogs was ambivalent. It was a great insult to call anyone a dog. When Piers Gaveston, the chief favourite of Edward III, nicknamed Guy, Earl of Warwick, 'The Black Hound of Arden', Guy was furious. 'Let him call me hound,' he threatened, 'one day the hound will bite him.' He kept his word; when he got Gaveston into his power he had him beheaded at Blacklow Hill, a mile or so away from Warwick Castle, that mediaeval fortress for man and dog. The twelfth-century forger who compiled the 'Laws of Howell the Good' obviously regarded the epithet 'cur' as an insult so grave that it could only be revenged by the utmost brutality on the part of the husband to whom it was uttered. The average dog was a discarded outcast, a member of a pariah pack only tolerated because they were a protection for the village and a reserve supply of food in hard times. During the reign of Thomas of Lancaster, the supplanter of Edward II, the famine was so severe that dogs were eaten in England.

Yet as much as dogs in general were reviled, certain favoured dogs were revered. The dog appeared as a heraldic charge, it fought on the battlefield, somehow it even entered into the iconography of religion as a dog-headed saint. It was so much associated with its master that it was looked on as the genius of his destiny. When Richard II has an interview with his supplanter, Henry Bolingbroke, the king's greyhound, Blemach, which has hitherto been the patient and uncomplaining companion of his misfortunes, leaves his side and goes to fawn on the usurper. For the first time Richard's heart sinks as he realises his star has fallen.

It is only when we read stories such as this one from Froissart and when we walk through the aisles of an old church, that we fully realise the nobility of the ideal which some mediaeval dogs achieved. On the tombs in the church lie the sleeping figures of the knights and their ladies. Their eyes have closed but the eyes of the dogs at the foot of the sleepers are open, for to slumber, even for a moment, would be a betrayal of trust.

3

The Renaissance

With the advent of the Renaissance the story of the dog comes out into completely open country, though it is true that a little mist hangs over the valleys here and there. There is copious information about English dogs, information not, as in the past, derived from a royal huntsman writing for a very narrow circle of aristocratic friends, but from a famous physician and a well-known scholar who write for an international audience, confident that Europeans as well as English folk will want to read about English dogs.

Not all the information that can be acquired is pleasant. Nobody would want to dwell, for its own sake, on the horror of the bull-baiting ring, yet it cannot be omitted because it is from bull-baitings that the most famous of all English dogs, the bulldog, is eventually to emerge. It is hardly surprising that the Tudor monarchs who were passionately attached to bull-baiting, were very lukewarm dog-lovers. Yet where their affection blew cold, it was more than compensated for by that of their subjects. The love of English people for their dogs during the sixteenth century became a matter for comment by moralists. Not content with native dogs, they had become collectors of foreign breeds, such as the Icelandic dog which was the first direct import to England from another continent. If English owners made their name as amateurs of new breeds, a role played to the end of this survey, they also gave America its most important breed during this era, the great bloodhound used by the Spaniards to subdue rebellious Indians and track runaway slaves. This splendid dog is the descendant of English bloodhounds, acquired by Philip II while consort of Mary and sent to the Americas. As if to round off this wonderful era fittingly, the dog for the first time becomes the inspiration of great poets.

There was no visible sign in the England of 1485 that the Middle Ages had ended and modern times begun, but one proof that the England of the Tudors was a completely different kingdom from what it had been during the reign of the Plantagenets was that subjects had now possessed themselves of that cherished royal privilege, game enclosures for hunting deer. As in the days of King Canute, every gentlemen 'could enjoy his own hunting in his own grounds'. There were many Englishmen who did little or nothing else. In 1559 Henry Lord Berkeley

... came with his wife and family to Callowden, his house by Coventry, when the first work done, was the sending for his buckhounds to Yate in Gloucestershire. His hounds being come away goeth he and his wife on a progress of buckhunting to the Parks of: Berkswell, Groby, Bradgate, Leicester Forest, Tiley, and others on this side of his house, and after a small repose, then the Parks of Kenelworth, Astley, Wedgnock, and others, on the other side of his house, and this was the course of this Lord, more or less, for the thirty next summers at least.

England had become a country of fallow deer, deer parks, oak palings and oak trees, where hunting was the only thing that mattered. 'There be more parks in England than in all Europe beside,' said Andrew Bourde, the shrewd physician who was the origin of our own term 'Merry Andrew'. Fynes Moryson noted that

... the King's forests have innumerable herds of red deer, and all parts have such plenty of fallow deer, as every gentleman of five hundred or a thousand pound rent by the year hath a park for them enclosed with pales of wood for two or three miles compass.... I will boldly say, that England (yea perhaps one county thereof) hath more fallow deer than all Europe that I have seen.

By the end of the sixteenth century the extent of the deer parks had become matter for moralists such as William Harrison.

In every shire of England there is great plenty of parks, whereof some here and there appertain unto the Prince, the rest unto such of the nobility and gentlemen as have their lands and patrimony lying near unto the same. I would gladly have set down the just number of these enclosures to be found in every county, but since I cannot do so, it shall suffice to say, that in Kent and Essex only are to the number of an hundred, wherein great plenty of fallow deer is cherished and kept.... Our parks are generally enclosed with strong palings made of oak, of which kind of wood there is great store cherished from time to time in each of them, only for the maintenance of the said defence and safe keeping of the deer from ranging about the country. The circuit of these enclosures in like manner contains many times a distance of four or five miles, and sometimes more or less, whereby it is to be seen what store of ground is employed upon that vain commodity which brings no manner of gain or profit to the owner, since they commonly give away their venison, never taking a penny for the same, because venison in England is neither bought or sold by the rightful owner, but maintained only for his pleasure, to the no small decay of husbandry and diminution of mankind. For, when in times past, many large and wealthy occupiers were dwelling within the area of one park, and thereby there was great plenty of corn and cattle to be seen, and ... besides a larger population, by which the country was always provided with suitable recruits for the army, now there is almost nothing there but wild and savage beasts, cherished for pleasure and delight. And yet the owners, still desiring to enlarge these grounds, do not hesitate to extend them daily, saying that we have already too large a population in England, that people get married too young, and instead of benefiting the country by doing so, fill it full of beggars. . . . Certainly, if it is not God's curse, to have our country converted in this way from being a nursery of men, into a game park, I do not know what is.

William Harrison wrote the first draft of his preface to *Holinshed's Chronicles* in 1577 and revised his work ten years later. His writing career thus spans what was probably the most crucial era in English and indeed in Atlantic history, the climax of the great struggle at sea between England and Spain. Though there were other factors which secured English victory in that struggle, the essential one was a supply of oak timbers for the fleet. Ever since Henry VII had invented the gunport, the fire of an enemy ship had been concentrated not on sweeping the deck of her opponent but on sinking her opponent by a well directed shot just above the waterline. A ship built of any material other than oak was extremely vulnerable to such fire; it also rapidly became a hell of flying splinters, more deadly than the enemy's fire as the planks cut from more open woods shattered in all directions. Aboard an oak-built ship the force of enemy fire, though still serious, was contained by the nature of the material of which she was built. Cannon-balls embedded themselves in the stout timbers or, if they cut them, went through with a clean hole. Oak-built ships could take an enormous pounding. Four years after Harrison revised his preface, Sir Richard Grenville fought the *Revenge* for fifteen hours against an opposing force of fifteen Spanish galleons. A ship built from fir or deal would have gone to the bottom in the first shock of the encounter.

The English ships which fought the Armada were the end of a biological chain which began with the buckhounds that every gentleman of substance kept. The quarry for these hounds was the herds of red and fallow deer kept in the deer parks. To keep in these deer and to keep out deer poachers the whole of the park was enclosed with vast palisades of oak, for a brick wall of four or five miles in length was beyond the means of any save the most princely sportsmen. In order to provide wood for these palisades, oak trees were grown, as Harrison reminds us. Towards the end of the century, the cost of inflation forced many gentlemen park owners to decide whether it would be their social prestige or their income which went to the wall. Most chose wisely and determined to make their estates pay for themselves. One noblewoman even sold her husband's venison to the pastry cooks, greatly to the scandal of Harrison. Others sold their rabbits or their butter, but most got rid of the expensive, and non-productive, deer parks. 'This prodigal age,' wrote Fynes Morison, 'hath so forced gentle-

men to improve their revenues, as many of these grounds are by them disparked, and converted to feed cattle.' The oaks, now no longer required for
palings round the now disparked parks, became available for shipbuilding, just at the time when they were needed most.

England's neighbour, Scotland, also indulged a brief dream of becoming a great maritime nation at about the same time that Henry VII began to
build up the English navy. James IV of Scotland (1473–1513) constructed a
fleet which included the flagship, the *Great Michael*, to make which all the
woods in Fife were felled. Under the Scottish admirals Sir Andrew Wood
and Sir Andrew Barton this fleet won signal victories against Henry VIII's
navy. Scotland's naval superiority was brought to an end not merely by the
national catastrophe of Flodden in 1513, but by the fact that she had simply
run out of timber. Because hunting was carried on in quite a different kind
of way in Scotland, with the great Highland deerhounds which coursed
the deer, or running-hounds which pursued them *à force*, there was no
need for deer parks and, consequently, oaks to pale them. James' shipbuilding programme left the country almost denuded of timber, in the
regions where it would have been useful for shipbuilding. A later observer
wrote rather sourly that if Judas had lived in Scotland he might have found
repentance, but not a tree to hang himself on.

The private parks for deer were of considerable importance to the
English countryside, particularly with regard to those countrymen who
kept dogs (such as young William Shakespeare, as will be seen). Between
the years 1515 and 1518 Richard Chambyr, Park Keeper of Framlingham in
Suffolk, noted down the game that had been killed in this park belonging
to the Duke of Norfolk. Chambyr made careful records of the deer he had
killed on his master's orders to send to friends of his and how other friends
of the Duke's had come to the park to kill deer themselves. He also noted
down the losses of the herd in fawning time and through disease. When it
came to the ravages wrought by dogs, whether accompanied or not by
their masters, he always made a note of how he had dealt with these four
and two-legged poachers. John Pulsham the elder rode past the outer
boundary of the park. A doe had escaped from the park and his dog killed
it. Thereupon Pulsham, no doubt on the insistence of Chambyr, hanged
the dog. Hanging was then and for centuries after the usual way of putting
down unwanted dogs, hence Shakespeare's line: 'Let gallows gape for
dogs, let men go free.'

Not all dog-owners were so complacent as Pulsham. Walter Warnere,
the son of Anne Warnere of Denyngton, 'forestalled my lord's deer when I
was setting them home and put his bitch to her and brought her in to the
park and killed her.' Chambyr was unable to exact any penalty from Walter
Warnere, who may have been supported by some noble who was a rival to
the Duke. He was unsuccessful in dealing with a number of other deer-
stealers who were accompanied by their dogs.

Dogs wandered into deer parks by themselves and their masters were held responsible for the damage they committed – if those masters could be found. Chambyr noted that he had lost a fawn, killed by 'a mastiff bitch and a spaniel', and that no fewer than eleven deer had been killed by dogs in 1518. In the following year, 'the Monday before Michaelmas Day, came in a dog of Johnson's of Denyngton, the shoe maker, and killed two does, and there the dog was taken up, and I sent to him to know whether he would have the dog again, and he sent me word, "No." And then I hung it on a tree.'

Chambyr's records throw a very interesting light on the relationships of dogs, their owners, the deer in the park and their owner, the Duke. First of all it seems obvious that poaching was quite common and that the deer parks were a magnet for poachers, who were not all humble countryfolk by any means. Chambyr found the parish priest of Tangton, John Bowse, with his arrow at the bow, ready to bring down a buck he had singled out. Though it seems very strange, it is difficult not to conclude that even a powerful nobleman like the Duke of Norfolk found it impossible to secure punishment for the poachers who took his deer. Then again, many people became involuntary poachers when their dogs started hunting on their own account. Dog-owners who offended in this way, such as shoemaker Johnson, seem to have been sensible that trouble awaited them if they turned up in the area of the park again.

It is with the information supplied by Richard Chambyr's records that we might attempt, tentatively, to solve one of the greatest mysteries of the sixteenth century, the question of why William Shakespeare should have had to leave his native town of Stratford and go to London to seek refuge from his enemies. One of the most substantial traditions that have gathered around Shakespeare's life is that, in 1584, he suddenly left Stratford and fled to London to escape the consequences of a poaching affray on the estates of a wealthy Warwickshire landowner, Sir Thomas Lucy. Sir Thomas Lucy turns up in *The Merry Wives of Windsor* as Justice Shallow, with the dozen white louses in his old coat – a punning allusion to Sir Thomas' coat-of-arms, which bore 'luces' or fish. Obviously, the incident of the poaching affray must have wrankled with Shakespeare, seeing that he mentions it in a play written sixteen years after it happened. It might well wrankle. Young Will had been forced to leave his beloved Warwickshire and bury himself in the noisome slums of Elizabethan London, where he would have to engage in all sorts of obscure pursuits to scrape a bare living. He had left his old father in the direst poverty. He had also left his wife, Anne, who had just given birth to their first child Susanna.

Many lovers of Shakespeare have felt that the poaching affair was inconsistent with the Shakespeare that we know from the plays. It seems almost incredible that the greatest dramatist who ever lived should have been a petty criminal. Curiously enough, no one who has investigated the Thomas Lucy affair has been inclined to attach any weight to the fact that John Shakespeare, the father, was a butcher and that young Will helped him with the business. John Aubrey even says explicitly that he killed calves for his father. Considering the disastrous state of the elder Shakespeare's affairs, it would have been a very unfilial son who refused what help he could give the old man. There can be no question that every butcher must have owned a mastiff, probably several. Cattle bought for slaughter were not delivered by the farmer in those days, they had to be collected from him and driven to the butchery, in the way that Edward, Duke of York described for us in the previous chapter. My solution to the Lucy affair, such as it is, is that Shakespeare was driving in cattle back to John Shakespeare's butchery with the family mastiff and was passing the Lucy park when suddenly the mastiff broke away, dashed into the park and made one of those rapid tours of destruction inside the palings which Richard Chambyr so dolefully describes in his park records. This seems a much more likely explanation to me than that young Will should have voluntarily jeopardised the welfare of his whole family. Once the mastiff had run its course, Shakespeare had no choice but to flee to London. He was poor and without those aristocratic supporters who were so essential to personal security in Tudor times.

Did this escapade with the mastiff take place at night? If it did, a puzzling line of Shakespeare may, like his reference to Sir Thomas Lucy, be a reminiscence of the affair: 'When night dogs run, all kind of deer are chased.'

This explanation would also go far to explain another problem which has long puzzled Shakespeare lovers. He speaks of dogs frequently in his plays but rarely, if ever, with affection. If my reconstruction of what happened is correct he had no grounds for affection. For the animal which had forced him to flee from all his loved ones. It was to be more than ten years before he felt sufficiently confident to return to Stratford from his involuntary exile in London. Shakespeare's adventures with dogs were not over by any means. We shall see later how the greatest English pastime, bull-baiting, imposed the design of the bull-ring upon the Shakespearian theatre and thus modified the construction of his plays.

Meanwhile we must look at the sport that was being sought in the deer parks of England by innumerable country gentlemen, such as Sir Thomas Lucy, and their dogs. Deer-hunting had changed drastically from what it had been in the Middle Ages. Most of the formalities and ceremonials had been cut out, while those left seem a little bizarre. 'Fewmets' or droppings of the deer were still presented to the sovereign in the huntsman's horn or on a large leaf. From the condition of these fewmets conclusions were drawn about the particular stag which was hiding in the covert. If it was decided to give chase, it would be tracked down by a limer or bloodhound, put up by the same dog, chased by running-hounds or coursed by greyhounds and either pulled down by the dogs if it were being coursed or, more usually, shot with a crossbow in a pre-arranged battue. Hunting in England had become a very tame affair compared with the wild scurry of hunters galloping after the hounds as they streamed in pursuit of a stag across the wildest country during Early Middle Ages.

For some of this tameness, the blame must be laid at the door of the reigning dynasty. Though not exactly parvenus, the Tudors were certainly less fond of sport than the reigning houses which had preceded and were to follow them. The only pastime which really pleased them was much too cruel to be dignified with the name of sport at all, it was bull-baiting.

Various Tudors went to great lengths just to prove how unsporting they could be, if they wanted to. Henry VII ordered his horse to be starved for twenty-four hours before he went on a procession through London, just in case it might get too restive to control easily. He also, says William Harrison, ordered all mastiffs to be hanged 'because they dare presume to fight against the lion, who is their king and sovereign'. Harrison recounts how this same monarch ordered a splendid falcon that had dared to engage alone with an eagle to have its neck wrung, 'saying that it was not meet for any subject to offer such wrong unto his lord and superior, wherein he had a further meaning.' Harrison means to imply that Henry was trying to read a lesson to the unruly and overmighty barons and remind them that their duty was to obey the king not fight him. It is unlikely that he ever carried out such a massacre of mastiffs as Harrison describes, though he may have issued an order to that effect, as a symbolic gesture, and then rescinded it. If he ever did order mastiffs to be killed it was not because they had committed 'treason' against that king of beasts, the lion, but because they were very useful allies on the battlefield.

Henry VIII was equally apathetic so far as sport and dogs were concerned. He made a great parade of hunting in his youth and tired his mounts so quickly that he had to have a relay of eight horses for every day's hunting, but he soon became so heavy in the saddle that he gave up riding altogether, confining himself to the murderous drives of deer which will be described in a moment. Not content with giving up hunting for shooting, he proceeded to spoil the sport of all deer park owners in England by ordering them to keep mares in their parks, so as to promote the breed of horses. By this act, passed in 1536, 'every man that has a park of his own . . . of the compass of one mile shall keep in the same two mares, and every man that has a park of the compass of four miles, shall keep four mares.' Though this act fell into disuse, it was revived by Elizabeth in 1577 and it was one of the factors that contributed towards the decline of deer-hunting in England as a national sport.

Henry went farther than any king of England would ever have dared before him. He banned dogs at court. One of the regulations for the Royal Household reads: 'No dogs to be kept in court. The king's highness also directly forbids anyone, whoever they are, to presume to keep at court any greyhound, mastiff, hound or other dog, except for some small spaniels for ladies and other folk, nor to bring dogs to court, except by the King or Queen's order.'

As might be expected, this prohibition did not apply to the king's own dogs, because he in fact kept quite a large number. He was often given dogs as presents and he watched them course against those belonging to other courtiers in the park at Eltham Palace. He may have done this to determine the greyhounds' qualities and thus assess how grateful he ought to be to the donor. Henry had a pet spaniel called 'Cutte' and there are at least three payments on record, of ten shillings, five shillings and four and eight-pence, to people who brought 'Cutte' home when it had got lost.

Another dog, 'Ball', was also returned after it had strayed into Waltham Forest and the finder compensated. Henry, however, may have been just as grateful to get back the dog's collar as the dog itself. Most creatures and objects which he owned were usually lavishly ornamented with gold and gems, at least during his prosperous years, and his dogs were probably not an exception to this rule.

Henry apparently enjoyed watching dogs working. When he was staying at Ashridge he gave four shillings and eightpence to a man who had trained dogs to draw water. Hertfordshire was apparently famous for these dogs. William Harrison, writing towards the end of the century, tells us that: 'in many places our mastiffs . . . are made to draw water in great wheels out of deep wells, going much like unto those which are framed for our turnspit dogs, as is to be seen at Royston, where this feat is often prac-tised.' One of the royal mastiffs, which is described as a 'carrier', may have been a trained working-dog. Possibly it had been trained to carry letters, like the one belonging to Sir John Harington a godson of Queen Elizabeth, who took great pride in his letter-carrying dog 'Bungey'.

All in all, Henry seems to have admired intelligence in dogs. He once gave twenty shillings, a large sum in those days, 'to the fellow with the dancing dog'. Yet there can be no doubt that the dogs in which he most delighted were his bear-baiting mastiffs who, complete with bears and bearward, figure in the royal accounts. To Henry's better known cruelties must be added this lesser known one of being the first important royal patron of the cruellest pastime in which dogs have ever figured. Unfortu-nately this was almost the only respect in which his two daughters, Mary and Elizabeth, took after him. They too were lukewarm about dogs. Mary owned a spaniel which she bought for fifteen shillings and she appears in a portrait now in Woburn Abbey, by Sir Antonio More, along with two small white dogs with long ears, pointed noses and belled collars. Elizabeth, too, liked lap-dogs well enough but was little concerned with other breeds.

Now that the Tudor coolness towards dogs has been mentioned, it is easier to accept the fact that they played a very small part in the official life of the court, even when it went hunting. The ideal Tudor hunt was a shoot on a fine day, aided by nets, beaters, dogs and a plentiful supply of ready loaded crossbows, and preferably in a subject's park, not a royal one. The following account is from Smyth's *Lives of the Berkeleys*.

Queen Elizabeth in her progress, in the fifteenth year of her reign, came to Berkeley Castle, where at this time Henry Lord Berkeley had a stately herd of red deer in a park near the castle called 'The Worthy', of which Henry Ligon was the keeper. During the time she stayed there she made such slaughter that twenty-seven stags were killed in the nets in one day and many others on that day and the next day stolen and havocked. When this lord, who was then at Callowden, heard about what had happened, he suddenly and impulsively ordered that 'The Worthy' should be disparked, because he had greatly delighted in this herd of game.

A battue like the slaughter of the Berkeley herd was carried out from special shooting-platforms called 'pavilions'. These were placed well out of danger from deer at special vantage points where the animals had to pass as they were driven along narrow lines of palings. As the deer passed, the courtiers shot them with steel crossbows which were handed to them, ready loaded with heavy bolts with metal heads. The best shots, amongst whom must be numbered Henry VIII and Elizabeth, waited until the pursuing greyhounds driving the deer had brought them within range and then killed with a clean shot through heart or throat. Bad shots missed altogether or killed a pursuing greyhound. The unskilful also tended to wound, rather than kill, the deer, but there was no prospect of the poor animal lingering in its misery, as it would be pulled down by the buckhounds which accompanied the hunt. They would get the deer by the ear, drag it to the ground and hold it till a hunter ran up to cut its throat with a hunting-knife. Then the deer would be brought to the royal pavilion where the monarch would be invited to make the first incision which would begin the process of 'breaking up' the animal. Someone so exquisitely dressed as Elizabeth probably never handled the breaking-up knife herself, any more than she touched the fewmets offered to her. Instead she stood, shading herself with a leafy bough, till it was time to take her crossbow and bring down another fat buck.

Occasionally the shooting of deer would be enlivened by coursing them with greyhounds. In 1591 the Queen arrived at Cowdray Park in Sussex, the seat of Viscount Montague.

On Monday, August 17th, at eight of the clock in the morning, her Highness took horse, with all her train, and rode into the park, where there was a delicate bower prepared, under which were placed her Highness' own musicians. After a sweet song, a girl dressed as a nymph gave the Queen a crossbow so that she could shoot at the deer. There were about thirty of them, in a paddock, and of this number she killed three or four and the Countess of Kildare one. Then her Majesty rode to Cowdray for dinner, and about six o'clock in the evening, from a turret in the house, she saw sixteen bucks, all having a fair start, pulled down by greyhounds on the lawn.

Coursing deer was every bit as artificial a sport as pigeon-shooting with clay pigeons. It was divided into paddock or forest coursing. In the former kind, part of a park about a mile long was fenced off with the palings placed about a quarter of a mile apart at the beginning of the ground, then gradually widening towards the end so as to accommodate more spectators. Posts marked off various stages of the course. The first was the 'law post' where the deer were started on their course and it was placed a hundred and sixty yards from the dog-house where the greyhounds were kennelled. The next was the 'Quarter of a mile' post, then came the 'Half mile post', the 'Pinching post' and finally a ditch, placed so as to save those deer which had run the course from being pulled down by the greyhounds. Greyhound-coursing was eventually to evolve from the sport of deer-coursing and it also had an important effect in keeping up the breed of greyhounds.

All that could be said that Tudor sport was that it still required the help of dogs but it did little to sustain the existing breeds, much less improve them. Almost any kind of dog could accompany a deer-shooter. When a stag, wounded by Burghley's crossbow, had taken to the water, Burghley sent in a water spaniel after it and another, smaller, hunting companion, a bitch which Leicester had given him. The only kind of dog which was really indispensable in a deer-shoot was a limer, which, as has already been noticed, was used to snuff out the hiding-place of the quarry and drive it out of cover.

Hunting was a pursuit that could be followed by old gentlemen of scholarly and sedentary tastes, like Burghley. You rode to the park, then dismounted and either ran on foot or stood on a stand for the shooting. English deer-hunting provoked no reaction in sportsmen trained in the traditions of the royal French or royal Scottish hunt except a yawn, diplomatically concealed by a flourish with the toothpick. 'The English are not so skilled in taking the stag as they are in maritime matters,' wrote the Marshal de Vielleville, Ambassador to England from France's Henri II. 'They took me to a great park full of fallow deer . . . and in company of forty or fifty lords and gentlemen we hunted and killed fifteen or twenty beasts. It amused me to see the English ride full tilt in this hunt, the short sword in their hand, and they could not have shouted louder had they been following an enemy after a hard won victory.'

Yet if the deer-hunt was too tame, the other principal English pastime in which dogs figured, the bull-fight, was only too exciting. Once again a foreigner – the young German Paul Hentzner, who visited England in 1598 can give us an eye-witness account.

There is still another place, built in the form of a theatre, which serves for the baiting of bulls and bears. They are fastened behind, and then worried by great dogs, but not without risk to the dogs, from the horns of one and the teeth of the other, and it sometimes happens they are killed on the spot. Fresh ones are immediately supplied in the place of those that are wounded or tired.

As has been noticed earlier, bull-baiting was a very long-established English institution, but bear-baiting seems to have originated with the Tudors. As early as 1506 Erasmus had noted in his *Adagia* that many herds of bears were maintained in England for baiting. Some considerable time later, Shakespeare refers to 'Russian bears' indicating that they were being imported. The sea route to Russia had been discovered by the Tudor explorers and so England was in a good position to import bears from that country. They continued to appear in England till the seventeenth century at least and before they disappeared the connection between Russia, and 'the bear' had become firmly implanted in the English mind.

Animal combats with English mastiffs had never been so popular in England as they became during Elizabeth's reign. While still young and a prisoner at Hatfield House, she and her sister Mary had watched an exhibition of bear-baiting 'with which their Highnessess were right well content'.

At liberty and a queen, Elizabeth continued to be well-content with baitings, and those who wished to please her arranged them for her benefit, as did the Earl of Leicester when she visited Kenilworth Castle in 1575. Here thirteen bears, which was certainly a large number, were assembled for her amusement. 'It was a sport very pleasant,' wrote a spectator, 'to see the bear with his pink eyes leering after his enemy's approach, the nimbleness and waiting of the dog to take his advantage, and the force and experience of the bear again to avoid the assaults.' Elizabeth showed so much a fancy for baitings herself that it became part of good diplomacy for ambassadors credited to her court to make a point of patronising them.

After being regaled with a bear-baiting at court in 1559, which lasted from the end of dinner till six o'clock at night, the French ambassadors went to one of the specially constructed London amphitheatres where baiting took place. All of them were on the south bank of the Thames and so the ambassadors 'took barge at Paul's wharf, and so to Paris Garden, at Bankside at Southwark, where was to be another baiting of bulls and bears, and the Captain with an hundred of the Guard, kept room for them against the time they came, so that they might have place to see the show.'

Nothing can indicate more forcibly just how much Elizabeth's subjects shared her taste for seeing blood flow than the fact that it took a large military detachment to ensure that they were able to reserve their places for the ambassadors. The Paris Garden was a real amphitheatre, a wooden circle with rising tiers of galleries, and accommodation for more than a thousand spectators. It had been erected in 1526 under royal patronage. The fee for admission was a penny and twopence had to be paid for a good place in the gallery. Animal-baitings were very much under royal patronage. When in 1570 a second amphitheatre was added at Paris Garden, for bull-baiting, it too had to have a royal licence issued by the Master of Game (the successor to that Edward Duke of York who introduced us to bull-baiting in the first place). Although bull-baiting played a much smaller part in the amusements of the Paris Garden than did bear-baiting, with only three bulls to twenty bears, yet the same dogs were used for both kind of combats, the incomparable English mastiffs.

Elizabeth supported the sport not merely because she liked it, but because animal combats were a popular crowd-attraction on Sunday, the working man's only holiday. It was better she felt that crowds should throng to a bull-ring and find an outlet for their savage natures in watching a baiting than they should form idle crowds which could be manipulated by someone with treasonable ambitions. So the 'official' view of the pastime was that it was 'a sweet and comfortable recreation, fitted for the solace and comfort of a peaceable people.' The Privy Council ordered theatres to close on Thursdays because they drew away the crowds from the fights on that other bear-baiting day – which may also help to account for the disillusioned attitude that Shakespeare often exhibits towards dogs. The Queen carried patronage to its utmost limits when in 1599 she actually visited Paris Garden herself. She never, so far as I know, attended a performance of a play at a public theatre, thus showing clearly where her preference for amusements lay.

In the whole of the Queen's realm there was only one group of people who had the courage to tell her what they thought about her views of baitings – the Puritans. 'What Christian heart,' asked Philip Stubbes in his *Anatomie of Abuses*, published in 1583, 'can take pleasure in seeing one poor beast rend, tear and kill another, and all for his foolish pleasure? . . . And to be plain, I think the devil is the Master of the Game, bearward and all. A goodly pastime, forsooth!'

Many Puritans felt that it was a righteous judgement when, on Sunday, 13th January 1583, the scaffolding of the amphitheatre at Paris Garden collapsed 'when the dog and bear were in the chiefest battle'. Five men and two women were killed, indicating that Elizabeth's tastes were shared by others of her sex. The Corporation of the City of London was strongly Puritan and it would have liked to close down the amphitheatres, particularly Paris Garden, but they were outside its jurisdiction. Nonetheless it lost no opportunity of pointing out to the government that bear-baiting helped to spread the plague and brought about the decline of archery. Puritans hinted that baitings were a very sinful pastime in that they produced a mood of intense excitement, in mixed company, to the accompaniment of a great deal of drinking. 'The general drink is beer,' wrote Paul Hentzner, 'strong and what soon fuddles.' In any case, said the Puritans, everyone should be in church on a Sunday. Eventually in James I's reign their views were to prevail and the Sunday baitings were abolished.

Since the days of Henry VIII, more secular-minded moralists had felt that the poor should be compelled to relinquish a luxury which they could ill afford:

> What folly is this, to keep with danger,
> A great mastiff dog, and a foul ugly bear?
> And to this one end, to see them two fight,
> With terrible tearings, a foul ugly sight.
> And yet, methinks, those men must be most fools of all,
> Whose store of money is but very small.
> And yet every Sunday they will surely spend,
> One penny, or two, the bearward's living to mend.
> At Paris Garden each Sunday a man shall not fail,
> To find two or three hundred for the Bearward's vale.
> One halfpenny a piece they use for to give,
> When some have not more in their purses, I believe.'

There was nothing to choose between the cruelty of bull-baiting and that of bear-baiting. From the point of view of a combat between animals and mastiffs, it was a very unequal contest whether bull or bear was involved. As has already been noticed, London animal-fights concentrated on the bear rather than the bull. The characteristic defence of the European bear is not biting or clawing, but the crushing to death of its victims between its forearms and its chest. Against this defence the mastiffs had little hope of survival. They could and did wound the bear frequently, sometimes lacerating its jugular veins, so that it bled to death, sometimes blinding it (so that it could be served up as a 'special turn' at the next session of Paris Garden) but more frequently inflicting on it merely minor wounds which the bear-ward would patch up as best he could.

The superiority of bear versus mastiff can be seen in the survival of numerous veterans which became 'stars of the bull-ring'. These bears, animals such as 'George Stone', 'Harry Hunks', 'Tom of Lincoln', 'Sackerson', 'Ned of Canterbury' and 'Don John', survived dozens of fights and became popular idols. They retained so much force and vitality, in spite of their numerous combats, that sometimes they broke the chain that tethered them and ran loose among the crowd of spectators. At this point the more daring among the bull-ring audience would try to seize the chain so that they could be re-tethered. Abraham Slender, the foolish suitor of Anne Page in *The Merry Wives of Windsor*, makes the improbable boast that he had seen Sackerson loose twenty times and taken him by the chain, among the frightened shrieks of women onlookers.

Though the bull sometimes had its horns muffled in straw, or trimmed short, it was still too formidable an antagonist for a fair fight between it and the mastiffs. Its horns, even though blunted, could send the mastiff flying high into the air to land among the spectators; its hooves took deadly toll of the dogs that were gathered right beneath it.

Nothing can speak more eloquently in favour of the pluck of the English mastiff than the fact that it was prepared to tackle such formidable adversaries. Englishmen were so proud of their mastiffs that they assumed that all foreigners had heard of them if they had heard of anything English at all. In *Henry V* the following dialogue takes place between the French noblemen waiting for the Battle of Agincourt to begin:

> *Rambures*: That Island of England breeds very valiant Creatures; their Mastiffs are of unmatchable courage.
> *Orleans*: Foolish curs that run winking into the mouth of a Russian bear, and have their heads crushed like rotten apples.

Not surprisingly, mastiffs make a very important showing in the two accounts of dogs writen by Elizabethan historians which we must consider in a moment. Caius (Dr Kaye) said that 'it is a kind of dog capable of courage, violent and valiant, striking cold fear into the hearts of men, but standing in fear of no man, in so much that no weapons will make him shrink, nor abridge his boldness.' William Harrison remarks that the mastiff 'is a huge dog, stubborn, ugly, eager, burdenous of body, and therefore but of little swiftness. . . . The force which is in them surmounteth all belief, and the fast hold which they take with their teeth exceeds all credit'.

The ghoulish monsters who frequented the bull-ring realised that the contest could be 'improved' if the mastiff could be considerably altered by breeding. In the very specialised circumstances of the Tudor animal-fight, the mastiff was really very much at a disadvantage. It had never been bred, originally, as an animal-fighting dog at all. It was a hunting-dog. Philip Sidney, talking to Camerarius in 1576, said that mastiffs were ideal dogs to use against wolves, they were also employed against foxes and badgers and to drive wild or tame swine out of the crops. They were also widely used as house and yard dogs, hence William Harrison's rather far-fetched derivation of their name from 'mastiff' meaning 'masterthief'. Often kept chained up, from which custom another of their names, 'ban dog', was derived, it was no wonder that they were slow in action when released in the arena.

The mastiff was large, it offered a good-sized target for the clutching paw of the bear or the stamping hoof or twisting horn of the bull. Its long throat was extremely vulnerable, even when covered with a metal collar. Above all its massive body and slow action did not permit it to exercise against its opponents what would have been the most effective tactic, an instant dart to inflict a wound and a lightning retreat. A new kind of dog was obviously required for the ring.

The form of the bull-ring, an amphitheatre designed to accommodate as many spectators as possible, was in turn to be imposed on the Elizabethan theatre. The first important English amphitheatre, the Bull Ring in Birmingham, had been merely a large open spot in the centre of the town. At Banbury, in Oxfordshire, bull-baitings were carried out in what was apparently an old Roman amphitheatre. The ring design of the Paris Garden was again based on an amphitheatre design. It was this layout that actor James Burbage chose for his new theatre in London when he began to build it in 1576. Rejecting the design of the old square inn courtyard with galleries, in which the first plays had been performed, he built a circular theatre with galleries rising one above another. There was a jutting-out apron stage in the middle of the ring, but this was movable and, if it were taken away, Burbage's new theatre was very like Paris Garden.

The choice of this design, inspired by that of the dog-fighting arena, enabled Burbage to crowd in an audience of as many as 1,500 for every performance, thus ensuring the prosperity of the undertaking. The design, which Shakespeare referred to as 'the wooden O', also helped to mould his plays. It was not so much that the new theatre lent itself to particular kinds of stage business, though obviously it did. The convention of the Shakespearian soliloquy seems less unreal when the actor delivering it walks to the end of the apron stage, far from his fellow actors but nearer to the audience. What was important in the change wrought in play construction was that, in a theatre which seemed like a microcosm of the round world, Shakespearian drama becomes, not a peep into a domestic scene from which the outside wall has been removed, but rather a theatre extended infinitely above, in which it is easy to accept the appeals which the dramatist continually makes to those forces which drive, not merely his characters, but the whole universe.

The enthusiasm felt by Englishmen for their dogs, and especially their mastiffs, was so communicative that it attracted the attention of foreign scholars. Conrad Gesner, a Swiss naturalist, wrote to Dr John Caius asking him what he could tell him about English dogs. Caius was delighted to oblige, for he was a prolific author, as well as a man of rare accomplishments. Caius had been born in 1510 in Norwich. He had studied divinity in Cambridge, at what was then Gonville College, then travelled over the Continent, taking a medical degree at Padua. He had written a number of books, not all of which had been printed, and some of which have now disappeared, and become court physician successively to Edward VI, Mary and Elizabeth.

Caius replied to his friend's request by sending him a long letter which was really a monograph in disguise. He subsequently published the letter in 1570 with the title *De canibus Britannicis*. He wrote in Latin because his correspondent, Gesner, did not understand any English, but unfortunately he did not take the trouble to translate his work back into English for publication. The result was a rather inaccurate and misleading translation by Abraham Fleming, published in 1576.

Caius' work was the first book published in England to be devoted entirely to dogs and the first in any language to try to work out a scientific classification into which they could be divided. First, said Caius, there came 'Generous or thorough-bred' dogs. They included 'Hounds' and inside that category were to be found terriers, harriers and bloodhounds. Then there were 'Hunting' dogs, including the gazehound, greyhound, limer and tumbler. The 'Hawking or Fowling' dogs included spaniels, setters and water spaniels. Next came 'Delicate' dogs, a category confined to the 'Spaniel Gentle or Comforter'.

The 'Country' dogs included the shepherd's dog and the mastiff or bandog. Last came a category which Caius labelled 'Degenerate'. This included the 'wappe' (a barking dog kept to guard the house), the turnspit (used as will be seen to turn the roast in front of the fire in the kitchen) and the 'dancer' which we would now call a dancing-dog.

Because Caius wrote in Latin and was translated badly it is by no means easy to relate everything he says about dogs to the breeds that we may assume to have been in existence in the England of his day. Nevertheless, with the help of the review of his book made by William Harrison in his edition of Holinshed's Chronicles not long after Caius' death it is possible to seize at least some of his meaning. It is not necessary to say anything about his comments on mastiffs, which have been already dealt with, or on bloodhounds, which will be mentioned later.

Caius' account stresses the incredible variety of dogs that might be encountered in England. There were terriers, used to pursue the fox and badger underground and bring them to the surface. Gazehounds were employed, especially in the north, to hunt the hare and fox, while greyhounds were also used for the chase of the fox, though their principal quarry was the deer. Then there were limers. The function of this dog may be summed up in a sentence quoted from a letter by the Duke of Württemberg's secretary, who described how in 1592 the Duke, on a visit to England, shot a fallow deer with a crossbow bolt. 'The latter deer we were obliged to follow a very long while, till at length an unleashed limer or bloodhound as they are called, by its wonderful quality and peculiar nature, singled out the deer from several hundred others and pursued it so long, till at last the wounded deer was found on one side of a brook, and the dog, quite exhausted, on the other.' The limer was, in fact, a bloodhound in its military capacity and a limer in its civil sphere. Caius says that it was a fast-running hound, but apparently this is wrong and he is corrected on this point by the Victorian dog-historian George R. Jesse who says 'It is plain from these, and some other remarks of Caius, that with all his learning, he knew little of dogs, or the chase.'

Caius mentions the dog described by the Scots historian, Hector Boece, which fishes on the rocks for lobsters. Though such dogs might exist, he says, he has not heard of them, though he has heard of otter-hounds. Tumblers are a kind of dwarf greyhound used for rabbiting. There are special poachers' dogs (lurchers?) which are trained to course rabbits at night for their masters without barking. Spaniels are in use for fowling on land and water and quite recently a new French breed of spaniel has been brought to England, all white with black spots, because the English are so fond of novelties. Spaniels trained as setters or pointers will show the presence of game birds such as partridges and quails in undergrowth in time for the fowler to throw a net over the right spot. Then, at a command from its master the dog will start the birds from cover so that they become hopelessly entangled in the meshes. Water spaniels are indispensable for retrieving anything from water, not merely a shot bird, but an arrow that has gone astray. Sheep dogs or 'shepherds' curs' will drive their flock wherever it is wanted, just on the command of the shepherd, a command conveyed often by a whistle through the clenched fist of the shepherd. Then there are pack-dogs which carry tinkers' wares.

So far so good, but when Caius comes to the foreign dogs in England (which are not, after all, in his terms of reference) his indignation rises.

The third sort of dogs of the gentle kind is the spaniel gentle, or comforter, or, as the common term is, the 'fistinghound', and those are called 'Melitei' of the island of Malta, from where they are imported. They are little and pretty, proper and fine, and sought out far and near to deceive the nice delicacy of dainty ladies, and wanton woman's will, instruments of folly to play and dally with, in trifling away the treasure of time, to withdraw their minds from more worthwhile activities. . . . The smaller these puppies are, the better they are liked, particularly if they have a little dent in the forepart of their heads . . . Their mistresses carry them in their bosoms, keep them for company in their bedrooms and sleep with them in bed. They feed them at table, let them lie on their laps and even allow them to lick their faces as they ride about, like the young goddess Diana, in their coaches. . . . They often feed these dogs of the best, while the poor man's child at their door can hardly get the worst kind of food.

Nor did Caius have anything better to say bout that other popular imported dog, the Icelandic. 'We have curs daily brought out of Iceland, which are made a great deal of because they are petulant and fond of snarling. They also give extremely painful bites, and are very fond of eating candles, like the human inhabitants of Iceland.'

In a final snarl, Caius hits out at dancing-dogs:

The last kind of fancy dogs are called dancing-dogs, mongrels which are taught to dance in measure to the sound of an instrument, such as a drum, citharne, or harp. They have many tricks, such as standing on their hind legs, lying flat on the ground, turning round in a ring holding their tails in their mouths, making bows and begging for food, taking off a man's cap from his head, and other tricks of this sort, which they learn of their idle roguish masters.

Caius' catalogue of dogs is more than a little disappointing, but it does show that at last learned men were beginning to take an interest in them; and poets too were singing their praises. Before we turn to dogs in Tudor poetry, however, it is worth looking for a moment at what is in many ways the most interesting Renaissance dog, the bloodhound. We last met the bloodhound in the form of the mediaeval Talbot. So well had this breed become established in England (if indeed it were not a completely native dog) that nowhere else could such good bloodhounds be found. The hound was in constant use on the Scottish border. As the Scots made a foray across the 'Debatable Land', and returned driving stolen cattle before them, the English landowners and farmers who had been harried would pursue them with hounds on leash. These hounds would follow the blood trail, or the 'dry foot', bloodless trail keeping on the track of the fugitives even though they had passed through great crowds of folk and done everything else they could to throw their pursuers off the scent. Caius says that they were kept in dark kennels during the day and only allowed to run loose at night, so as to accustom them to hunt in the darkness, but this seems very improbable as part of their hunt would certainly have to be carried out in daylight.

James V of Scotland wrote on 8th January 1526 to the Archdeacon of the East Riding of Yorkshire, Thomas Magnus, asking for 'three or four brace of the best raches in the country, to hunt foxes, harts or any other greater beast, along with a brace of bloodhounds, of the best kind that are good and will ride behind men on horseback.'

James' request was supported by his mother, Queen Margaret, the daughter of Henry VII, and Magnus replied to their majesties by enclosing a letter from the Duke of Richmond. In it he told the royal mother and son:

I think I can do no less but to furnish your grace with your said honourable request, and for that purpose do send to your said grace at this time, ten couples of hounds of the best kind that I have tried out for myself. So as to make sure that they arrive I have sent also to your grace Nicholas Eton, my yeoman of the hunt, whom I have commanded to remain for a fortnight or a month with you, at your pleasure to show how hunting is carried out with these hounds.

I have no limer hounds that can ride pillion at present, but as soon as I can get some from my friends, I will send them to your grace.

These letters about bloodhounds which could accompany a rider on his saddle puzzled dog-historian George R. Jesse considerably. He suggests that they 'were perhaps to be taken up when the tracks of the marauders were plainly visible in soft ground.' A marauder who ran across ground soft enough to leave a plain trail, or for that matter ran on any ground where a horseman could follow him, certainly deserved to be caught.

Everybody on both sides of the English and Scottish border knew that a bloodhound never made a mistake. There was no possibility of its ever seizing on the wrong person and Hector Boece, Canon of Aberdeen in the early sixteenth century (who was mentioned a short time ago by Caius as the authority for the existence of lobster-catching or fishing-dogs), says 'he that denies entry to the sleuthhound in time of chase and searching of good shall be held to be an accessory to the crime and theft committed.' Boece remarks that the bloodhounds used in Scotland are red, or else black with spots. John Lesley, Bishop of Ross, confirms this description and adds:

> ... these are endowed with such great sagacity and fierceness that they pursue thieves in a direct course without any deviation, and this with such ferocity of nature that they tear them to pieces even if they chance to be lying down with many others, for from the first scent it gets ... it is never confused.... Only in passing rivers are they at a loss, because there they lose the scent.... Nor has it imbibed this art from Nature alone, but has learned it of man, who, with much labour, forms them skilfully to this. Whence comes it that such among them as excel are purchased at a very high price.

Lesley's words are particularly interesting because Philip II of Spain, sometime consort of Queen Mary, purchased some English bloodhounds which he sent to the Spanish Indies. There these dogs earned a great reputation for tracking down any kind of fugitive, Indians, runaway slaves, criminals black or white. Later we shall see the descendants of these bloodhounds being enlisted in English service for a campaign against revolted blacks in the West Indies. The trainers of the dogs assured the British officer who commanded the punitive detachment that if they caught someone, they would simply hold him down till help arrived, but as the bloodhounds could only be restrained from eating the officer, his coachman and coach-horses by the greatest exertions on the part of the trainers, there seems some doubt on this point.

Controversy also existed as to whether bloodhounds ran silent or barked when they were on the track. Though it had emerged from the troubled conditions of the Middle Ages and the Anglo-Scottish bickerings of the sixteenth century, the bloodhound, fortunately, did not become an extinct breed once James VI of Scotland became James I of England. It lingered on in its old home on the borders, at least till the eighteenth century. The Duke of Buccleuch kept these hounds on his estate. One of his tenants, at Eldinhope in Ettrick Forest, had an allowance of oatmeal for keeping a ducal bloodhound and while the shepherd watched the flock at night, the dog watched alongside him.

Another interesting breed beside the bloodhound was still in existence, but very little was heard of it. This was the great Irish hound. In 1562 Shane O'Neil wrote to Lord Robert Dudley sending him two horses, two hawks and two greyhounds and imploring his favour with Queen Elizabeth. In 1591 another Irish notable, Brian O'Rourke, brought two hawks and two 'great dogs' to James VI in Scotland, only to be arrested by that monarch as a rebel to his rightful Queen, Elizabeth.

The poets of the dynasty were aware of the change that had come over English people's attitudes to dogs. Edmund Spenser mentions mastiffs, ban-dogs, hounds, limers, spaniels, shepherds' curs and curs in his great poem, *The Faerie Queene*. He does not mention the great Irish hound, though much of his poetry was written in Ireland. Perhaps he never saw any Irish hounds, they were probably in hiding with their masters on the hills and crannogs (lake islands). Spenser's introduction of the dog into his poetry is natural and there seems no darker meaning behind his words.

In Shakespeare's works, on the other hand, bitterness seems to haunt even the mention of the word 'dog'. In *Macbeth* one of the murderers says to Macbeth, 'We are men, my Liege.' Macbeth replies that he knows the speaker is a man, or accounted such, just as every kind of dog is put down in the catalogue as a dog, and he runs over a list of the best-known kinds. Macbeth seems to imply here that some dogs are as vile as murderers. No dog-lover would ever subscribe to this sentiment, any more than he would write:

I spurn thee like a cur out of my way.	*Julius Caesar*
And foot me, as your spurn a stranger cur Over your threshold.	*Merchant of Venice*
Slave, soulless villain, dog!	*Antony and Cleopatra*
They flattered me like a dog.	*Lear*
In killing creatures vile, as cats and dogs.	*Cymbeline*

Was Shakespeare representative of his age? I do not think so. He must have had his own reasons for crying 'Avaunt you curs!' What they were we will never know for certain, but apart from his youthful misadventure in Charlecote Park, he must have felt a lifelong resentment against the dogs of Paris Garden (in whose near neighbourhood he lived) both for the noise that they kept up, 'like a bear garden', as we would say, and also because they were a great rival attraction to his own plays.

Perhaps more representative of the British dog-lover was that grand-daughter of the Queen Margaret of Scotland who had written to Archdeacon Magnus to ask him to get her son some bloodhounds which could ride pillion. Mary Stuart, Dowager Queen of France and Queen of Scots, was, like Shakespeare, one of the great spirits of the sixteenth century. At the age of thirteen she had maintained a thesis in Latin before Henry II of France, his Queen and court, that it was befitting for a woman to know Latin and the liberal arts. She spoke six languages, was a great patron of poetry and always set aside two hours a day for study while she lived in France. So Mary was not the kind of person who could be described as 'just a doggy woman'.

It is therefore noteworthy that, at her execution, Mary sought solace in the company of a lap-dog. It may have been a spaniel, it may have been a French griffon, like the ones which appear beside her in the first engraving to portray her. This is Perrissin and Tortorel's view of the death-bed of her father-in-law, Henry II. She stands beside his bed, with the rest of the royal family, the two dogs are on the floor at the foot of the bed. Though the print was published in 1569–70, ten years after the event depicted took place, it is probably correct in most essentials.

Mary had been aware that sentence of death had been passed on her some three months before the execution took place. Elizabeth had contrived to denude her of virtually all her friends and associates and it is not surprising that she felt the need of a companion for the last journey. She walked to the scaffold with slow steps, keeping pace with the dog which was concealed under her long skirts and petticoats. Even after the axe had fallen the dog did not move. It was discovered by the London hangman, Bull, and his varlet, who had orders to remove everything splashed with Mary's blood so that it could be washed clean: 'for fear someone might dip a piece of linen in it, as several of this country have done, who keep it as a relic of this act, to incite to vengeance those concerned for the death of the dead person. 'While untying her garters, which in those days were tied at the knees, Bull noticed the dog. It had to be dragged out by main force and refused to leave the body, lying between the severed head and neck. Eventually it was carried away, washed, because it too was now covered with the Queen's blood, and given to a French princess who asked for it as a memorial of her friend.

4

The Seventeenth Century

The calm of the Tudor deer park was now shattered, for good, by the thunder of the hooves of a Spanish barb, mounted by a rider whose mettle equalled his horse and ridden at a pace which was something new to English folk. As he galloped o'er hill and dale, the cavalier hallooed to his dogs, all of which he knew by name, to cheer them on.

This dashing rider, whose attitude to dogs and hunting was such a contrast to that of the stately Elizabeth, was none other than James I. It seems almost incredible that a man whose timidity was a commonplace throughout European courts should have been one of the great hunters of his day, a man whose example was to transform the English hunting-field and turn us into a nation of hard riders striving to keep up with fast-running hounds. James was only really afraid of being assassinated; he no more minded breaking his neck while out hunting than had his mother, who had once been swept from her saddle by the bough of a tree and nearly killed. James had more than inherited his mother's love of hunting and of dogs. He had been brought up in the hell-for-leather traditions of French court hunting, traditions that had become firmly implanted in France's political dependency, Scotland. 'Hunting . . . with running hounds,' he told his son, Prince Henry, 'is the most honourable and noblest sort thereof, for it is a thievish form of hunting to shoot with guns and bows, and greyhound hunting is not so martial a game.' James' first portrait shows him as an assured falconer of about eight or nine. He hunted up to the year of his death, in 1624. Throughout his long reign he became a sort of apostle of hunting in England. 'It is notorious to all our subjects,' he wrote in a proclamation against deer poachers in the royal parks, 'how greatly we delight in the exercise of hunting, as well for our recreation, as for the necessary preservation of our health.'

Indeed it was only on the hunting-field that James' painstaking attempts to educate his subjects in his own often enlightened ideas bore any fruit. 'Hunting,' wrote Robert Burton, 'is the sole, almost, and ordinary sport of all our noblemen . . . it is all their study, their exercise, ordinary business, all their talk, and indeed some dote too much on it, they can do nothing else, discourse of nothing else.'

The first thing that James did, once safely arrived in Whitehall, was to set up a vast hunting establishment, on a scale that made that of Henry VIII, the last hunting king, look like the equipage of a petty squire. Henry had owned a pack of beagles and greyhounds for coursing, as well as buck-hounds and the spaniels which were the indispensable companions of the falconer. The large brown and white spaniels with long heads and ears accompanied their masters to the field and retrieved those birds struck by the falcons which were not easily recoverable. 'A good spaniel,' wrote George Turberville in his *Book of Falconry* (published in 1575) 'is a good jewel.'

Henry does not appear to have owned any terriers, dogs imported from the Low Countries round Artois, or bred in England, because, as we have seen, there appear to have been terriers here since Roman times. In the six-teenth century terriers were indispensable for putting into foxes' or badgers' earths to drive them out. The shaggy-haired and straight-legged terriers and the smooth and bandy-legged animals were both well spoken of.

James decided that if he was going to hunt in England in the French style, *à force*, it might be as well to import some French hounds to begin with. He sent to King Henri IV for some royal French hounds and some huntsmen to instruct his hunters in the rules of the chase.

Henri complied by despatching the hounds and the Marquis de Vitry, one of the most celebrated huntsmen of the day. Vitry was in turn replaced by M. de Beaumont, M. du Moustier and M. de Saint Ravy, who became Anne of Denmark's chief huntsman. The recruitment of new huntsmen, new dogs and new ideas made a complete change in English hunting. Saint Ravy even went so far as to import forty or fifty red deer from the Forest of Fontainebleau for the king's especial enjoyment.

In contrast to the rather modest hunting establishment kept by his great uncle, Henry VIII, James owned: buckhounds, harriers, otter-hounds, greyhounds, liam-hounds, hawks (and of course spaniels to go with them) sleuth-hounds, great Irish hounds, water spaniels, boar-hounds, setters and beagles. He virtually lived in the saddle, partly because on foot he looked supremely ridiculous. He had weak legs which bent under his weight so that he had to lean against someone; whenever he began to walk he contrived to go round in a circle, his fingers making strange gestures as he moved. So James put in all the hunting he could. Once more, as under the Angevin dynasty, England was governed from the hunting-field, only nowadays the centre for the royal hunt was nearer to London, at New-market.

The king's love of dogs was to have the most important historical conse-quences. Wherever the royal hunt went, a stream of orders and demands preceded it. When James went to hunt the deer or to hawk the crow, magpie, heron, or partridge, in Hertfordshire, the farmers would be ordered not to plough their lands in narrow ridges, not to suffer swine to wander about without rings on their necks to prevent them rooting out holes 'to the endangering of his Majesty and the Prince in hawking and hunting'. Occupants also had to take down high bounds between lands, which hindered his Majesty's ready passage, and to put up gates, to which the king should possess the only key, to prevent him having to break down the fences. All millers were commanded to stay their water courses during the otter-hunting season.

If the country folk writhed under these severe instructions, they felt doubly aggrieved at James' attempts to deal with deer-stealers, according to the letter of the law. We have already noticed that he issued a special proclamation against deer-stealers. He once even wrote personally to the Surrey Justices to get justice done against one Taddy Farnwall, who had killed a red deer in Windsor Forest.

The demands for food and forage for the royal hunt became insufferable. Once, one of James' favourite hounds, 'Jowler', went missing. It turned up the following morning, just as the hounds were going to the field. The King, noticing a paper tied round its neck, pulled it off and read it.

'Good Mr Jowler,' read the letter. 'We pray you speak to the king, for he hears you very day, and he does not hear us. Ask that his Majesty be pleased to go back to London, or else this countryside will be undone. All our provision is used up already, and we are not able to entertain him any longer.'

James, who could be very obtuse when he wanted, took this as a joke. Yet it was past a joke, as far as most Englishmen were concerned, when he asked not merely for food and provender but dogs as well from his subjects. In 1605 he had annulled the commissions issued by Queen Elizabeth in the past 'for the taking up of hounds, greyhounds, spaniels and dogs of other sorts, accustomed for hunting, falconry, or other sports of princes.' In 1616 he renewed the lapsed commissions in the person of Henry Mynours, Master of the Otterhounds. Mynours was authorised 'to take for us and in our name in all places within this our realm of England . . . such and so many hounds, beagles, spaniels and mongrels, as well dogs as bitches fit for hunting the otter as the said Henry Mynours shall think fit. . . . And we do also hereby authorize the said Henry Mynours to seize and take away all such hounds, beagles, and other dogs as are or may be offensive to our game and sport.'

This was not the only demand of James for dogs: as we shall see in a moment, he was always demanding mastiffs as recruits for the bull-ring as well. As far as the English country gentleman was concerned, the Stuarts were trying to turn back the clock to what it had been in the days of bad King John. James I even began to re-establish the royal forests, not for hunting but for revenue, and his son was going to follow in his footsteps.

In the new kind of hunting, the royal huntsman assembled his pack of twenty to thirty hounds, which were then loosed on the track of some deer selected from a herd. Then hounds and horsemen followed the quarry till the kill. The hunt travelled at a speed which made it impossible to avoid considerable damage to any property that lay in between, such as fences. A chance remark by Marshall Bassompierre, an Alsatian in the service of Henri IV, tells us that English horses were the fastest in Europe. He always used to call crown pieces *alezans* (the French name for the newly imported fast English mounts) because the crown pieces left him at such speed the minute he began to gamble.

James was always telling his nobles that they should go and stay at their country houses. This was good advice; in his case, he would have been more popular if he had stayed in London. Elizabeth had carried on her hunting in the stately and decorous way in which she did everything else. James made quite a different impression on his subjects as he rode out after his beloved hounds, and because he was hunting in open country, not in a deer park, like Elizabeth, he came in contact with many more spectators than Elizabeth had ever done. The Queen's hunting had been paid for by her nobles. If they dared to complain about the cost of having the queen as an uninvited guest, Elizabeth had a very short way with them. When, for example, Elizabeth and the court descended on Berkeley Castle and slaughtered Henry Lord Berkeley's deer herd, the latter had the imprudence to 'suddenly and dispassionately dispark that ground'. Elizabeth's response to this was characteristic. She let Berkeley know that she had been brought to the castle, against her better judgement, by the Earl of Leicester, that the Earl disliked Berkeley and would probably like to get his hands, not merely on his deer, but on his castle as well, so she advised Berkeley to keep a close watch over his words and actions in future.

James' hunting expenses fell not merely on the nobility and gentry, but on the common people as well. They had to find beaters and provisions for the whole hunting establishment of the king. As James' huntsmen and falconers were very numerous (he had twenty-four falconers with the due number of horses and dogs) the expense was a ruinous one, especially as the King was continually hunting.

There was nothing about the appearance of the King as he rode out hunting that inspired respect in his subjects. Slouched in the saddle, his hat set just at the angle at which it had been clapped on his head by the hunt servant, and hiccuping from the effects of the strong Greek wines which accompanied him to the field on 'the king's bottle horse', James cut almost as comical a figure as he did on foot.

His subjects reacted to the oppressions caused by the royal hunt in two ways. One was to begin poaching the king's deer on a grand scale. James felt compelled to issue a 'Proclamation against hunters, stealers and killers of deer within any of the King's Majesty's forests, chases, or parks' as early as 1609. With his invariable tendency to rub salt in his own wounds, he says that the poachers would never have attempted such depredations in the old Queen's day, and that 'the transgressions that are done ... do proceed ... out of an insolent and disrespectful attitude to our person, no way to be endured.'

The other attack on royal hunting came from the Puritans. Hunting was ungodly, they told the King; Nimrod, that mighty hunter, had been expressly condemned in the Old Testament. One Puritan preacher even told the King to his face while he was out hawking in Hertfordshire that the fowls of the air and the beasts of the forest were intended by God for man's delight and not for slaughter.

Occasionally, the court indulged in shooting deer with a crossbow or longbow, though, as has been seen, James had discouraged this kind of hunting as unsportsmanlike. In 1613, while hunting in this way, James's queen, Anne of Denmark, shot his favourite dog, 'Jewel', by mistake. The King raged and stormed, but was soon pacified and sent Anne a diamond worth £2,000 as a peace-making gift. Nonetheless James did not forget his favourite hound's death and he referred to it eight years later when there was another accidental shooting in court circles. This time the victim was a man, a keeper of Lord Zouch at his park at Bramshill, and the bad shot was the person next in precedence to the royal family, George Abbot, Archbishop of Canterbury. James tried to console the prelate by telling him 'that an angel might have miscarried in this way' and that 'he was not to discomfort himself, as such an accident might befall any man, and his Queen in like sort killed him the best brache he ever had.'

James' efforts to console the unfortunate archbishop (who had been ordered to hunt for exercise, by his doctor) had no effect. Abbot brooded over his unintentional manslaughter until his concern became obsessive. A special court met to decide the question of whether a homicide could continue to exercise the functions of archbishop. It divided equally, unable to condemn, or exonerate Abbot. James, a kindly man with more real charity than Abbot's clerical colleagues, gave his casting vote in favour of the archbishop and granted him a royal pardon.

For the rest of his long life, till 1633, Abbot remained out in the wilderness, absent from the council, away from court, and finally suspended from his functions by Charles I. During his enforced inaction the Church of England fell under the baleful influence of the Bishop of London, William Laud, the man whose 'reforms' were to split the Anglo-Saxon race in two by driving the Pilgrim Fathers to leave England. If only Abbot had been content to follow the new fashion set by James of 'hurrying incessantly after the dogs until they have caught the game', William Laud could never have run on unchecked until he had brought about, not merely the American Colonies, but the English Civil War as well.

Altogether, dogs were to play a great role in James' reign. Before we turn once more to the horrors of the bull-ring let us note, during that reign, the creation of a particularly English literary form, the dog biography.

Sir John Harington, godson of Queen Elizabeth and poet and translator of Ariosto, sent the biography of his dog 'Bungey' to James' eldest son, Prince Henry. 'Bungey' also enjoyed another unique distinction, in that its portrait was the first (so far as I am aware) to figure as an illustration in a printed book. The title page of Harington's *Orlando Furioso*, published in 1591, shows him as a large spaniel, or setter, shaggy in front and clipped short behind, like a poodle. The poodle-cut originated because poodles were originally waterdogs, and a clipped back and sides enabled them to throw off the water more easily as they emerged from a river or pond.

'Having good reason,' wrote Harington to Prince Henry, 'to think your Highness had good will and liking to read what others have told of my rare dog, I will even give a brief history of his good deeds and strange feats. . . . Although I mean not to disparage the deeds of Alexander's horse, I will match my dog, Bungey, against him.'

'Bungey' was certainly a remarkable dog. It had retrieved Harington's purse, full of gold, when he had dropped it. With a satchel of letters tied to its neck, it made the incredible journey between Bath, in Somerset and the Palace at Greenwich just outside London. Once it had delivered the letters at Greenwich, Queen Anne of Denmark, or some other princely correspondent of Harington's would send it back to Bath or to another of Harington's houses at Kelstone with other letters in reply.

'Neither must it be forgotten,' wrote Harington, 'how he was once sent with two loads of sherry from Bath to my house by my servant Combe, and on his way the harness slackened, but my trusty bearer now bore himself so wisely as to secretly hide one of the bottles in the rushes, and take the other to the house, in his teeth. Afterwards he went out and brought back the other bottle.'

'Bungey' was so highly trained that once, when it had been stolen and sold to the Spanish Ambassador, his master was able to prove ownership by making it go through its repertoire:

In a happy hour after six weeks I did hear about him, but such was the court that he did pay to the Don, that he was just as much liked there, as at home. Nor did the household listen to any claim or challenge of mine till I rested my suit on the dog's own proofs, and made him perform such feats before the assembled nobles as to put it past doubt that I was his master.

I sent him to the hall at dinner-time, and made him bring thence a pheasant out of the dish. This created a lot of mirth, but they laughed even more heartily when, at my order, he went back to the table and put it back into the same dish. At this point the company was content to allow my claim, and Bungey and I were well content to accept it and go home.

If James's fondness for hunting-dogs did nothing to make him liked by those countryfolk who had to support the expenses of the royal hunt, his addiction to bear- and bull-baiting infuriated the growing number of Puritans in England. The greatest concession that James would make to the Puritans was to prohibit bull- and bear-baiting on Sundays, in his *Book of*

Sports, issued in 1618. Not content with the normal animal-baitings of the day, James also arranged combats between English mastiffs and lions. He had been intrigued to discover that lions were kept in the Tower of London and one of his courtiers reminded him that Abraham Ortelius, a sixteenth-century travel writer, had declared that the English mastiff was just as courageous as any lion. James ordered Edward Alleyn, the great impresario of bull-baiting of the day, to bring his three fiercest dogs to Paris Garden. They were loosed on the lion one by one and the third dog succeeded in biting the great carnivore so severely that it retired to its den, licking its wounds. This third mastiff was the only one that survived. Prince Henry ordered Alleyn to bring the mastiff to him at the Palace of St James. There he formally charged the bull-baiter not to fight the dog again, for a mastiff which had fought a lion ought never to be matched against any inferior creature. He told Alleyn to make much of the dog and look after him.

Edward Alleyn combined the apparently irreconcilable vocations of arranging animal-fights and being a noted philanthropist. He had accumulated a fortune much more through his activities as a bull-fighting impresario than as an actor-manager and with this wealth he built and endowed Dulwich College. Alleyn's career shows what profits could be made as a manager in this very lucrative pastime and also how unpopular bull-fighting must have become to dog-owners, who were obliged to provide their mastiffs, free of charge, to be slaughtered in the arena, on the order of the royal official who controlled the amusement.

Alleyn and his father-in-law Philip Henslowe divided their interests between producing plays and organising baitings on the Bankside. In 1604 they jointly purchased the mastership of the royal game of bears, bulls and mastiff dogs and monopolised it for seven years. More will be said later about the Master of the Game, the official who controlled the baitings. Alleyn's share of the purchase money, which amounted to £450 in all, was £250. His earnings during the sixteen years he held the patent were £60 a year, amounting to £960 in all. In 1610 he was able to sell his share to Henslowe for £580. Allowing for a payment of £200 to a Mr Burnaby, Alleyn's profits had, by 1610, mounted to £1,590, which for those days was a princely fortune.

Alleyn's wealth had been built up by the mass-slaughter of mastiffs, dogs which, in many instances had been torn from their masters under the terms of the royal patent which he held. A letter to Alleyn from an associate, William Fawnte, throws an oblique light on the short life of a mastiff in the bull-ring:

Mr Alleyn, my love remembered. I understood by a man who came with two bears from the [Paris] Garden that you had a desire to buy one of my bulls. I have three western bulls at this time, but I have had very ill luck with them, for one of them has lost his horn to the quick, so that I think he will never be able to fight again. He is my old 'Star of the West'. He was a very easy bull. Then there is my bull 'Bevis', he has lost one of his eyes, but I think if you had him, he would do you more harm than good, for I think he would either throw up your dogs into the galleries of the amphitheatre, or else dash out their brains against the gratings put up to protect the spectators in the pit. . . . I have a bull which came out of the west, which is worth twenty nobles . . . a marvellous good bull . . . and one that I have played thirty or forty courses before he has been taken from the stake, with the best dogs which half a dozen freights had.

The royal officer who controlled the pastime on a national level has been already mentioned. He was the 'Chief master, ruler and overseer of all and singular games, of bears and bulls and mastiff dogs and mastiff bitches.' Like most court offices the Mastership was for sale and that was how Alleyn and Henslowe had acquired it. The Master had unlimited authority to seize dogs suitable for the ring. This power, whether exercised by the Master in person or by his officials, was an odious one which many dog-owners resisted, rather than give up their faithful protectors and cherished companions. Officials were set on and beaten and local justices refused to bring the offenders to trial. Some towns compounded with the Master, agreeing to send dogs for the king's service so long as none of the hated officials set foot in their boundaries. Manchester agreed with the Master to send him yearly 'a mastiff dog, or bitch, to the bear garden, between Midsummer and Michaelmas.'

Besides resistance by private dog-owners, Henslowe and Alleyn complained to James I that provincial bear-wards or bear-owners flouted the Master's authority:

There are diverse vagrants and persons of loose and idle life that usually wander through the country with bears and bulls, without any licence, and for aught we know, serving no man, spoiling and killing dogs for that game, so that your Majesty cannot be served, but by great charges to us, fetching them very far, which is directly contrary to a statute made in that behalf, for the restraining of such persons your Majesty would be pleased . . . to renew unto your petitioners our patent and to grant us and our deputies power and authority to apprehend such vagrants and convene them before the next Justice of Peace.

Charles I's accession brought no relief from the bull-ring, for Charles, like his father, was a devotee of the cruel pastime. He had a taste for wild animals and even despatched animal catchers to Virginia to supply his collections. Apart from mastiffs, other dogs were now affected by Charles' policy of strong government. They were no longer welcomed in church, though in the Middle Ages, as we have seen, they had been regular church attenders with their masters; in the sheep countries of England, special benches had been provided at the back of the church where the shepherds could sit with their dogs. 'There happened in the town of Tadlow a very ill incident on Christmas Day, 1638 by not having the Communion Table railed in,' reports Stevens in his *History of Downing College*. 'For in sermon time a dog came to the Table and took the loaf of bread prepared for the Holy Sacrament in his mouth and ran away with it.' To prevent incidents such as this the Bishop of Norwich had ordered, in 1636, that a rail should be made before the Communion Table so thick with pillars that a dog could not get between them. A Puritan writer noted how at Canterbury 'one of the great Canons or Prebendaries, in the very act of his low bowing towards the altar as he went up to it in prayer time, was, not long since, greeted by a huge mastiff dog, which leapt upright on him again and again and pawed him in his bowing progress to the altar, so that he was forced to call aloud: "Take away the dog." '

As part of the Laudian Reformation worshippers were discouraged from bringing dogs to church and were sometimes fined if they did. The activity of the 'dog whippers', lowly church officials whose task was to drive dogs out of church, was also intensified and they came to be provided not merely with whips but with lazy tongs with spiked teeth which could grip a recalcitrant dog and drag it out from under the benches.

Yet the ecclesiastical dislike for dogs was as nothing compared with the work of the city officers known as 'dog-killers', who destroyed dogs every year during the 'dog days' of the hot summer months, particularly in August. By the seventeenth century men had begun to realise that there must be some connection between dogs, rats, cats and the plague. They were unable to demonstrate just what that connection was – of course it was the plague-carrying flea, which was liable to infest dogs as well as humans. Accordingly, in the summer months, and particularly when the plague reached epidemic proportions, great massacres of dogs took place. Whenever the dog-killer appeared, the dogs recognised him, as Ben Johnson tells us, and began to bark. One reason why they recognised this local government official was that he wore a special uniform, apparently made out of dog skins. Sir Kenelme Digby, after noting the antipathy that dogs had for dog-killers, goes on to mention their identical antipathy for glovers. 'We daily see,' he wrote, 'that dogs will have an aversion to glovers, who make their goods out of dog skins. They will bark at them, and be aggressive to them, and cannot bear to come near them, though they never saw them before.' When the plague was at its worst, in 1666, no fewer than 40,000 dogs and five times as many cats were destroyed by order of the Lord Mayor of London.

By the middle of the seventeenth century dissatisfaction with the new Stuart dynasty had reached its peak and had culminated with the deposition and execution of Charles I. With this dissatisfaction dogs had had not a little to do. James I's great hunting establishment, his packs of buck-

'A Couple of Foxhounds', 1791, by George Stubbs (1724-1806). Formerly with Spink and Son.

Spanish Pointer, an illustration from the Rev. W. B. Daniel's *Rural Sports*, London, 1801, from the painting by George Stubbs, engraved by John Scott.

Foxhound, from an illustration to *The Sportsman's Cabinet*.

Terriers, also from an illustration to *The Sportsman's Cabinet*.

Bull Baiting

Badger Baiting.
Both drawn by Henry Alken (1750-1825), engraved by J. Clark,
published by T. McLean in 1820.

Above: King Charles Spaniel.

Opposite: A Staffordshire Bull Terrier.

Below: A White Poodle, 1842. All by Sir Edwin Landseer (1802-1873). Formerly with Spink and Son.

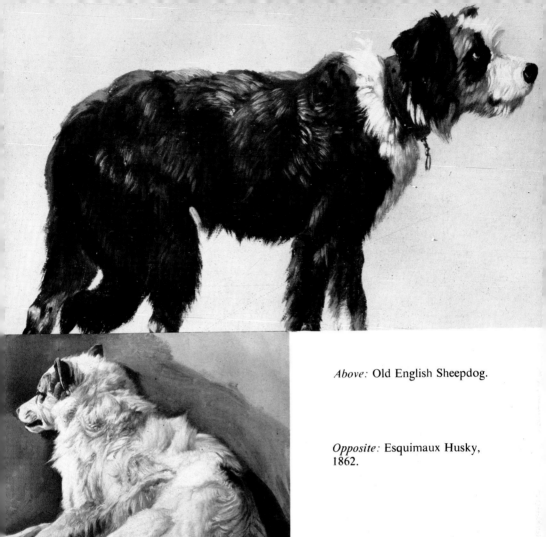

Above: Old English Sheepdog.

Opposite: Esquimaux Husky, 1862.

Below: A Hound
All by Sir Edwin Landseer
and formerly with Spink and
Son.

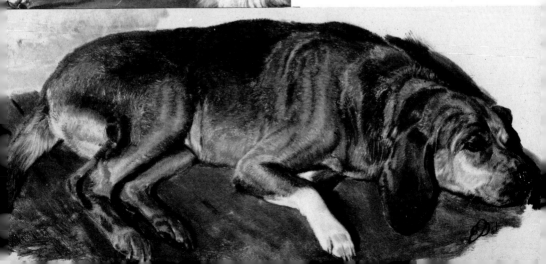

Water Spaniel, from *The Sportsman's Cabinet*.

Harrier, also from *The Sportsman's Cabinet*.

The Dalmatian, from
The Sportsman's Cabinet

'Danish Dog' (Great
Dane) drawn by H. Weir
and engraved by Dalzeil
for J. G. Wood's *The
Illustrated Natural
History*, London (no
date).

Turnspit,
drawn and
engraved by
W. R. Smith
for Edward
Jesse's
*Anecdotes of
Dogs*, London,
1846.

hounds, boar-hounds, harriers, otter-hounds, greyhounds, liam hounds, sleuth-hounds, water spaniels, beagles and mongrels were partly dogs requisitioned from his subjects and partly those contributed unwillingly as gifts. The whole of England had been called upon to contribute these dogs. As the contemporary writer Gervase Markham pointed out, the best sport could only be obtained with a pack which represented the different regions. Slow hounds, which were 'a large, great dog, tall and heavy', were bred in the West Country, Cheshire and Lancashire. The middle-sized hound, which was much faster, was raised in Worcestershire, Bedfordshire and other counties. The 'light, nimble, swift, slender dog' which was also indispensable for good hunting was a native of the north, especially Yorkshire, Cumberland and Northumberland. Finally there was the little beagle 'which may be carried in a man's glove, and are bred in many countries.'

Many of the people who contributed dogs to James's packs must have done so with a very bad grace, such as the Puritan uncle, godfather and namesake of Oliver Cromwell, who presented the king with 'swift and deep-mouthed hounds', horses and hawks. When gifts were not forthcoming, James and Charles put requisitions into effect. The Master of His Majesty's Leash, Lord Compton, was given a commission in 1628 to seize 'greyhounds and other dogs for his Majesty's sport and recreation.' He was also licensed to seize all greyhounds or beagles that might interfere with the king's sport.

It is not difficult to imagine the feelings of country squires who found themselves the unwilling patrons of the royal hunt. Hunting was all that the country squires cared about. If one country gentleman wrote to another without mentioning sport, his friend's reply might well contain the words: 'In all your letters I find not one word of horse, hawk and hound.'

Yet the great grievance felt by many country gentlemen against the king was not his requisitioning of dogs, but his extension of the royal forests. Charles already owned sixty-eight forests and his attempt to restore the boundaries of the old ones which had lapsed centuries ago was carried out to improve his revenue, by troublesome fines and exactions, and not his hunting. Nonetheless, dog-owners suffered again because one of the rights of the king's foresters was to expeditate large dogs such as mastiffs by cutting out the ball of the feet and lopping the three foreclaws. Though landowners within the revived forests might have enjoyed hunting rights there that dated back for hundreds of years they now found that their hounds must be put down, or mutilated, that they might not go out hawking, or hunting or even attempt to control vermin such as foxes and wild cats.

In the battles of the Civil War which now broke out, many of James's hunting countries were to be ridden over by the cavalry of both sides. It was small comfort for the Royalists that the Jamesian Revolution in the hunting-field had produced a matchless cavalry force. The Cavalier commander of horse was Prince Rupert, whose dog soon became the most famous animal in the war. Rupert had been captured during the Thirty Years War in Germany by the Imperialists. He was fighting to try to recover the Palatinate for his mother, James I's daughter Elizabeth. While a prisoner of war at Linz, in Austria, he was able to put in a lot of hunting, including the chase of the fox, an animal which at this time was by no means the favourite quarry of English sportsmen. He also acquired a white dog of uncertain breed which, it has been conjectured, was a poodle. This animal became Rupert's mascot and as it always accompanied its master to the battlefield 'Boy', as the dog was called, became the bugbear of the Parliamentarians. Rupert appeared to be unbeatable and the Puritan pamphleteers accused him of being a wizard and said that 'Boy' was his 'familiar.'

Then, at Marston Moor, 'Boy' was killed and the Parliament army hailed his death as a sign that Rupert's luck had turned. They were right, as the battle ended in a crushing victory for Cromwell from which Rupert was only able to escape by the skilful horsemanship he had acquired on the hunting-field. Soon afterwards he was dismissed by his cousin the king because he had sensibly suggested that Charles try to get terms from his opponents.

The great Civil War profoundly affected sport, with which dogs have always been intimately connected. The deer of the royal forests were almost totally destroyed and so were those belonging to the Cavaliers. Parliamentary Commissioners ordered the slaughter of those in royal parks, while soldiers carried out wholesale poaching. Royal huntsmen were forced to go into hiding, taking with them what remained of the royal hounds. Not merely the deer, but the trees as well disappeared during the Parliamentary interregnum. When William Cavendish, Duke of Newcastle, returned from exile at the Restoration he found that. . . .

of eight parks that he was possessed of before the wars, all but Welbeck Park, were quite destroyed. . . . Clipston Park, wherein he had formerly taken much delight, it being seven miles in compass, rich of wood . . . was quite defaced, there being not one timber tree left in it, though it had had the tallest in the country, valued at £20,000. When he beheld the ruins of this country seat, though he was remarkable for his patience under misfortunes, the Duke was observed to be much troubled, but he only said, he was in hopes to have found it not so much defaced.

Buckhunting, once the primary English field sport, now had to give way to coursing and hare-hunting. Even the Puritan Cromwell enjoyed hunting the hare and owned a favourite greyhound called 'Coffin-nail'. Gervase Markham, a writer who has already been mentioned, published his book *Country Contentments* in 1651, under the Protectorate. He gave practical advice to his readers on how to choose a greyhound which would run well. Avoid round, fat and compact puppies he advises and instead choose rawboned, lean and gangling whelps, which will make the best coursers.

Markham's advice to foxhunters is a little like Mr Punch's advice to young people who want to marry. The sport is a waste of time, he tells his readers. There is very little excitement in the pursuit of a quarry whose scent is so rank that there are 'very few dogs but will hunt them with all eagerness.' Yet during the Protectorate many country gentlemen may well have turned to foxhunting instead of the now defunct buck-hunting and, in view of the scratch packs that were all that they could raise during this troubled period, come to regard the rank scent of Reynard as an asset, not a liability.

The Cromwellian period also brought a temporary respite for the mastiff and for a new breed of dog, the bulldog. The latter kind of dog had been evolved in response to the need for a speedier animal which could dart in below the guard of the bull, or the bear, inflict damage on it and then retire equally swiftly. In 1631 an English merchant's agent, a man called Prestwick Eaton, wrote to a friend in London from St Sebastian in Spain:

Procure me two good bulldogs and let them be sent by the first ship. . . . Let them be good at the bull and cost what they will, but let them be fair and good curs ... good brother, procure them at the Bear Garden. They are better esteemed and go farther than a greater present.

After a Cavalier rebellion in Wiltshire, Cromwell divided England into eleven districts with a major-general at the head of each, who was helped by a garrison to control the area. The major-generals proceeded to ban horseracing – which brought bodies of royalists together as spectators – bear-baiting and cockfighting. The latter sports entailed gatherings in which the young might be corrupted by older bad characters and they entailed cruelty to animals. In a way, this was the first governmental action to stop cruelty to animals though, as we shall see, it was carried out in a cruel way. It was very forgiving of Cromwell to give the poor mastiffs a respite because he had apparently nearly been killed by two mastiffs while he was a student. According to Ralph Thoresby, 'in the ingenious Dr Sampson's manuscript is an account of Oliver Cromwells' being set upon when at Cambridge by two mastiffs, whereupon he set his back against a tree, and taking his head with both his hands, as if he would have flung it at them, frightened them away'.

The trick of pretending to throw your head at a dog is referred to in

William Shakespeare's *King Lear*:

> *Lear*: The little dogs and all;
>   Tray, Blanche, and Sweetheart, see they bark at me!'
>
> *Edgar*:Tom will throw his head at them:
>   'Avaunt, you curs!
>   Be thy mouth or black or white
>   Tooth that poisons if it bite.
>   Mastiff, greyhound, mongrel grim,
>   Hound, or spaniel, brache or lym,
>   Or bob-tail tike, or trundle-tail
>   Tom will make them weep and wail.
>   For with throwing thus my head,
>   Dogs leap the hatch and all are fled.'

Colonel Pride, the same officer who 'purged' Parliament, proceeded to put the new regulations about bear-baiting into effect with his own hand. He marched a detachment of soldiers to the bear pit at Bankside and there personally shot all the bears while his men made the round of the cockpits, wringing the birds' necks.

Cromwell's aversion to bull-baiting ensured that it would be one of the institutions which would be revived with the restoration of the monarchy, although Charles II took very little interest in bull- and bear-fights and James II hated them.

Bull-baiting also figured prominently in one of the most important anti-Cromwellian polemics. Samuel Butler, the Cavalier poet, celebrated Charles II's return to England by writing the longest comic poem in the English language, *Hudibras*, which appeared, in an unauthorised edition, in 1662. The Puritan anti-hero of the poem, Hudibras, and his squire Ralph attack a party of bear-baiters and their bear, which is called 'Bruin'.

> He was by birth, some authors write,
> A Russian, some a Muscovite,
> And 'mong the Cossacks had been bred.

Hudibras, which was immensely popular, undoubtedly helped to re-inforce the connection between Russians and bears which was already strong in the English mind. Marching in the procession with Bruin was a very motley crowd consisting of Crowdero, a lone-legged fiddler with griz-zled hair and long beard, Orsin the bear-ward, carrying an iron-tipped truncheon, leading Bruin, equipped with a nose ring and a triple-fold leather gorget round the neck for protection against the dogs. Following the leaders of the procession, who include the trollop, Trulla, come the country folk:

> The numerous rabble was drawn out
> Of several countries round about . . .
> Came men, and mastiffs, some to fight,
> For fame and honour, some for sight.

Hudibras and his squire attack this mob, but are routed.

The effect of meetings between the country dogs and the bears must have been to more than decimate the dog population. A dog attacking a bull faced an enormous risk, as John Houghton pointed out in 1695:

The bull circulates to watch his enemy, which is a mastiff dog, commonly used to the sport, with a short nose, that his teeth may take the better hold. This dog, if right, will creep upon his belly that he may, if possible, get the bull by the nose, which the bull as a carefully strives to defend, by laying it close to the ground, where his horns are also ready to do what in them lies to toss the dog, and this is the true sport.

But if more dogs than one come at once, or if they are cowardly and come under his legs, he will, if he can, stamp their guts out. I believe I have seen a dog tossed by a bull thirty, if not forty feet high, and when they are tossed either higher or lower, the men about strive to catch them on their shoulders, lest the fall might mischief the dogs. They commonly lay sand about, that if they fall upon the ground it may be easier. Notwithstanding this care, a great many dogs are killed.

Yet in spite of the losses in the bull-ring, dogs were always forthcoming, though good ones were hard to get. Breeders were eager to obtain the money prizes offered for dogs which made a good score against the bull. They wanted dogs which would win them bets and which would also make money if sold to other fanciers.

If they did nothing else, the heavy losses in the ring helped to eliminate the old breed of mastiff in favour of the two kinds of dogs which were just emerging, the bulldog, which is the 'short nosed mastiff' mentioned by Houghton, and the bull terrier, which is still some way into the next century.

Though Charles II tried to re-stock his deer parks from the estates of Parliamentary noblemen such as the Earl of Essex, and even sent as far afield as Germany to replace the deer destroyed in Windsor and Sherwood Forests, the lack of runnable stags made him abandon buckhunting as a bad job and transfer his attention to horseracing, coursing and keeping dogs for pleasure. He spent most of the racing season at James I's old hunting centre, Newmarket, which now became the capital of England for much of the year. Though he showed no interest in foxhunting, his courtiers began to hunt with the select Charlton Hunt, which met at Charlton, hunting-box of the Earls of Arundel, near Midhurst. Amongst other notables, the hunt included the Duke of Monmouth, who was later to learn about the other side of hunting by being tracked by the royal bloodhounds after Sedgemoor.

Charles showed a mild interest in dog-racing which was not, however, in spite of royal patronage, to become a popular sport until it was introduced from America in the 1920s. Writing in April, 1679, the Marquis of Ormonde described the 'Hampton Court Olympic, where the King honoured the pastimes with his presence, and thousands followed his example, so that the breadth of the paddock course was fain to be divided with stakes and ropes.' Matches were made between different dogs, while heavy betting went on. Winners included 'a fallow dog of that excellent poet, Ned Howard, whose dog, having better feet than his verses, won his match.'

Hitherto small pet dogs had been an exclusively female prerogative, the only exceptions being 'mitten beagles', which were small enough to fit into the large-cuffed riding-gloves that were then worn. Mitten beagles could serve as a companion for the ladies at home 'and in the field will hunt as cunningly as any hound whatsoever, only their music is very small, like a reed.' One reason why ladies liked lap-dogs was that they acted as a magnet for the fleas that would otherwise settle on their persons, producing unsightly red punctures on the shoulders and breasts that were revealed by the exaggerated *décolletage* which was then the fashion. As early as the days of Dr Caius people had also believed that invalids would be comforted by lap-dogs. They would strengthen a weak stomach and they would also absorb the disease of a sick person if they were carried in the bosom.

Charles II was the first male dog-owner to make a real fetish of lap-dogs. Only a king could have sanctioned this departure from tradition. When Henrietta of Orleans brought a toy black and white spaniel to court Charles fell in love with the breed, which was later called after him. A pair of red and white spaniels sent to John Churchill, later the Duke of Marlborough, as a present from China were christened 'Blenheim' spaniels. These tiny spaniels could be used as working-dogs, though not all of them did work. They would be employed in low and close growing covert to spring woodcock, hence their name of 'cocker spaniels'.

Charles's spaniels overran the palace. 'God save your Majesty, but God damn your dogs,' one of his courtiers once remarked. Charles played with a spaniel during Council to the scandal of the other Councillors and the neglect of business. When his dogs were stolen the king was inconsolable and in 1660 he inserted an advertisement in the *Mercurius Publicus*, a newspaper of the day, which he had apparently composed himself:

> We must call upon you again for a black dog, between a greyhound and a spaniel, no white about him, only a streak on his breast, and his tail a little bobbed. It is his Majesty's own dog, and doubtless was stolen, for the dog was not born or bred in England, and would never forsake his master. Whosoever finds him may acquaint any at Whitehall, for the dog was better known at court than those who stole him. Will they never leave off robbing his Majesty? Must he not keep a dog? This dog's place, though better than some imagine, is the only place which nobody offers to beg.

Four years later poor Charles was forced to advertise again, for another stolen pet. The vile calling of the professional dog-thief had now become an established one. Just as they had shared his life, so spaniels shared Charles' death-bed, greatly to the indignation of Bishop Burnet. The royal tradition of having dogs 'in at the death' was to be observed at Queen Victoria's death-bed as well.

If it were possible, Charles's brother James was even fonder of his pets. Once, travelling in a ship off the Scottish coast with the future Duke of Marlborough, he was compelled to abandon ship and ordered the crew to: 'Save the dogs and Colonel Churchill.' Perhaps all the rest of the ship's complement were sailors and could therefore save themselves.

The only possible contender for first place as favourite lap-dog with the spaniels was the pug. It became popular in Holland, to which it had supposedly been brought from China. In Holland, it had become almost a royal emblem because one of the breed had awakened the Prince of Orange just before a night attack by the Spaniards. The Prince always kept several of these dogs about him and so did his friends and followers. The pug became established in England with the arrival of William of Orange and the last but one of the Stuarts, Mary. More than any other English dog, however, it seems to have suffered from fluctuations of popularity. The principal reason that it never became a real favourite was that, until very recently, there was a prejudice against any dogs which were not working ones and nobody could make a pug hunt anything.

5

The Eighteenth Century

The landscape of the eighteenth-century dog is quite different from anything that we have seen before. Never before have there been so many breeds in view, some of them hailing from very far afield indeed, from places such as Newfoundland, Labrador and the Arctic. Many of the dogs we see are obviously kept, not for work, but for their masters' pleasure. They have no sporting connections, unless it is to run alongside their masters' carriages or sit with them in the driver's seat. Yet if there are many dogs kept just for pleasure there are, alas, many others to whom life must be anything but a pleasure, worker-dogs such as the transport animals that we can see in long teams dragging heavy carts along the roads, with feet that leave a bleeding paw mark at every step. Help is at hand for these poor industrial slaves, as well as for the patient turnspits, in the humanitarian movement just beginning which aims to lessen some of the burdens on dogs.

The movement for greater kindness to animals is very much associated with the sportsmen of England, men whose constant association with dogs has interested them in their lot. We can see these sportsmen and their dogs: wildfowlers with their spaniels and waterdogs, and many kinds of gun-dogs preceding the guns. Then there are the foxhunters, with hound and horse travelling at a speed which would have been thought incredible in the previous century. Other packs are in view, shaggy, fierce otter-hounds, harriers and the very last (or so it seems) of the stag-hounds. There are still far too many sports being pursued which are not so much cruel as sadistic, such as bull-baiting and badger-drawing, and we note with sadness that dogs figure in all of them. But at least their days are now numbered, thanks in part to the pleas for better treatment for dogs put forward by the first major writer on British dogs, William Taplin, whose work is compiled in this century but published in the next.

In the eighteenth century we begin to see the first notable breeders, men of immense force of character and a monomaniac desire for perfection, such as Lord Orford, Colonel Thomas Thornton, and Hugo Meynell.

It is difficult to decide which was the most exciting eighteenth-century sport in which dogs figured, but coursing seems to stand out as the greatest sport of the age and the greyhound as its most exciting dog. No crowd ever attended a meet of foxhounds equal in number to that which waited at Carshalton to see the match between Mr Durand's greyhound 'Bellissima' and Colonel Thornton's greyhound 'Major'.

The match was for a thousand guineas, 'the largest stake ever offered upon a match with greyhounds'. The meeting was to be held at Carshalton simply because it would have been impossible to control the crowds at Mr Durand's house, near Epsom, where the contest had originally been arranged to take place. Epsom was so near to London that so many Londoners were likely to attend 'that the curiosity of the multitude would totally prevent any possibility of trial, or sport'.

Even at the new venue of Carshalton there was a great line of carriages and 'little less than five hundred horsemen'.

The great crowd, which numbered everybody from costermongers in their donkey carts to peers in their carriages, watched agog as Thornton appeared on the scene to contest the wager of a thousand guineas. As his chaise marine drew up on the ground, there were led from it first 'two brace of greyhounds, adorned with blue and buff sheets . . . followed by 'Major' sheeted in rich buff colour, on the right side of which were embroidered the armorial bearings of the Thornton family; on the left, in letters of gold embroidery: '*Major, aut ne plus ultra*' (a punning Latin verse which can mean 'Major, or no more', or else 'Greater or no more').

When stripped, 'Major' appeared 'fine, gay, airy, and in good condition, though eleven years old.' Then, instead of the great contest which everyone had been waiting for there was a terrible anticlimax: Durand agreed to pay the bet without a trial of the two dogs. So as to give the crowd something for their trouble, Thornton agreed to let 'Major', accompanied by a lively little bitch, chase a boxed hare. This was certainly not so exciting as the contest between 'Major' and 'Bellissima' would have been. William Taplin, the author of the *Sportsman's Cabinet*, who was in the crowd with all the rest of sporting England, said that it bore about as much relation to the real thing as exchanging salmon fishing in Loch Lomond for stickleback fishing in the Paddington Canal.

Colonel Thomas Thornton (1757–1823) was one of the creators of the modern greyhound, Lord Orford being the other. George Walpole, Lord Orford, (1730–91) was the grandson of the Robert Walpole who had been England's first Prime Minister. Even when in London, Robert Walpole had assiduously hunted Richmond Park with a pack of beagles. He preferred to be painted in sporting clothes and he always opened his gamekeeper's letters before any others in the mail. All Robert's sporting enthusiasm had been inherited by his grandson and he decided to devote his life to coursing. Although this had been a popular sport during the seventeenth century, as has been noticed, it was by no means carried on at a national level. The foundation, by Orford, of the Swaffham Coursing Society changed this by opening a new era for the pastime. The society's Rules

And Regulations covered the way in which coursing was to be run and they also took two steps of the outmost importance. They provided for a silver cup, to the value of twenty-five guineas, which was to be run for at the November meeting, and they established a panel of Lady Patronesses of the Society. Coursing was to have an enormous social importance in that it was the first respectable sport attended by women.

The foundation of the Swaffham Society produced so much interest that soon other clubs began to be formed: the Ashdown Park Meeting at Lambourn in Berkshire, the Bradwell and Tillingham Club in Essex and, greatest rival to Orford's society, the Flixton Wolds Meeting in Yorkshire, set up under the leadership of Colonel Thornton and Major Topham.

Orford decided that to become a successful courser the existing greyhound must be taken in hand and completely remodelled. Greyhounds had good looks, but they lacked the speed and stamina required by the ideal hound which, so far, existed only in Orford's mind. Other breeds must be woven into the existing genetic pattern to provide the greyhound with the speed and staying-power, the quality that eighteenth-century folk called 'bottom', that it needed to make it a real courser.

Nobody was in a better position to recast the greyhound than Orford, he was in touch with every sporting man in Norfolk, from the peer to the poacher. His eccentricity as well as his burning passion for the sport allowed him to seek for advice wherever it might be found. Nobody looked less like a great landowner than he did, as he rode after his beloved greyhounds 'mounted on a stump of a piebald pony (as uniformly broad as he was long) in a full suit of black, without either great coat or gloves, his hands and face crimsoned with cold, and in a fierce cocked hat facing every wind that blew.'

Poachers amongst his acquaintance would not have been slow to praise to him the qualities of the lurcher, a companion of every poacher, and a worker as opposed to a working-dog. Lurchers had to catch hares and rabbits for their masters, for a living. They had to do it in record time, before the gamekeeper arrived, and without making a sound, or an error. Orford took the hint. Taplin records that, starting with his existing greyhounds, about a hundred in number,

... he went still farther in every possible direction and introduced every experimental cross, from the English lurcher to the Italian greyhound. He had strongly indulged an idea of a successful cross with the bulldog, which he could never be divested of, and after having persevered (in opposition to every opinion) most patiently for seven removes, he found himself in possession of the best greyhounds ever known, giving the small ear, the rat-tail, and the skin almost without hair, together with that innate courage which the high-bred greyhound should possess, retaining which instinctively he would rather die than relinquish the chase.

Something has already been said about one of the ancestors of the Orford greyhound, the bulldog; more will be said shortly about the lurcher; but it is worth explaining what was an Italian greyhound.

These dogs were comparatively unknown in England and Taplin says of them repressively:

this diminutive breed ... seems only calculated to soothe the vanity, and indulge the frivolities of antiquated ladies.... They are so deficient in the spirit, sagacity, fortitude and self defence of every other sort of the canine race, as not to be able to officiate in the services of domestic alarm or protection, and in consequence are dedicated only to the comforts of the tea-table, the fire-side carpet, the luxurious indulgencies of the sofa, and the warm lap of the mistress.

Italian greyhounds were really toy dogs and were considered too delicate to be easily reared in England. Owners of these dogs wrapped them in warm clothing during the cold months before taking them out. Statistics about eighteenth-century dogs are not easy to come by, but during the following century the Revd J. G. Wood said that the weight of an Italian greyhound ought not to exceed eight or ten pounds, while good examples might weigh as little as six. At that time the dog stood at 14¾ inches and the favoured colour for its coat was a uniform black. This was not the colour desired in Taplin's day, as his illustration shows.

Wood admitted that a cross between the Italian and the larger greyhound 'takes away the heavy, clumsy, aspect of the head which is caused by the bulldog alliance and restores to the offspring the elastic grace of the original greyhound.'

Every new strain that was brought into the greyhound made it slightly more difficult to manage. Thus the bloodhound cross gave Orford's greyhounds a tendency to hunt by the nose, whereas true greyhounds always hunt by sight.

Orford persevered; he had a wonderful knowledge of and feeling for animals. In his zoo at Houghton the park was 'curiously and infinitely stocked with every original in beast and fowl of almost every country from the African bull to the pelican of the wilderness.' George IV, who as Prince Regent was a frequent visitor to Houghton, was impressed by the Earl's collection. Orford's taste for the exotic in animals once nearly put an end to his efforts to breed new greyhounds for good. Taplin writes:

Amongst his experiments of fancy was a determination to drive four red deer (stags) in a phaeton instead of horses, and these he had reduced to perfect discipline for his excursions and short journeys upon the road. But unfortunately as he was one day driving to Newmarket, their ears were accidentally saluted with the cry of a pack of hounds, who soon after crossing the road in the rear, immediately caught scent of the 'four in hand', and commenced a new kind of chase with breast high alacrity. . . . In vain did his Lordship exert all his charioteering skill, in vain did his well trained grooms energetically endeavour to ride before them, reins, trammels and the weight of the carriage were of no effect. Off they went with the celerity of a whirlwind, and this modern Phaeton, in the midst of his electrical vibrations of fear, bid fair to experience the fate of his namesake. Luckily, however, his Lordship had been as accustomed to drive this . . . set of fiery eyed steeds to the Ram Inn, at Newmarket, which was most happily at hand, and to this his lordship's fervent prayers and ejaculations had been ardently directed.

Into the yard they suddenly bounded, to the dismay of ostlers and stable boys, who seemed to have lost every faculty upon the occasion. Here they were luckily overpowered, and the stags, the phaeton, and his lordship were all instantaneously huddled together in a large barn, just as the hounds appeared in full cry at the gate.

Besides his fondness for animals, Orford's scientific attitude towards breeding stood him in good stead. He would never part with a single dog till it had been given a fair trial. His position as Lord Lieutenant gave him an immense influence in obtaining stud-dogs and information about breeding, while his vast estates made the walking out of his innumerable greyhounds an easy matter.

In the end, it was coursing that killed Orford. During his second attack of insanity which had been brought on by the death of his mistress, he managed to elude his keeper, jump out of the window, saddle his pony and ride to the coursing match which he knew was taking place. There his best bitch 'Czarina' was running. As the old man appeared amongst the crowd, they made way for him, and no one ventured to take him back to Houghton. Instead the match, which was an important one, was begun. In his excitement Orford rode after the greyhounds and tumbled from the saddle just as 'Czarina' won. He was killed instantly.

The mantle of Lord Orford now fell on Thornton. At Tattersalls, he bought 'Czarina', 'Jupiter', and some more of the best dogs, paying for them a mere thirty or fifty guineas. This was not a large price when it is considered that about this time a Cumberland greyhound fetched a hundred and fifty guineas.

Established in Yorkshire, the Norfolk greyhounds found it quite difficult to chase the hares of the High Wolds. When the hares turned short on the hillsides, the hounds, 'unable to stop themselves, frequently rolled like barrels from the top to the bottom.'

Thornton decided to cross the Orford dogs with his own breed of East Riding greyhounds. These were the descendants of the wolfhounds with which the inhabitants of Flixton, Stackston and Folkton had been accustomed to hunt down the last-remaining English wolves. The wolves 'used to breed in the cars below amongst the rushes, furze and bogs, and in the night time come up from their dens, and unless the sheep had been previously driven into the town, or the shepherds indefatigably vigilant, great numbers of them were destroyed.'

The Wolds greyhounds were long-haired, curly-tailed dogs, with straight, firm legs, round hard foxhound feet and incredibly swift powers of closing up on the prey. As William Taplin commented:

That a dog of this description should sufficiently gratify the coursing sentiment of that day, is by no means surprising. The uncultivated face of the country, covered with brakes, bushes, wood and infinite obstacles, may readily account for it. In running their game, they had to surmount these impediments, and to dart through thorn hedges . . . which covered eighteen or twenty feet in width, and frequently to kill their object of pursuit in the middle of them.

The cross between the Yorkshire and Norfolk greyhounds which Thornton effected resulted in 'perhaps the three best and most perfect greyhounds ever produced in one litter.' 'Major', whose portrait sketched by Reinagle by permission of its owner, is given as an illustration, and 'Sylvia' were never beaten. 'Snowball' won ten large pieces of silver plate and more than forty matches against other greyhounds. When it died it was buried under a tomb consisting of a Grecian urn and pedestal. Its master, Major Topham of the Wold Cottage, Yorkshire, wrote an epitaph which begins:

He who out-bounded time and space,
The fleetest of the greyhound race,
Lies here! At length subdued by death,
His speed now stopped and out of breath.

So far as I know 'Snowball''s tomb was the first erected for a dog in modern times, though the ancient Greeks had buried their pets under inscribed monuments. Tombs for famous dogs such as 'Snowball' were going to lead to the provision of cemeteries for dogs in the next century.

Thornton long upheld the highest standards of coursing, until the mania which had beset the Earl of Orford began to attack him as well. His dress became more and more flamboyant, his manners more and more eccentric. Even his wife, often the steadying part of the partnership in a sporting couple, began to ride as a female jockey in a costume devised by her husband. Conduct such as this shocked Thornton's fellow sportsmen as much as running a boxed hare 'amidst whiskies, buggies and gingerbread carts' on Epsom Downs had shocked Taplin.

Thornton's expenditure on sport, always excessive, became so prodigal that even his career as a successful punter was insufficient to pay his expenses. He made tours in France and in the Highlands of Scotland that seemed more like royal progresses. Everywhere he went his retinue of huntsmen, falconers, grooms, keepers, his hawks (which included four cormorants), his hounds and horses, as well as his private menagerie and wagons loaded with choice vintages, accompanied him. He hunted white bucks with bloodhounds and chased ribbon-clad deer with garlands attached to their antlers.

By 1819 the career of the greatest sportsman in England had ended. Thornton had to sell his remaining possessions and move to France to escape his duns. The man who had trained the greatest coursers in England ended his course in a seedy French hotel.

Thornton's departure was probably a relief for his fellow greyhound-owners. The sport became more and more popular and ladies attended coursing matches, not just as patronesses but as participants. A Miss Ann Richards of Compton Beauchamp, Berkshire, never missed a day in the season, following on foot and often walking twenty-five miles in a morning. Her epitaph, written by herself, says that 'all her joys was Ashdown Park'. Women were not to appear on the foxhunting-field until the 1850s, by which time coursing had been firmly established as a national sport. In 1858 the National Coursing Club had been set up, while by 1882 an official Greyhound Stud Book set the recording of pedigrees and the registration of ownership on a regular footing. The keeping of greyhound pedigrees had already been begun in William Taplin's time.

Coursing was magnificent sport but everybody was too enthusiastic about it.

Immense sums changed hands as the greyhounds hurled themselves after the hare at speeds of twenty miles an hour or more. Owners of dogs felt almost compelled to bet on their greyhounds and the attraction of the sport became not so much the silver collar which was the prize for the best courser but a successful book made on a coursing match.

The greyhounds were too enthusiastic as well. Taplin who, as he himself tells us, was a gynæcological surgeon, inserts details about dogs which ran themselves into such a state of exhaustion that they had to be bled to recover them. Needless to say this treatment would be no more effective with dogs than with humans but it was the recommended one at the time. Other greyhounds were carried over a cliff in their wild pursuit or hurtled into one another and broke their necks.

The objections that could be made against coursing, that it lent itself to ruinous betting and was cruel to the dogs, could not be laid at the door of the most characteristic of eighteenth-century dog sports, foxhunting. The rise of foxhunting to become an important English sport was totally due to improved foxhounds, a new kind of dog bred by the famous Hugo

Meynell. There seems little doubt that it was through foxhunting that the dog exercised its greatest influence on English history. The hunt, as the most recent historian of hunting, Professor David C. Itzkowitz, has pointed out, 'came to be looked upon as one of the chief promoters within a country district of unity, stability, harmony, and devotion to traditional deferential values.' It was foxhunting men, much more than Methodist preachers, who saved England from a French Revolution, by keeping the different classes in constant and amicable contact. Foxhunting also made an incredible improvement to the breed of English horses. Until the early nineteenth century it was the ambition of every gentleman to be first at the kill so that he could obtain the coveted fox's brush. Then in the nineteenth century this privilege was found to cause reckless riding and it came to be awarded at the discretion of the Master. Yet because only a fast horse would take a rider within grasp of the brush the custom of riding horses that had more and more Arab blood in them had developed. Blood horses began to be used not just by foxhunters but by cavalry troopers and the art-illerymen of the 'Flying Artillery' devised during the Napoleonic Wars. After Waterloo Frederick Halsey of the Inniskillings was told by a French-man that English cavalry horses were as good or even better than those employed by the French upper classes for riding or carriage-horses.

The services rendered by foxhunting to the cavalry and the Royal Artil-lery have been obscured by the fact that in the greatest battle of the Napol-eonic period, Waterloo, the horsemen were ridden off the field by superior numbers. It was only the English foot that were left. But fortunately in England sport has never been the prerogative of this class, or of that and as the French cavalry moved in on the British squares, they were received by countrymen trained in the hard tradition of the rural poacher.

It is a paradox that the foxhound, which ended the century by becoming the purest bred dog in existence, started it by being very much of a mongrel. The packs of the early eighteenth century contained specimens of all kinds of sporting dogs, such as the Old Southern hound, now com-pletely extinct in England but fortunately surviving in America as the Pennmarydel hound. Though foxhound pedigrees had been begun at least as early as 1717, much earlier than the oldest race-horse pedigrees, which start in 1791, the background of many packs was purely conjectural.

The Old Charlton Hunt, for example, which was mentioned in the pre-vious chapter, was a case in point. It met at a hunting-box of the Earl of Arundel near Midhurst in Sussex from the 1660s onwards and belonged to the second Duke of Richmond, son to Charles II by Louise de Kerouaille. The stud groom, a Monsieur St Paul, came from Louise's estate of Aubigny in France. Because of the French background of the Richmonds it has been surmised that the Old Charlton may have begun life with a French pack and that it included the Normandy hound, descendant of the Black and White St Huberts and the French dun hound. Impossible to prove or dis-prove, this conjecture certainly emphasises the composite picture of the

English foxhound. Even inside the Old Charlton change was constantly being carried out, change often dictated by quite impractical considerations. As a poet advised the Charlton Master:

> The Spanish colour or the brown reject.
> The black tanned dog does never take the eye.
> The all-white hound of snowball kind don't please.
> The black-pied dog, with bright tanned edges round,
> With buff or yellow head, and white the ground,
> Of such compose thy pack.

Many of the qualities sought for in his hounds by a Master were about as practical as the qualities demanded by a breeder of fancy pigeons in Spitalfields. As can be seen in the above quotation, Masters were concerned about colour and the way it was distributed and other completely irrelevant factors such as the shape of the ears.

Foxhounds had started the century under enormous disabilities. The eighteenth-century foxhunters did not breed hounds especially for foxhunting but went in search of the fox with whatever hounds they had, usually harriers. These dogs were slow, with good scenting powers and sufficient stamina to kill a hare, but without the strength required to run down that tireless trotter, the fox. In an attempt to catch fast foxes with slow hounds, hunts met very early in the morning, at dawn, hoping to find the fox with a belly that was still full after his nocturnal depredations, hit his scent by chance, without drawing for him and run him down in a short burst. Failure to put this plan into operation involved a long, slow hunt that lasted many hours and which was often ended by the escape of the fox as the winter's dusk drew down.

There were other drawbacks. The fox was scented not by the whole pack, but by a few tufters. The very mixed pack found it impossible to travel at an equal pace. Apart from the terriers, there were fox beagles, which could easily outrun the larger and slower Southern hounds, with their good nose and cry, or the Northern hounds, with their superior stamina.

The principal difficulties under which hounds laboured, however, arose from the conduct of the Master, huntsman and hunt-servants. All sorts of habits, strange to us, then pervaded the hunting-field. It was believed that if a cat were tethered to a tree no fox would be able to pass it and this would ensure that hounds would find. Many if not all packs ran their hounds coupled together at the start of the century. Masters were preoccupied with killing their fox, even if it meant waiting for hours at the earths while the terriers and the spade did their work. The second Duke of Buckingham had fallen a victim to this practice in the previous century, having died of pneumonia after a long dig in 1687.

Better days dawned for hunting when Hugo Meynell was born in 1735. At the age of eighteen he took a lease on Quorndon Hall, in Leicestershire, and began to build up the hunt which, under the shortened name of 'Quorn', was to become famous all over England. Meynell was able to hunt because his elder brother had been disinheritted and he inherited the family property in 1753.

In every respect save one Meynell was a rather conservative Master. He liked hounds to take their own time in finding a fox in covert and he liked them to hunt at their own speed, without being hallooed on to the fox. When the scent was lost, he never cast the pack but let them wander round till they had found it again. He was rather unusual for the time in that he was indifferent to killing foxes. If a fox escaped, so far so good, it would be there for him to chase another day. Like most Masters he was very considerate to his hunt-servants, horses and hounds and refused to hunt more than three days a week. He had no need to please anyone save himself, as the hunt was run from his own pocket and for his own amusement.

Where Meynell was unusual, however, was in his approach to breeding. He realised that existing foxhounds could not put on enough speed to catch a fox, which relies much more on speed than cunning, and he set out deliberately to breed fast hounds. Under his care a new kind of Quorn foxhound began to develop, fast, hard-running, a patient hunter with a good nose and a voice that was raised only at the right moment. The new foxhounds revolutionised the sport by making it far more exciting and making it possible for hounds to meet at ten or eleven in the morning, rather than at dawn. Fashionable young men, who would have jibed at leaving their beds before the sky was red, now began to attend the Quorn.

They included a Mr Childe of Kinlet, nicknamed 'Flying Childe' on account of his hard riding and because there was a famous race-horse called: 'Flying Childers'. Around 1780 Childe, mounted on his 'half bred' Arabian, began to jump hedges and ditches hard on the heels of the hounds and even in front of them. Meynell, who had always looked for a good gap in the hedge and kept a decent distance between himself and his hounds, was scandalised. By 1800 Childe had found plenty of imitators, gallopers like Lord Jersey and Cecil Forester. Meynell complained bitterly that since foxhunting had turned into fox-racing he 'had not a day's happiness'. Nonetheless he accommodated himself very well to the change because he knew that the twin changes of faster hounds and faster riders had made the Master of the Quorn the most famous sportsman in England. Meynell began taking subscriptions from the Quorn members, reckoning that anyone who could afford to buy a blood Arab could certainly afford to pay for his hunting – and for his keep while at Quorn Hall, which was now his property.

The Quorn foxhound now rivalled the greyhound and the race-horse for the title of the fastest domesticated animal. Travelling in a little cart pulled by a team of foxhounds, a cripple called 'Old Lal', about whom more will be said later, could outpace the fastest transport vehicle then available, the stage-coach. A stage-coach travelled at a speed of about thirteen miles an hour, but only at certain stages of its run. Foxhounds sometimes averaged speeds far in excess of that of a stage. Colonel Thornton owned 'Merkin' a foxhound which once ran four miles in seven minutes, a speed of upwards of 36 miles an hour, and one which would have seemed absolutely incredible but for the fact that Thornton was, as usual, trying to win a bet and the dog's speed was carefully verified.

On 24th February 1800, the Quorn ended a run of 28 miles in two hours 15 minutes, at an average speed of 12 miles an hour. Even in an age of such successful genetic pioneers as Bakewell and Colling, Hugo Meynell had earned not merely his title of 'the father of foxhunting' but that of one of the most eminent of biological experimenters.

The new foxhound needs no description because it is admirably portrayed in Reinagle's pictures, which were drawn from life. Contemporaries commented on the features which made it a big change from earlier hounds, the straight legs, round feet, wide chest, broad back, small head, thin neck and bushy tail.

The nineteenth-century hunt did little more than stamp its seal of approval on the genetic pattern established by Meynell, though Masters continued to be extremely fussy about the colour of their hounds. The packs of the Belvoir and the Peterborough, the fashionable hunts of the nineteenth century, bore their pedigree on their back in the shape of the fashionable 'Belvoir' tan. Yet it was estimated that by 1820 half the hounds in England were descended from Hugo Meynell's 'Guzman' and the other half from Lord Yarborough's 'Ranter'.

As indispensable to a hunt as the thirty-five or forty couples of hounds which were usual at the time was its terriers. There were always two of these at least, one smaller than the other so that it could penetrate foxes' earths with small openings. The terriers hurried after their larger colleagues, the hounds, catching up with them whenever there was a check and arriving at the finish, ready to go underground.

The fox's retreat might be an unstopped earth or some natural crevice. Undaunted by the severe bites it received from its enemy, the terrier would pursue it into the earth, its furious barking a guide to the hunt-servants who were trying to dig down to uncover the fox. In the earlier part of the century terriers had worn collars with bells to guide the diggers, but many must have been choked by their collars catching on an obstruction, just as many buried themselves alive in their eagerness to throw up the earth while enlarging the passage in which they were digging, or died in a crevice of solid rock, locked in a last deadly embrace with the fox.

A terrier needed what the Revd W. B. Daniel called 'coat and courage'. His thick wiry covering of hair helped to protect him in part against the savage bites that he was sure to receive from the fox. He must not be too small or else he could not hope to follow with the hounds, nor must he be too large or else he could not hope to penetrate where a fox had gone. Black and white were the preferred colours. 'Those that are altogether of a reddish colour,' wrote Daniel, 'awkward people may mistake for a fox.'

Careful training was needed to make a foxhunting terrier. The young were entered at about ten months old, with old terriers to show them how to go to work. If they killed (they were often given the cubs to pursue after the adult foxes had been killed by the adult terriers) they were given fox's lights fried with cheese as a reward.

Daniel thought that the best recipe for a terrier was a cross between a beagle and a mongrel mastiff, or between a beagle and a drover's dog. A drover's dog was a larger and more ferocious version of the sheepdog. It usually had a docked tail – which in the latter part of this century was to avoid the dog tax. Taplin felt that it was a cross between the sheepdog, lurcher, mastiff and Great Dane. It was black or dingy coloured, with a white belly, face and legs, a sharp nose and pricked ears, with a long and usually matted coat. Drovers' dogs, which were also called 'curs', were usually ferocious, as a visit to Smithfield Market or any of the other London cattle markets would demonstrate. They were invariably badly treated by their masters. Taplin wrote:

> This dog ranks but low in society, submitting to degrading rebuffs, blows and kicks innumerable, with the most humiliating and philosophic patience. Notwithstanding which severities, he is a serene and faithful follower of fortune with his employer, and is seldom without the power and ability to render assistance in any little poaching excursion that may be occasionally entered into at certain seasons of the year.

Failing a cross with a drover's cur, Daniel recommends his readers to try a cross with a beagle 'or from any small, thick skinned dog that had courage'.

There were evidently plenty of breeds of terriers about, even if they had not yet been named or sorted into their regional types. 'Terriers of the best blood,' wrote Taplin, 'and most determined ferocity, are now, by the prevalence of all colours, red, black (with tanned faces, flanks, feet, and legs) and brindled, sandy, some few brown-pied, white pied and pure white.'

The most familiar type of terrier was undoubtedly the bull terrier. Originally it had been a rough, wire-haired breed, known for its good-biting qualities. Subsequently, 'this breed,' writes Taplin, 'has been so enlarged and repeatedly crossed in and in with the bull dog, for the favourite sport of badger baiting with the lower classes, that they are increased in size, strength and stimulus for that particular purpose.'

The bulldog had been evolved in the previous century. It was a breed intended to retain the best qualities of the mastiff, ferocity and an unbreakable grip, and to introduce new qualities of lightness, nimbleness, speed, and compactness. 'Its sudden fury in silently advancing,' wrote Taplin, 'and its invincible perseverance in maintaining its hold, are very far beyond the conception of those who have never been witnesses to their malevolent and destructive exertions. . . . Puppies will attack a bull, and give ample proof of their breed and courage, when no more than six or seven months old, and if permitted to continue the combat, will suffer themselves to be destroyed rather than decline the contest.' Frequently bulldog puppies were sacrificed in this way against a bull so as 'to demonstrate the purity of the blood, and to prove there has been no chance or improper cross.' Generally speaking though, young bulldogs were not entered until they were at least fifteen months old and even then were not considered mature till two years old and not in their prime till four or five.

Nowadays the most distinctive characteristic of the bulldog is its bandy legs, but it was not this that made it a national symbol for Englishmen. Taplin wrote:

It is a distinguishing and an invariable trait in the true-bred bulldog to attack the animal in front, and never to make a cowardly attempt at the extremities. . . . The dog whose breed has been preserved genuine and uncontaminate aims at and makes most ferociously for the face of the bull, and sinking closer to the ground the nearer he approaches, makes a desperate effort to seize upon the lip . . . failing in which he relaxes not in his efforts, but with the most incredible and determined fury fastens upon the tongue, the eye, the under-jaw, the throat, or some parts about the head or face (never degrading his character by making a pusillanimous attempt behind) where having secured his hold, he retains it beyond the power of description, in opposition to every energetic and desperate effort of the bull to get himself disengaged from so furious and a bloodthirsty an opponent.

Hunting the badger as opposed to 'drawing' the badger, the sport for which bull terriers were most used, took place by moonlight. A trap was set up and placed inside the earth of a badger once it had left it. The trap consisted of a sack extended into a hoop by a bent willow wand. A pack of dogs was then loosed into the cover, whereupon the badger immediately scurried towards its earth, where it became tangled helplessly in the trap. It was then collected and sold to the badger-drawers.

'Badger-baiting,' wrote Taplin, 'is a sport . . . exceedingly common in every part of the country where they can be procured . . . but more particularly with butchers and the lower orders of society in and round the metropolis, for whom a constant supply of badgers, from the woods of Essex, Kent and Surrey are sure to be obtained.'

The badger was a formidable opponent:

He is so rapid in his motions, that the dogs are often desperately wounded on the first assault, and compelled to relinquish the contest. The looseness of the badger's skin enables it to turn easily round when seized, and gives it an opportunity of wounding its adversaries in their most tender parts, and the thickness of the skin, added to the length and coarseness of the hair, defends it much from the bites of the dogs, no species of which will fight the badger so resolutely and fairly as terriers, of which there are two kinds, the one rough, short-legged, long-backed, very strong, and most commonly of a black or yellowish colour mixed with white, the other is smooth-haired and beautifully formed, having a shorter body and more sprightly appearance, is generally of a reddish-brown colour or black with tanned legs. Both these sorts are the determined foe of all the vermin kind, and in their encounter with the badger, very frequently meet with severe treatment, which they sustain with great courage, and a thorough-bred, well-trained terrier often proves more than a match for his opponent.

Badger-baiting was still legal throughout the whole of the eighteenth century but Taplin, who like many dog-lovers of the time was an animal-lover as well, keen to improve the lot of all animals, points out to his readers that the badger is a useful animal which does no harm to agriculture. He refers approvingly to the action of the magistrates of Islington and Tottenham Court Road, in London, who 'most laudably exerted themselves to put an end to a business of brilliancy, which brought together an infinity of the most abandoned miscreants with their terriers and bull dogs from every extremity of the town.'

Unfortunately Taplin's words had little, if any effect. Badger-hunting was a lucrative business. Alive, the badger could be sold to the baiters. Dead, 'their fat is in high estimation with rustics for ointments and salves', while the skin was used for making pistol holsters and sporrans for Highland dress. The hair was also used for painters' brushes.

Even Taplin could find nothing good to say for the other enemies of the terrier, vermin such as polecats, weasels and stoats. These animals would rob the game-preserver of all his birds if they were not checked. Taplin got Reinagle to 'draw his white-pied' (terrier) bitch in the act of pursuing a polecat to ground.

As terriers would put up rabbits for shooting as well, they were obviously an all-round sporting-dog, yet the reason why many people kept them was not for sport, but for pleasure. Taplin told his readers that he had never been without two or three since 1780. He could sell the puppies of his terrier bitches 'Doxey' and 'Gipsey' for as much as three pounds each – a good round sum in those days.

A terrier, he says, is not merely an affectionate pet, but a courageous protector of its master, and in support of this assertion he quotes a newspaper account of 1796. A young gentleman named Hardie, passing through St Andrews Square, Glasgow, was attacked by a footpad armed with a club. Hardie's terrier seized the robber by the throat, whereupon Hardie snatched the club and ran for safety. 'The terrier soon after followed him home, bearing in his teeth, as a trophy of his courage, nearly half of the man's waistcoat, in the lining of which half-a-guinea was found carefully sewed up.'

A dog which brought home half-guineas was likely to be very popular in Scotland and no one was fonder of terriers than Sir Walter Scott. As a lawyer, he made his debut at the bar by successfully defending a guilty burglar. In exchange the burglar gave him a useful piece of advice: 'always keep a small dog that makes a noise rather than a big one which goes to sleep.' Scott took the advice and became a great collector of terriers, especially the 'Dandie Dinmonts', which were named after a character in one of his novels, *Guy Mannering*. Though Scott had never met the real life prototype of Dandie Dinmont, James Davidson of Hindlee, before he wrote the book, the latter's fortune was made, as fanciers clamoured for puppies from his terriers, all of which were named 'Pepper' or 'Mustard'.

Scott kept big dogs as well and the biggest was 'Maida' a half-Pyrenean half-Scottish wolfhound. 'Prodigious' exclaimed two American visitors, dressed in suits of Royal Stuart tartan, who had dropped in for lunch uninvited, when they caught sight of 'Maida'. Scott's novels undoubtedly helped to popularise the keeping of terriers as pets. They also created the role of the dog as a character in fiction. The dogs in the Waverley Novels, dogs such as Sir Kenneth's giant Alaunt 'Roswal' in *The Talisman*, helped to make their creator's literary fortune. When, in the following century his financial fortune disappeared in the wreck of his publisher's business and there was only his literary fortune left, his bitterest thought was that he would have to part with the animals he loved. 'My dogs will wait for me in vain,' he wrote in his diary. 'It is foolish, but the thoughts of parting from these dumb creatures have moved me more than any of the painful reflections I have put down. Poor things! I must get them kind masters!'

Until the advent of the Quorn, the most popular pack sport had been hare-hunting. It continued to be very popular and in 1849 some sportsmen were surprised to read that there were now more foxhounds than harriers. The balance had gradually been tipping in favour of the fox, as some packs of harriers took to hunting the occasional fox as well. When William Lee Antonie changed his hounds from harriers to foxhounds in 1796, a move already anticipated by many other packs, a sportsman wrote to the Duke of Bedford: 'I cannot think but Mr Lee's changing his Hare-hounds into Foxhounds will give general satisfaction and be highly approved of by all his neighbours.'

Not everyone shared this satisfaction because not every sportsman wanted a neck-or-nothing gallop over the fences in the Quorn manner. Hare-hunting was a gentle amusement, suitable for the elderly or the timid. It required no great outlay on bloodstock, because no hare ran so far or so fast as a fox. There were so many checks while the unwindings of the hare were unravelled that there was plenty of time to chat with a nearby member of the hunt, or admire the countryside. There was, too, plenty of amusement to be had from hare-hunting, in a quiet way, because it was a very scientific pursuit.

The purpose of hare-hunting was not to kill the hare, but to have a good run. 'It is a fault in a pack of harriers to go too fast,' wrote Peter Beckford, 'for a hare is a little timorous animal which we cannot help feeling some compassion for, at the very time we are pursuing her destruction. We should give scope to all her tricks, nor kill her foully and over matched.'

In order to allow the surviving packs of harriers to compete with fox-hounds, the process of hunting hares was speeded up somewhat during the eighteenth century. At the beginning of the century the pack left the kennel at dawn, reaching the ground when there was just enough light to ride with safety. Days were short as hares were hunted in the spring or autumn, after harvest. The huntsman would lead his hounds to search for the 'trail' or winding path of the hare that led to where it lay concealed at present. None of the field beat the ground, but maintained a religious silence. When the hounds had found the scent they went along it at their own pace, slowly and carefully casting back when they were checked. In woods the twists and turns of the trail led to interminable delays, tiresome to horses and young huntsmen alike. Eventually the hounds approached the 'form' where the hare lay hidden and the huntsman drew them off for fear they should kill her before the chase had even begun. Once the hare had got away, with a good start, the chase could begin and an exciting, if short, pursuit followed.

After 1760 several changes took place in hare-hunting that were deplored by Taplin, a man of the old school. The hunt started much later in the day, to attract the fashionables, which meant the scent was colder. So men called 'hare-finders' were often brought in to find hares sitting. The pack would be brought up to them in a more direct way, so that they were often killed on their form. Wide casts with the hounds were made, to cut short the windings of the trail, and they were often hallooed on to the hare by the hunters, who also occasionally turned back the hare on to the hounds and certain death. Nor were harriers content with just a brace of hares any more. They wanted kills.

Much thought and much blood had gone into the harrier packs. They included Southern hounds, the breed which Whitaker, the historian of Manchester, asserted was the Ancient British hound. Others suggested an origin from the Gascon hound brought to England from France during the Middle Ages.

The Southern was a big hound, about 22 inches high, with a long body, deep chest and thick lips with drooping ears which suggested a bloodhound ancestry. It was slow, but had great powers of scent and a full musical cry. Except in districts of England which were marshy or moor covered, and where hare-hunting was bound to be a slow affair in any case, the slow speed of the Southern hound had sent it on the way to extinction by the end of the century. The term 'Southern' had nothing to do with regional location: Southern hounds were apparently most popular in the north. In Manchester, one of the two packs of harriers supported in 1775 was a Southern one. The subscribers wore blue, with white cuffs and capes. They were glad to take their pleasure at a reasonable pace, because all round Manchester the hunting country was a maze of coal pits and peat moors. One local pack, Mr Wild's, even had a huntsman who operated on foot with a pole to help him clear obstructions.

In spite of its obvious defects, the Southern hound was greatly prized. A north-country gentleman of the family of Osbaldestone was thrown out of the house by his father, because he had dared to marry a female servant. With a lingering touch of kindly feeling, the father allowed his disinherited son to take with him a Southern hound bitch which was big with pups.

Young Osbaldestone succeeded in getting a job as a lawyer's clerk and was thus able to support his wife and what proved to be a numerous family. In his spare time he kept the accounts of butchers, who allowed him offal on which to feed the hound and her progeny. With his Southern hounds Osbaldestone started his own pack of harriers, hunting over the land of gentlemen who winked at his catching the odd hare because they knew of his unfortunate circumstances.

The second of the Manchester harrier packs which were mentioned a moment or two ago were the beagles. Subscribers had a hunt uniform of scarlet, with silver buttons and green velvet capes. Of all types of harriers, beagles seemed ideally suited to conditions in Lancashire. 'The small, busy, indefatigable beagle,' wrote Taplin, 'is evidently intended by nature for those steep, hilly, and mountainous countries where it is impossible for the fleetest horses, with the boldest riders, to lay constantly by the hounds.'

Beagles shone in gorse and thick cover. Many varieties were developed, including Cotswold beagles, famous for dash and speed, North Country beagles, which were to develop into the third most popular hare-hound, the 'Harrier' (with a capital for distinction), and Peak District beagles. The latter are described by Peter Beckford as being 'too lively, too light and too fleet'.

The Harrier proper was a north-country beagle, though it looked much more like a miniature foxhound than anything else. It was about eighteen inches high, and had a small head, thin neck, bushy tail, a wide breast and a deep chest. The craze for speed which had spread from foxhunting to hare-hunting had promoted the rise of Harriers as the most popular hare-hound, though some sportsmen felt they went unmercifully fast for the poor hare. Harriers were only at their best in suitable country. 'Harriers of a superior description,' wrote Taplin, 'are only adapted to display their superiority in those open countries where, for want of a covert, the hare goes five or six miles to an end without a turn.' At the time of their greatest popularity during the eighteenth century, Harriers were considered to be a double-cross between the small beagle, the Southern hound and the dwarf foxhound.

Hare-hunters might disagree about which was the best dog with which to pursue their quarry, but they were all agreed that they would much rather be out pursuing 'Puss' as the hare was called, than having a day with the stag-hounds, in chase of a carted deer. 'At the present day,' wrote the Revd W. B. Daniel, speaking of the year 1801, 'as an object of chase to the sportsman, the stag requires but cursory mention. Those, indeed, who are fond of pomp and parade in hunting, will not accede to this opinion.'

One English sportsman who certainly did not accede was George III. His stag-hounds – the Royal Buckhounds, as they were called – were kept at Swinley, by Ascot Heath in Windsor Forest. Besides this pack, to which the king was passionately attached, the only other packs that William Taplin felt worth mentioning were those kept by the Earl of Derby at his seat at The Oaks, near Epsom in Surrey, and a subscription pack kept going by the London sportsmen near Enfield Chase in Essex.

In defence of foxhunting Daniel wrote:

At present very few hounds (except those of the Royal Establishment) are kept for this amusement exclusively and were the King once to see a fox well found and killed handsomely, he would in all probability give a decided preference in favour of Foxhounds, for what a marked difference is there between conveying in a covered cart, an animal nearly as big as the horse that draws it, to a particular spot where he is liberated, and cheerfully riding to the cover side, with all the ecstasy of hope and expectation.

George III did not take the hint though his son, later to be George IV, did ride to foxhounds. He would probably have defended his chosen sport on the grounds that nothing beat the excitement of watching buckhounds pursue their prey. His Majesty was not to blame for the substitution of a carted deer for a wild one. His forests and those of other landowners had barely recovered from the effects of the civil wars of the previous century before they began to be depredated by highly organised poaching gangs.

At the beginning of the century Queen Anne had sat on a grassy bank at Lippock about half a mile from Wolmer Pond and had there seen, 'with great complacency and satisfaction,' the whole herd of red deer in Walmer Forest, about five hundred head, driven past her.

Half a century later there were no deer to be seen in Wolmer at all. 'It is now more than thirty years ago,' wrote Gilbert White in 1788, 'that his Highness [the Duke of Cumberland] sent down an huntsman and six yeomen-prickers, in scarlet jackets laced with gold, attended by the stag-hounds, ordering them to take every deer in this forest alive, and convey them in carts to Windsor.'

Cumberland's decision to remove the deer had been made because they were being poached persistently by White's parishioners' fathers. White wrote:

Most men are sportsmen by constitution, and there is such an inherent spirit for hunting in human nature, as scarce any inhibitions can restrain.

Hence towards the beginning of this century, all this country was wild about deer-stealing. Unless he was a *hunter*, as they affected to call themselves, no young person was allowed to possess of manhood and gallantry.... Our old race of deer-stealers are hardly extinct yet. It was but a little while ago that, over their ale, they used to recount the exploits of their youth, such as watching the pregnant hind to her lair, and when the calf was dropped, paring its feet with a penknife to the quick to prevent its escape, till it was large and fat enough to be killed, the shooting at one of their neighbours with a bullet in a turnip field by moonshine, mistaking him for a deer, and the losing of a dog in the following extraordinary manner.

Some fellows, suspecting that a calf, new fallen, was deposited in a certain spot of thick fern, went, with a lurcher, to surprise it, when the parent hind rushed out of the brake, and taking a vast spring with all her feet close together, pitched upon the neck of the dog, and broke it short in two.

More will be said about the poachers' dogs – lurchers – in a short while. Meanwhile it must be noted that it was not merely in Wolmer Forest but in other parts of England as well that deer-poaching reached epidemic proportions. The 'Waltham Blacks', an organised band of desperadoes, cleared Waltham Forest of its deer. A special 'Black Act', the statute of 9 George I, c. 22, was passed in 1722–3 to deal with deer-poachers and several were hanged.

Even at the end of the century, however, the king had the chagrin of seeing Windsor Forest poached under his very eyes. At High Wycombe, in Buckinghamshire, a countryman shot the stag in the heat of the chase, while George was following the buckhounds. At Mapledurham, in Oxfordshire 'one of the best running deer in the King's collection,' according to Taplin, 'was most wantonly and inhumanly shot, as he lay in a willow bank, near the Thames, two days after he had completely beaten the hounds. Yet it is publicly known, in the forest and its district, that no steps whatever were taken to prosecute or punish the offenders.'

It is small wonder that George III followed the precedent, established in 1728, of chasing a carted deer, which could be reclaimed at the end of the run. The first carted run had not been after an English deer, but an American elk. Paradoxically, George III's hunting would have been much more approved of today than it was in his time. All the runs were bloodless, unless the poachers got there first. The hunted stag was cornered, captured and saved from the hounds before being put into a cart and sent back to its paddock. George particularly commended those hunters who had shown the greatest zeal in preventing the hounds from harming the deer. Although most sporting writers could find little to excite them in the Royal Windsor Hunt, William Taplin, a follower of the hunt for thirty-five years, gives us a description of a typical chase that shows that the royal buck-hounds could give plenty of excitement to their followers, especially, Taplin points out, as there was never a check or fault. Hounds ran so fast that only a real rider on a blood horse could keep up with them; everyone else was left behind.

By ten o'clock in the morning George III, who was always punctual to the minute, could be seen riding up to the field. He was dressed in the uniform of the Royal Windsor, light blue coat with black cuffs, and accompanied by his Master of Horse and two equerries-in-waiting. Ready to greet his Majesty were the Master, Lord Sandwich, the huntsman, Johnson, and six yeomen prickers 'richly apparelled in short hunting jackets of scarlet and gold'.

Half a mile away was the carriage containing the deer from the paddocks at Swinley, where the royal deer were kept. They were fed regularly on corn and the deer to be chased would be given a special feed. One of the king's favourite deer was called 'Moonshine', because he usually kept the Royal buckhounds running till nightfall.

As soon as George had dismounted from his hackney, and mounted a hunter, the deer would be liberated. Then minutes would elapse to give it a good start, during which the French horns carried by the yeomen prickers would sound. Two of them would then start in pursuit of the deer, one to its left and the other to its right.

Now the hunt, which consisted of more than a hundred and fifty horse-men, would draw away from the carriages containing the ladies and set off in hot pursuit. Soon only a dozen hunters mounted on the finest horses would still be within sight of the two yeomen-prickers, who marked the flight of the deer, while the rest tailed behind. From time to time the hounds would be checked by the huntsmen to allow the king, who rode at eighteen stone, to catch up. Obviously Taplin's comment that the hunt ran with never a check did not apply to days when the king hunted himself.

After a run of between an hour and a half to two hours the stag, complete-ly blown, would take to the water if a stream or pond were nearby and fight off its pursuers, the hounds, till the huntsmen could arrive and beat them away. The French horns would sound the end of the hunt, the deer would be led off to a neighbouring farmhouse or other place of safety and George would mount a hackney to take him to the nearest town where he could find a post-chaise to bring him back to Windsor.

There can be no doubt that there had never been a time when pet dogs had been more important. The choice of pets and of guard-dogs and worker-dogs as well was going to fluctuate considerably during the eight-eenth century. New breeds were adopted and old ones became less popular. Breeds which had existed in the previous century were often re-bred to such an extent that they showed little resemblance to their fore-bears. We have already noticed this process going on in the case of the foxhound. William Taplin gave another instance of a dog which had changed completely during his own lifetime. 'The Spanish pointer, for-merly so frequently seen, and so well remembered by the elder branches of the present generation, is so completely changed by the various specu-lative and experimental crosses . . . that one of the race, in its pure and uncontaminated state, is very rarely to be found.'

Another dog which had been completely changed by breeding was the mastiff. Though a few of the old strain were left, such as the Legh Hall mastiffs, the mastiff's occupation was gone as soon as a more efficient bull-baiting animal had been evolved, in the shape of the bulldog. Many fewer pure-bred mastiffs were kept. They were expensive to feed, a danger to inoffensive strangers and they had acquired a bad reputation for sheep worrying.

A mastiff belonging to Mr Snell, 'a gentleman of independent fortune in Gloucestershire', had lived a blameless life for years as a loyal protector of his master's property, until, towards the close of the century, it began to lead a Jekyll and Hyde existence. It left home at night, though to do so required leaping an eight-foot wall, and returned home just before day-break. Everyone in the house was asleep so nobody noticed the dog's absence and no suspicion ever attached to it of being the perpetrator of the mass sheep-worryings that took place in various parts of the county.

Then, one moonlight night, the mastiff was discovered by a farmer called Wood in a field near to his master's park. Round it were the bodies of sixty-three sheep and lambs. Snell immediately paid for all the damage that had been done, even before the farmer could ask for compensation. Then, 'after having had a painting taken of the dog in remembrance of so singular a transaction, he made a present of him to a Mr Wilcox, mercer, of Gloucester, whose servant having him with him, on a Sunday's walk to Cheltenham, he seized a woman by the leg upon the road, and tore it so severely that it was judged expedient to take away his life.'

Another sheep-worrying mastiff acquired national celebrity during the eighteenth century. It had been left behind by the crew of a smuggling vessel at Boomer on the coast of Northumberland. The dog had probably been carefully trained by its former owners never to approach strangers. At any rate, instead of simply turning up at the kitchen door of the nearest farmhouse in the hope of being fed, it began to prey on sheep. Soon it was killing such large numbers that it had become the terror of the farmers for twenty miles around. Instead of just killing a sheep and eating it, it bit a hole in the right side of the sheep it caught and contented itself with eating some of the fat near the kidneys. Some of the sheep which it attacked in this way are reported, rather incredibly, to have recovered.

The local farmers raised a hue and cry and hunted the mastiff with hounds, greyhounds and many volunteer hunters on foot and on horse-back. It escaped again and again by using a very simple technique. 'He lay fawningly down upon his back, as if imploring mercy from his pursuers, and in that position they never hurt him.' The mastiff was thus able to catch its breath and when the mounted hunters came within sight, it would trot off, at an easy pace, without the dogs pursuing it. Once the huntsmen had arrived, the hounds would once more be whipped on to the scent, only for the same procedure to be repeated again and again.

Once the mastiff was chased thirty miles from Howick, near which most of its depredations took place. It returned to Howick the following evening and killed more sheep. It was, says William Taplin, 'evidently demonstrat-ing sagacity, resentment, and revenge'.

With a grasp of strategy that many contemporary British generals might well have envied, the dog took up an unflankable position. 'After various fruitless pursuits,' wrote Taplin, 'his most constant residence was ascert-ained to be at the extreme summit of a rock, known by the name of Heugh Hill, near Howick, where he had an unobstructed view of the four distinct roads which approached it, and there he was, by a stratagem, waylaid and shot in the month of March, 1785.'

Ten years later yet another sheep-worrying mastiff created havoc in Northumberland. It struck at sheep again and again, near Wooller and on the Fells, taking a toll of as many as sixty sheep in one locality. On 6th June 1799 a hunt to put down the mastiff was advertised. Three packs of hounds and sharp-shooters were once more employed, while a reward of twenty guineas was offered to whoever killed the dog. Finally, in September, the mastiff's lair was discovered. It was chased from Carrock Fell, in a thirty-mile run which lasted six hours. A Mr Sewel of Wedlock lay in wait in Moss Dale and as the gaunt, wire-haired mastiff came within range, he was able to shoot it.

It was not just mastiffs whose numbers had dropped in Britain; other breeds had now become markedly less popular, notably the great Irish hound. So long as there still existed Irish wolves, the hound was indis-pensable. By the late seventeenth century, however, it was noted by Blount that 'wolves in Ireland, of late years, are in a manner all destroyed, by the diligence of the inhabitants and the assistance of Irish Greyhounds, a wolf dog.' In consequence, as Bishop Gibson noted, in this century 'The race is now almost extinct; there are not perhaps ten in the country.'

Other and much humbler breeds prepared to follow the great hound towards extinction. They included the turnspit, the best known represen-tative of those worker-dogs which had once provided power for various purposes, such as raising water from a well by working a treadmill.

Before the introduction of the turnspit dog, meat had been turned on the spit by a human turnspit, a small boy protected from the heat of the fire by means of a round woven straw shield, soaked in water. Even with this pro-tection, turning the spit must have been an unpleasant task, while the child spit-turners probably got in the way of the adult cooks, who had to be continually basting the meat with hot fat.

At some indeterminate time, during the Middle Ages, special treadmills were built near to the fires of large and important kitchens and dogs trained to keep them turning. The power developed by the treadmill was communicated to the spit. George R. Jesse describes two ways in which this might be done:

> At Caerleon, near Newport, Monmouthshire, in the kitchen of the Hanbury Arms Inn, two years since [1864] there was a turnspit-wheel, worked by a long-backed little dog. Indeed it probably still exists. The wheel was attached to the ceiling, and the dog worked inside it like a squirrel in its cage, consequently when once in motion he was forced to continue running.
> In former days, when this mode of turning a spit was common the wheel was in a line with the spit forming the axle of the wheel, but in the present one a chain passing round the wheel also wound round the spit.

The turnspit's task was not a sinecure. A large, solid piece of beef would take at least three hours to roast properly. While the roasting went on, the dog had to turn the wheel hundreds of times and if it stopped for a moment it might be scolded or beaten by the cook, whom the heat from the ovens kept in a perpetual mood of irritation. The poet Thomas Gay (1688–1732) knew all about the trials of a turnspit's life:

> ... The dinner must be dished at once,
> Where's this vexatious turnspit gone?
> Unless the skulking cur is caught,
> The sirloin's spoilt, and I'm in fault.'
> Thus said (for sure you'll think it fit
> That I the cook maid's oaths omit),
> With all the fury of a cook,
> Her cooler kitchen Nan forsook:
> The broom-stick o'er her head she waves,
> She sweats, she stamps, she puffs, she raves –
> The sneaking cur before her flies;
> She whistles, calls, fair speech she tries;
> These nought avail. Her choler burns;
> The fist and cudgel threat by turns.
> With hasty stride she presses near:
> He slinks aloof, and howls with fear.

Turning a spit was such hard work that families or households that employed turnspits kept two. The dogs worked on alternate days and each dog knew his day. This custom may have been the origin of the proverb: 'Every dog has his day.' (Apparently this proverb first appears during the turnspit era, in the works of George Borrow (1803–81)).

If a turnspit dog tried to avoid doing his day's work and his colleague was forced into the treadmill in his place, the dog might bite the cook's hand as a protest. It was not unknown for a dog imposed on in this way to rush out of the kitchen to round up the turnspit that was on duty at that time.

The invention of a clockwork roasting-jack spelled the end of the turnspit. Writing in 1822, the Revd Henry Crowe remarked:

I shall dwell but briefly on a use to which dogs, called turnspits, were formerly much applied, hoping that it will soon be totally discontinued, as it is now nearly so.... Enclosed in a wheel from which they cannot escape, overcome by a labour which admits of no pause (indeed the lash prevents any) and oppressed by the heat of the stove, their fate is well nigh that of Ixion, except that he was not doomed to toil by a fireside in hot weather. A kitchen joke, too, I understand, is, if they are lazy, to put into the wheel a hot coal as a stimulant to their feet, and this is said to be the method of teaching them originally their business.... Roasting jacks of various constructions are now everywhere common and cheap.

Soon turnspits were only to be found in old-fashioned parts of the country such as Wales and the West Country. Edward Jesse wrote:

How well do I recollect in the days of my youth, watching the operations of a turnspit at the house of a worthy old Welsh Clergyman in Worcestershire, who taught me to read. He was a good man, wore a bushy wig, black worsted stockings, and large plated buckles in his shoes. As he had several boarders, as well as day scholars, his two turnspits had plenty to do.

They were long bodied, crooked legged and ugly dogs, with a suspicious, unhappy look about them, as if they were weary of the task they had to do and expected every moment to be seized on to perform it. Cooks in those days were very cross, and if the poor animal wearied with having a larger joint than usual to turn, stopped for a moment, the voice of the cook might be heard rating him in no very gentle terms.

By the time Jesse had finished his book, *Anecdotes of Dogs*, in April 1846, the turnspit was almost extinct. As with other specialised breeds of dogs, its life had been dependent on having a job to do: once that job had disappeared so did the dog. Almost the only turnspits left were some in the royal kennels. Queen Victoria had recently married a German husband and these dogs were still used there. Jesse describes them further:

They are extremely bandy legged, so as to appear almost incapable of running, with long bodies and rather large heads. They are very strong in the jaws, and are what are called 'hard bitten'. It is a peculiarity in these dogs that they generally have the iris of one eye black and the other white. Their colour varies, but the usual one is a blueish-grey, spotted with black. The tail is generally curled on the back.

Somehow the turnspit did manage to survive at least till as late as 1870; by this time it was so rare that owners could earn more than 6d a day by hiring out their dogs. Writing at the middle of the nineteenth century, the Revd J. Wood noted that 'Just as the invention of the spinning jenny abolished the use of distaff and wheel, so the invention of automaton roasting jacks has destroyed the occupation of the turnspit dog, and by degrees has almost annihilated its existence.'

Yet if some breeds had fallen entirely out of favour, new ones had emerged to take their place. Prominent amongst the ranks of the newcomers was the Dalmatian and the Great Dane, both carriage-dogs acquired at this period.

In Denmark the Great Dane had been used as a pointer; in England, it came to the running footman which attended its master's carriage, ensuring that urchins did not scare or harm the horses and keeping watch on the rich pelisses of fur which were often left in the vehicle, for the groom who had driven with his master would be fully occupied holding the horses' heads while his master made a call on some acquaintance.

By the end of the eighteenth century there were three distinct breeds of Great Dane known in England: the bluish-grey marbled with black, the fawn and the harlequin. William Taplin commented:

The majestic and commanding aspect, bold muscular action, and elegant carriage of this dog would recommend him to notice, had he no other useful properties or points of attraction. Those he has already in possession we observe honoured in adding to the splendid pomp and magnificent retinues of the noble, wealthy, and independent, before whose emblazoned vehicles he trots or gallops with a degree of dignity denoting no small consciousness of the patronage he is under and the state of grandeur he is selected to precede and support.

The Great Dane accompanied so many carriages that it was known as the 'Coach Dog', unless the more common term of 'Plum Pudding Dog', was preferred. Though the spotted dog was often a direct importation from Denmark, many dog-owners must have regarded it as a purely British dog which had now returned to its native land. Buffon, the great French naturalist, had argued in words that convinced many that really the Great Dane was an Irish hound which had become acclimatised on the Continent.

'Water Dog', from *The Sportsman's Cabinet*.

Newfoundland Dog, an illustration from *The Sportsman's Cabinet*, by
William Taplin, London, 1803, painted by Philip Reinagle (1749-1833) and
engraved by John Scott.

Greenland Dog, from *The Sportsman's Cabinet*.

Springer Spaniel

Pointer.
Both from illustrations to *The Sportsman's Cabinet*.

Springer Spaniels, drawn by J. Wells and engraved by E. Evans for J. G. Wood's *The Illustrated Natural History*.

Cocker Spaniels, from the same publication.

King Charles Spaniel, also from the same publication.

Pointers, from *The Illustrated Natural History*.

'Scotch Colly', drawn and engraved by W. R. Smith for Edward Jesse's *Anecdotes of Dogs*, London, 1846.

'The mole-catcher and his terrier', by H. Alken, from Charles White's ('Martin-gale') *Sporting Scenes and Country characters*, London, 1840.

'The earth-stopper and his terrier, by T. Landseer, from *Sporting Scenes and Country Characters*.

The rat-catcher and his terrier, by T. Landseer, from the same source.

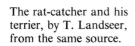

St Bernard Dog, one of the pair belonging to the lecturer and
novelist Albert Smith, drawn by H. Weir and engraved by Dalzeil
for J. G. Wood's *The Illustrated Natural History*.

'Old Lal and his team. Illustration by an anonymous artist in
M. E. Haworth's *Road Scrapings*, London, 1882.

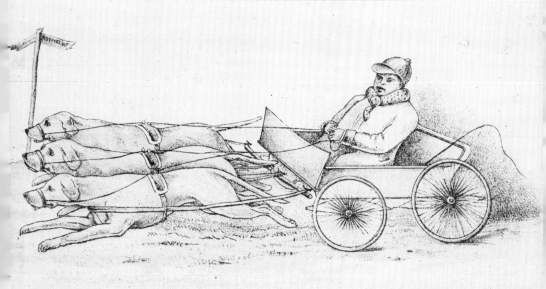

"THE DEFIANCE HAS GONE 10 MINUTES!"

Florence Nightingale cures her first patient. Engraving by anonymous artist in 'W. J. W', *The Story of Florence Nightingale*, London (no date).

The only possible competitor to the Great Dane as a carriage-dog was the Dalmatian. It was considered less aristocratic than the Great Dane, but it was popular, nonetheless. 'The Dalmatian, or common coach dog,' wrote Taplin, 'is considered a much more humble and subordinate attendant upon the horses, the carriages, and the servants.' The Dalmatian's popularity lasted from the end of the eighteenth century down to the early decades of the nineteenth. Even now, of course, it has many admirers. Unlike the Great Dane, it had no connection with sport but had been originally bred as a watch-dog or war-dog to give warning of the approach of enemies. Its name is apparently no misnomer, it did originally come from Dalmatia, a province of Illyria, on the eastern Adriatic coast. The Dalmatian was trained to run alongside horsemen in the field, one of the hardest tasks a dog can undertake, but one for which this magnificent animal was particularly suited by its stamina.

By the seventeenth century the original purpose of the breed had disappeared and it was being used in Italy, perhaps as a pointer. It appears twice in a picture painted by the Italian sporting artist Castiglione, who died in Venice in 1716.

By the end of the century the Dalmatian had reached England, and taken it by storm. Everyone liked them – except William Taplin:

They seem but little calculated for any useful, entertaining, or profitable purpose in this country, unless in contributing to the splendour of a stable establishment, the magnitude and magnificence of which has never before reached its present state of unprecedented elegance, and emulative opposition for a display of fashionable superiority.

The whole and sole destination of the Dalmatian is the individual attendance upon, and the protection of, the horses and carriage to which he belongs; to these it is his business to be invariably annexed, and to both he is so fervently attached, that they are never brought into use, either by night or by day, without his appearing in an official capacity as an indispensible part of the retinue.

His attendance upon the horses when in a state of inactivity, and his exulting consciousness of dignity in preceding the carriage (as if to announce its approach, with an authority to clear the way) seem to constitute the most superlative gratification of his existence.

Not everyone would have agreed with Taplin. To many, such as the naturalist the Revd J. G. Wood, the Dalmatian appeared the equivalent in the dog world of the Regency buck:

Its shape is very like that of a pointer, but the artificially shortened ears give it a different aspect. The ground colour of this animal's fur is nearly white, and is richly crossed with black spots, earning for it, in common with the Danish Dog, the title of 'Plum Pudding'.

The height of this animal is about twenty four or twenty five inches. Some years ago, the Dalmatian Dog was very frequently seen in attendance upon the carriage of its owner, scampering along in high glee by the side of the vehicle, or running just in front of the horses, apparently in imminent danger of being knocked over every moment. Now, however the creature has lost its hold on the fashionable world.

Carriage-dogs did indeed live a life of constant danger. One Dalmatian which followed the London to Brighton coach (one of the very last) in 1851 was killed as he jumped from the coach to take up his usual position, under the very high wheels which were fashionable for coaches. In his heyday, this dog had done the trip from London to Brighton on eight successive days, with a break for Sunday. Sometimes he rode, but usually he preferred to trot beside the coach. For a long time after his death his stuffed figure, in a glass case, was one of the attractions of a pub in the Edgware Road.

Although I have described the Dalmatian as not being a sporting-dog, in the usual acceptance of the term, it must not be forgotten that coaching was a sport, indeed for many it was *the* sport while it lasted. The Dalmatian was essentially a horse and stable dog. With his usual realism, Philip Reinagle has depicted it in a stable yard. It was rarely admitted to the house, probably chiefly because it was an excellent guardian of the horses and stable.

Not everybody kept coaches or curricles and so could sport a Dalmatian, but everyone could own one of the newly imported American dogs. The Newfoundland dog and the Labrador, also known as the St John's Newfoundland or the St Johns waterdog were the companions of wildfowlers and the worker-dogs of watermen, fishermen and smugglers, as well as being the friends and companions of all sorts and conditions of men.

Both these dogs suddenly became prominent in the very thinly inhabited yet vast island colony of Newfoundland, off the east coast of Canada. Labrador is that part of Canada which fronts Newfoundland across the Strait of Belle Isle and St Johns is the capital of Newfoundland. The name 'Labrador' is apparently a mistake because the dog was always associated with Newfoundland, not Labrador, though specimens of the breed were taken to Labrador.

The two dogs from the island colony were very different from one another. The Newfoundland was a large dog with a rough, shaggy coat and the Labrador was smaller and sleeker, with smooth, short hair, close and compact to the body. How had two quite distinct dogs originated in one island in such a short space of time, between the colonisation of Newfoundland by the Bristol merchant, John Guy, in 1610, and the middle of the eighteenth century?

The original inhabitants of the island, who are now extinct, had been the most mysterious of all Indian tribes, the Beothuks. They were very much in touch with the neighbouring Eskimos, spoke a language which contained many Eskimo words and even wore body armour of slats of bone or walrus ivory, just as the Eskimos did.

A notable feature of the Eskimo way of life, to which the Beothuks approximated so closely, was their possession of dogs. However, when Lieutenant John Cartwright, who visited Newfoundland in 1768, met the Beothuks, he said they had no dogs. Cartwright's statement is not an insuperable objection to the hypothesis that the Newfoundland originated from a dog kept by the Beothuks. In 1870 a Mr 'W.C.' of Halifax wrote that the Beothuks did have 'a dog, but that it was a small breed.' The absence of dogs on Cartwright's visit could have two possible explanations: the Beothuks might have hidden the dogs for fear of their being stolen, or they might have eaten them during a famine. In either case they would have had no difficulty in replacing their stock of husky dogs. Bruzen de la Martinière, a French geographer who wrote in 1763, mentions that the Eskimos from Labrador made regular visits to Newfoundland to trade.

If the Beothuk or Eskimo husky was one ancestor of the Newfoundland (and perhaps the Labrador as well) the Pyrenean Mountain dog might have been the other. The Pyrenean dog was a large, shaggy, all-white dog with a very Newfoundland-shaped head and face and a bushy tail, also like the Newfoundland.

The Pyrenean dog was employed in the reign of the Pyrenees as a sheepdog and guard-dog. It was from the very region where it was most popular that the other inhabitants of Newfoundland came – those French and Spanish Basques who made their way to Canada to fish and catch whales. The Beothuks apparently had contacts with these cod fishermen; John Guy found the hoops of casks in their deserted cabins, objects which they could only have got from the fishermen, by trade or theft.

Most French and Spanish fishermen carried a dog aboard. It would guard the nets and, as we shall see later, it might even be trained to deal with snapping codfish which slipped off the hook once they were dragged aboard the dory. In 1763, when de la Martinière wrote, there were no fewer than 250 French fishing-boats plying on the Grand Banks off Newfoundland. It would not have been very unusual if one of these dogs wandered off into the interior, or came ashore after a shipwreck.

The Newfoundland has a good deal of the appearance of the Pyrenean Mountain Dog, and yet its first appearance in history is that of a workerdog, doing exactly the same task as the husky. At some time after the arrival of the first English settlers in Newfoundland in 1623 it became the usual draught animal of the Newfoundlanders. At a very early age Newfoundlands were broken into harness by the coastal settlers. Three, four or five dogs drew a sledge across the frozen ice, often a sledge with a load of several hundredweight. They would go for miles pulling this burden, travelling by themselves without a driver to direct them. Once their sledge had arrived at its destination it would be unloaded and they would return home with the empty sledge to their owner's home, where as a reward they would be fed. 'The Newfoundland . . .' wrote Edward Jesse: 'is docile, capable of strong attachment, and is easy to please in the quality of his food, as he will live on scraps of boiled fish, either salted or fresh, and on boiled potatoes and cabbage.' Yet, according to Wood, the dogs never got enough to eat. 'The poor animals,' he wrote, 'are not only urged beyond their strength, but are meagrely fed with putrid salt fish, the produce of some preceding summer. Many of these noble dogs sink under the joint effects of fatigue and starvation, and many of the survivors commit sad depredations on the neighbouring flocks as soon as the summer commences, and they are freed from their daily toils.'

The journeys of the Newfoundlands usually took them in the direction of the sea. They were pulling lumber for fuel or for repairing the fish stages where the cod were salted and dried. They were also used to guard the stages and the wharves.

By comparison with the husky, a dog so fierce and intractable (when handled and trained by Eskimos at any event) that it took six months to accustom to the sledge and was even then so fierce that it would eat its owner if he gave it the chance, the Newfoundland was very docile and very intelligent. Taplin wrote of it:

He is easily taught almost everything within the power of the human mind to inculcate of which his own strength and frame are capable.

One Justice of Peace at Harbour Grace in Newfoundland, a Mr Garland, even succeeded in training his dog to accompany him at night carrying a lantern. The old dog was in the habit of carrying a lantern before his master at night, as steadily as the most attentive servant could do, stopping short when his master made a stop and proceeding when he saw him disposed to follow him. If his master was absent from home, on the lantern being fixed to his mouth, and the command given, 'Go, fetch your master,' he would immediately set off and proceed directly to the town, which lay at the distance of more than a mile from the place of his master's residence.

He would then stop at the door of every house, which he knew his master was in the habit of frequenting, and laying down his lantern, would growl and strike the door, making all the noise in his power until it was opened.

Before long the cod fishermen who were the principal English visitors to the island had discovered the virtues of the Newfoundland and had begun to carry it aboard their ships. Soon Newfoundland dogs were to be found in Britain, not merely near to the home ports of the cod fishers, but farther afield, in Scotland for example, where Burns refers to the Newfoundland in one of his poems.

The Newfoundland very soon showed its versatility aboard ship. It became so much at home on the water that many people of the eighteenth century really believed that it had webbed feet. It was an ardent retriever of naval property and naval personnel. If an oar fell overboard from a boat, the ship's dog would dive in and bring it back. If a sailor fell overboard – and this was an age when many sailors could not swim – the Newfoundland would be in the water trying to help him.

By the middle of the eighteenth century the Newfoundland had become the dog equivalent of the popular idol of the time – the heroic sailor. Once when a group of seamen and a woman were preparing to board a sloop of war in the Hamoaze from a shore boat, the boat suddenly upset. A Newfoundland which had been standing on the quarter deck of the sloop instantly dived into the water, seized one of the drowning seamen by the collar and held his head above water till help arrived.

Whole ship's crews were sometimes saved by a Newfoundland, which would leap into the raging sea with a rope's end between its teeth and swim ashore, so that a line could be hauled aboard the foundering vessel. Occasionally a dog might make the journey in reverse, out from the shore, through the battling surf, to the ship.

By the middle of the nineteenth century the life-saving properties of the dog had become so well known that Sir Edwin Landseer painted one and gave it the title 'A distinguished member of the Royal Humane Society'. (This was a society devoted to saving those in peril of drowning.)

In France the heroic qualities of the Newfoundland had been recognised much earlier. A corps of life-saving dogs was organised on the banks of the Seine, in Paris, and they were trained to save people struggling in the water by being exercised with special dummies made to represent men, women and children. One of these Parisian life-savers took his duties so seriously that he persistently tried to save ordinary swimmers as well, by drawing them to shore.

By the eighteenth century, the Newfoundland had become the mascot as well as the pet of many ships, whether in the Royal Navy or the Mercantile Marine. In 1789 a Newcastle ship went aground off Yarmouth and the captain's Newfoundland brought his pocket book ashore in its mouth. The crew of HMS *Bellona* had a Newfoundland called 'Victor' which stayed on deck during the Battle of Copenhagen in 1801, running fore and aft and growling defiance at the Danes. When the ship paid off after the Peace of Amiens, the sailors held a farewell dinner on shore. Victor was placed in the chair and ate roast beef and plum pudding. The bill was afterwards made out in his name.

Our opponents during the Napoleonic Wars, the French, had their mascot dogs too, usually poodles. The most famous poodle was 'Moustache' which once saved its regiment from being surprised by the Austrians and was very clever at detecting spies in the camp. It was killed during the Peninsular War. Many French dogs seem to have been acquired by English officers during this campaign as spoils of war.

The Newfoundland was not merely a life-saver and a mascot, it was a born protector as well. One sailor lay down in the middle of Piccadilly to sleep off a drunken orgy, confident that no one would dare to come near him as long as his dog was standing by. During the following century, a performance of *Jesse Vere* was being given at the theatre in Woolwich. In this play a villain manhandles a young girl. Fired with indignation at this proceeding, a Newfoundland in the audience jumped the footlights and was only pulled away from the actor impersonating the villain with the greatest difficulty.

It was a short step from the employment of Newfoundlands as ships' dogs to their use as working-dogs and pets. One captain in the 'Sea Fencibles', a marine Home Guard set up during the Napoleonic Wars, took his dog wildfowling with him whenever he had any leave. A Newfoundland was already a born retriever, and it could easily be trained to do everything a gun-dog needed to do.

Such an admirable dog could not fail to be acquired as a pet, even by owners who did not require working-dogs. Byron, who was keen on sailing, had a Newfoundland called 'Boatswain', of which he was extremely fond. He hoped to be buried beside Boatswain, which he described as the only friend he ever had on the inscription for the tomb which he built for it at Newstead Abbey. In fact events frustrated his hopes and he had to sell his house. Boatswain's tomb was perhaps the first nationally famous monument to a dog which was a pet and not a working-dog.

A contemporary of Byron's who was, like the poet, a Scot, a Mr Haldane of Stirling, tried employing Newfoundlands as private transport dogs. Every morning a team of two dogs would pull a specially constructed cart from his house to a baker's in the centre of Stirling. The baker, who had a key to the box fitted to the cart, would unlock it and put some hot rolls in, then lock it once more. Now the team would return home, calling on the way at the post office where they picked up any letters that might be waiting there for the family.

By the following century the Newfoundland was ranked second in the list of most popular dogs because of his 'courage, perseverance, and fidelity'. It had also become the most notorious of all British dogs because of the Macnamara and Montgomery duel. Although this occurred three years after the eighteenth century had ended, it might be mentioned here as we shall not be returning to the Newfoundland.

On 6th April 1803, at about four o'clock in the afternoon, Colonel Montgomery of the 9th Regiment and Captain Macnamara, R.N. were both riding in Hyde Park, each accompanied by a favourite Newfoundland. Suddenly, without any warning, the dogs began a battle royal. Their owners parted them, exchanging words in the process. Macnamara said he regarded Montgomery's words as arrogant, to which Montgomery replied, 'If you feel yourself hurt you know where to find me.' This, the captain decided, was a slight on his honour and he despatched a second to Montgomery to arrange a meeting. In three hours time the two men were looking at one another down the barrels of their pistols, at twelve paces. Both fired, simultaneously. Macnamara was wounded, Montgomery killed almost instantly. Duelling was illegal and the coroner's jury found no difficulty in reaching a verdict of: 'Guilty, for manslaughter, in shooting at Robert Montgomery with a pistol loaded with a leaden ball . . . whereby the said Robert Montgomery received a wound through the body of which he died.' The gallant naval officer was thereupon put on trial for his life.

Macnamara replied to the indictment in a speech which he had to read from a chair because of the weakness caused by his wound:

Gentlemen, I am a captain in the British navy. . . . To maintain my character in that station, I must be respected. When called upon to lead others into honourable danger, I must not be supposed to be a man who has sought safety by submitting to what custom has taught others to consider as a disgrace. . . . It is impossible to define in terms the proper feelings of a gentleman, but their existence has supported this happy country for many ages, and she might perish if they were lost.

Lord Nelson, Lord Hood, Lord Minto, Sir Hyde Parker, Admiral Hotham, General Churchill and a number of other witnesses testified that the defendant was a man of excellent disposition and mild character. Not brought out in the evidence, because it was common knowledge, was the fact that both the duellists belonged to the Anglo-Irish aristocracy who were dedicated duellists to a man.

This fact probably weighed with the jury, because in spite of a clear summing-up by the judge directing them to find Macnamara guilty, the jury declared the captain 'Not Guilty' to considerable applause.

Before the end of the eighteenth century, a new type of dog began to be imported from Newfoundland, the Labrador. Once more these dogs began to arrive in England aboard fishing-boats. The Labrador was an invaluable ally of the fisherman. On the Grand Banks, Labradors had been trained to jump into the water and retrieve any codfish that managed to get free of the hook and jump back into the sea after being landed in the dory. The origins of the Labrador remain obscure. One nineteenth-century informant said that it was 'a distinct breed . . . formerly they were only to be met with on that part of the coast of Labrador which to us is known as the South Shore of the mainland in the Straits of Belle Isle.'

Most writers who mention the Labrador, however, take just the opposite view, that it was a purely Newfoundland dog. 'The dogs sent to

England with rough, shaggy coats,' wrote De Boillieu, 'are useless on the coast, the true-bred and serviceable dog having smooth, short hair, very close and compact to the body.' Edward Jesse commended the Labrador as 'by far the best for every kind of shooting . . . oftener black than of another colour and scarcely bigger than a pointer. He is made rather long in the head and nose, pretty deep in the chest, very fine in the legs, has short or smooth hair, does not carry his tail so much curled as the St John's, and is extremely quick and active in running, swimming or fighting.'

By the 1830s the Labrador had attracted the attention of the second Earl of Malmesbury, who had brought dogs from Canada to join those already established in England. Many of the first Labradors in this country had been brought to the district round Poole Harbour. Under the Earl's hands, the Labrador was shaped into the most popular of all the retrievers.

The whalers and sealers which left Scots ports such as Dundee and Aberdeen for the Greenland seas apparently sometimes took dogs with them to help with the sealing. This at least might be inferred from a Victorian novel by Dr Gordon Stables, *From Greenland's Icy Mountains*, in which one of the heroes of the book is the mastiff 'Toro'. Whalers also brought back dogs from the Arctic, the huskies which were used by the Eskimos for sledging. These dogs never achieved the status of an established British breed, though individual owners such as a Mr Cleghorn of Edinburgh might keep them.

A close relative of the Eskimo dog, the Spitz, Fox-dog or Pomeranian, did however achieve real popularity in England during the eighteenth century. William Taplin described the breed as he knew it:

The dog so called in this country, is but little more than eighteen or twenty inches in height, and is distinguished by his long, thick, and rather upright coat, forming a most tremendous ruff about the neck, but short and smooth on the head and ears. They are mostly of a pale yellow, or cream colour, and lightest on the lower parts. Some are white, some few black and others, but very rarely, spotted, the head broad towards the neck, and narrowing to a muzzle, ears short, pointed, and erect, nose and eyes mostly black, the tail large and bushy, invariably curled in a ring upon the back.

In general opinion as a house dog he is held in but slender estimation, being by nature frivolous, artful, noisy, quarrelsome, cowardly, petulant, and deceitful, snappish and dangerous to children, without one predominant property of perfection to recommend him.

Perhaps Taplin had been bitten by a Pomeranian belonging to a patient, because the Pomeranian was very much a ladies' dog, and an aristocratic one at that, and Taplin was a gynaecologist.

The mistress of the Prince Regent, Mrs Robinson, whom he called 'Perdita', was so fond of her Pomeranian that she had it included in her portrait by Gainsborough.

The Pomeranian was a revival – though people did not know that at the time. It had been a popular dog in Roman Britain. Another and much stranger revival was the introduction, not to Britain, but to British service, of a dog which had once been a native breed, the Cuban bloodhound. It was a descendant of English bloodhounds imported to the Spanish Indies by order of Philip II. In America it was used for hunting down rebellious Indians, runaway slaves and buccaneers. The Cuban bloodhound had been used against the black rebels of Haiti by the invading French armies, who had imported them from either Cuba or the Spanish Main. One of Napoleon's field officers, General Boyer, had his cook eaten alive by them in the garden of Government House because the man had cheated him of a few *sous*. At a place in Haiti called 'Haut du Cap', the French fed them a live negro to make them more ferocious.

According to sixteenth-century accounts, bloodhounds had been known to eat their quarry alive in England as well and in a moment we shall see them attempt to eat a British general, his coach-horses and his coach-man. Yet the admirers of the Cuban bloodhound said that it was really a most docile dog, carefully trained never to harm the pursued fugitive – unless he turned at bay and attacked. Once the bloodhounds had run their man down, which they never failed to do, they barked at him till he stopped running and then crouched near him, terrifying him with their growls, till their dog-handlers came up.

Some credence seems to attach to this view of the bloodhound in that they successfully brought in a body of pirates whom they had chased. Spanish renegades who had been shipped aboard a British ship ran her aground on the north shore of Cuba and murdered the captain, the officers and all of the British hands aboard her. The renegades now took to the mountains, confident of being able to escape pursuit in the jungle, and hoping to make their way to some remote settlements on the southern coast.

The governor in Havana had now heard of the massacre however and he sent out twelve dog-handlers (called *chasseurs* or 'hunters' in Cuba) who brought in the whole party of murderers, alive and unharmed, so that they could be hanged.

A rigorous training prepared the man-hunters for their task. Every *chasseur* lived with his dogs and was inseparable from them. He was obliged by the government to keep three, though he could only hunt two at a time. Feeding the dogs was a considerable expense. Dogs and bitches, on leashes, were taken into the field together to hunt. They were helped by special 'finder' dogs which were good at hitting the scent. At home the bloodhounds were always kept chained up and abroad they were never allowed to go out unmuzzled. When they were let off their rope leashes they knew that this was the signal to attack and, as we shall see, they tended to attack anyone they saw.

In 1795 there was a revolt in Jamaica. A war broke out between the Maroons and the white settlers. The Maroons, who got their name from a Carib word that meant 'wild', were free blacks, descendants of African slaves who had fled to the mountains when Jamaica was captured by an English expedition in the seventeenth century.

The British commander in Jamaica decided to engage a force of Cuban bloodhounds, with their *chasseurs*, to put down the rebellion. The *chasseurs*, more than forty in number, were commanded by Don Manuel de Sejas, the *Alcalde Provinciale*. There were only 104 bloodhounds with the party, so obviously the dog numbers were below strength. A long and tedious voyage awaited the Cuban mercenaries. After embarking from Batabano in Cuba, it took them seven weeks to arrive in Jamaica, accompanied by the British Commissioner who had gone to fetch them.

As soon as the ship carrying the *chasseurs* reached Kingston, the mercenaries were ordered to land. From the moment the first bloodhound raced down the gangway, dragging its handler after it, and began to drag itself towards the nearest passer-by, barking ferociously, the streets began to clear as if by magic. Soon there was not a black man to be seen. Every householder shut and barred his door, and crowded to the window to gaze at the muzzled bloodhounds pulling at their heavy rattling chains, which were held by the wild-looking *chasseurs*.

The British commander, General Walpole, ordered an immediate review of the Cuban bloodhounds at a place called Seven Rivers. He arrived on the field in a post-chaise, at dawn, accompanied by Colonel Skinner, whom he had ordered to supervise the manoeuvres of the dogs.

The Spaniards soon appeared at the end of a gentle acclivity, drawn out in a line containing upwards of forty men, with their dogs in front, unmuzzled, and held by the cotton ropes. According to directions previously given, on receiving the command to fire, they discharged their fusils [flint-lock carbines] and advanced as upon a real attack. This was intended to ascertain what effect would be produced on the dogs if engaged under a fire of the Maroons. The volley was no sooner fired than the dogs pressed forward with the greatest fury, amidst the continued shouts of the Spaniards, who were dragged on by them with the most irresistible force.

Some of the dogs, maddened by the shout of attack, while held back by the ropes, seized on the stocks of the guns in the hands of their keepers, and tore pieces out of them. Their impetuosity was so great, that they were with difficulty stopped before they reached the General, who found it necessary to get expeditiously into the chaise from which he had alighted, and, if the most strenuous exertions had not been made to stop them, they would most certainly have seized upon his horses.

Word of the arrival of the Cuban bloodhounds soon reached the

Maroons. They hastened to give in and accept the Government terms. The *chasseurs* were paid off according to their agreement and returned to Cuba. Everybody was happy at the result, except perhaps the bloodhounds.

6

The Nineteenth Century

With the beginning of the nineteenth century our landscape, once so extensive, has now narrowed to the eye of the dog. As in past ages this reflects all the devotion that dogs feel towards men, but now it also shows dawning gratitude for man's kindness, as the dog begins to realise that, rather belatedly, man has begun to be its friend and ally rather than its exploiter and persecutor.

In many ways the history of the dog in nineteenth-century England was to mirror that of man. It was to be a great era of sport for dog and man, but sporting enjoyment was by no means unalloyed. The last sanguinary act of the drama which began with the Forest Laws was to be enacted, with squires and poachers, setters and lurchers arrayed against one another. It was to be an era in which many of the abuses of working life were to be removed and many working-dogs had their toil eased. It was to be an age of military expeditions overseas and dogs were to join in these as well, as mascots. In an age of drama, one of the most popular of all dramatic parts, 'Toby' in *Punch and Judy*, was to be taken by a dog.

Yet of all characteristics of the time, surely the most important was the growth of a love of dogs and with it a love of animals in general and a desire to spare them needless pain. Fondness for animals in England had arisen principally amongst those who kept dogs for sporting purposes or as pets. Critics, then and now, have accused the English of being too kind to dogs. The Royal Society for the Prevention of Cruelty to Animals considerably antedates the Society for the Prevention of Cruelty to Children which, as has often been pointed out, is even now not a Royal Society.

Animal-lovers had always existed in every country and during every age, but custom and public opinion had usually stifled the impulse to make life easier for the other half of creation. In nineteenth-century Japan, for example, dogs were looked upon as untouchable creatures, even though Japan had been a Buddhist country for more than a millennium and although the greatest Japanese novel, by Bakin, centred round eight dogs. Little Etsu Sugimoto, a Samurai's daughter, had a dog called 'Shiro,' but everyone in the family pretended it belonged to someone else because girls were not supposed to own dogs. When 'Shiro' was dying, Etsu tucked her brocade pillow under its head to make it more comfortable. Her father ordered the pillow to be taken away and burned by one of the servants because anything that had been in contact with a dog was polluted.

The advent of the omnipresent Englishman and his dog was going to change the views of the world as to how animals ought to be treated. Fondness for animals was to be one of the most important examples that England had to give to the world – though there are many parts of the world which are still very slow to follow it.

There was never a time when dogs were responsible for more class hatred than at the start of the nineteenth century. Even the possession of a sporting-dog by a poor Irishman might lead to a conviction for poaching, while in England, laws were equally severe. The Game Laws, which began to be enforced with increasing violence after Waterloo, forbade anyone not a landowner with an annual value of £100 or a tenant for life with a rent of less than £150 or the son or heir apparent of an esquire or person of higher rank from shooting game. Everyone else was a poacher – and the penalties that faced poachers were harsh indeed.

To be armed and present in a rabbit warren could mean hanging, though rabbits are not game. To possess a rabbit snare or net, whether it were used for poaching or not, could entail seven years' transportation. To be caught with a gun while poaching might mean fourteen years transportation, while if a poacher shot a gamekeeper who intercepted him, he would be very lucky if he escaped hanging even if he had merely wounded the gamekeeper. Two brothers called Lilley shot a gamekeeper; the gamekeeper subsequently recovered but they were hanged in the spring of 1829. Well might a poacher's widow in Charles Kingsley's *Yeast* exclaim:

> There's blood on your new foreign shrubs, squire,
> There's blood on your pointer's feet;
> There's blood on the game you sell squire,
> And there's blood on the game you eat.

Two views about poachers have prevailed in English history. The first, favoured by nineteenth-century game-preservers, was that poachers were organised desperadoes who worked in gangs to secure a large and immediate profit from stealing game. These gangs did exist, and the famous 'Waltham Blacks' of Epping Forest was the example that all nineteenth-century folk would call to mind. Poaching by these gangs partook of the nature of organised crime and the people who carried out poaching in this way were criminals, not ordinary countryfolk. Frequently they had no connection with the country whatsoever, but were townees, miners or ribbon-weavers, out to supply the fashionable poulterers of London with game and make themselves rich in the process. William

Taplin wrote about it:

No ghost need come from the grave to report the well-known fact that a large majority of the stage coaches upon all roads, but particularly the Norfolk and Western roads, come amply supplied for the demands of the London market. . . . a customer of decent and unsuspicious appearance may be accommodated with a sufficiency to furnish out a city feast. Even the round-frocked drivers of the common road-wagons (those staunch sympathising friends of the poaching fraternity) can execute an order, having a few days' notice, to any amount; and no traveller ever finds a difficulty, during a country tour, in procuring from the landlord, or waiter of his inn, a hare, pheasant, or leash of birds to send off to his friends in town on the following morning.

The contrary view about poachers – which is much favoured by social historians of today – is that they were driven by hunger to poach in order to eat. The Lilleys, for example, mentioned a short time ago, were poor labourers who had been unemployed for a long time and who preferred to poach than starve.

Both these views about the poacher err through over-simplification. It would be very difficult for poaching to be carried out just by organised gangs, they would make their presence in the countryside all too evident, despite the conspiracy of silence about poaching that was part of the country code. On the other hand game is certainly not the kind of food best adapted for stilling the pangs of hunger, as anyone who has picked his way through a partridge would agree. A turnip purloined from the field, which no one will miss, the innumerable wild herbs and roots that could be gathered from the hedgerows, such as the beech mast on which starving cotton-mill operatives in Lancashire lived during the 'cotton famine' of the American Civil War, would hold hunger at bay in a much more effective fashion.

The truth of the matter – as I see it – was that the English poacher broke the Game Laws because they were there. They were a challenge to all that the agricultural revolution had left him, his manliness, and it was a challenge he could not resist.

Charles White, who knew his countryside well wrote:

A poacher carries his life in his hand. Having little sympathy with his fellow men, and less of all the obligations due to society, he pursues his course with a fixed determination of purpose and a recklessness of consequences peculiar to himself, and worthy of a better cause. Tracing him from his sylvan haunts, he will be found the frequenter of the tap-room, the alehouse, and the beer-shop – the hero of the band with whom he associates, and listened to on all occasions, because he has surmounted extraordinary difficulties and braved extraordinary dangers.

What has been said about the poacher has been said to introduce his dog, without which faithful ally he would have laboured in vain to outwit the justices of peace, squires, mantraps and spring-guns that lay in wait for him. The poacher's favourite dog was the lurcher, a dog which had been developed as a courser and rabbiter at least as early as the Renaissance. A statute of James I, which was still in force in 1803 when William Taplin was writing about dogs, prohibited the possession of such a dog, along with other rabbit dogs, to anyone not possessed of land worth more than £40 a year. In an attempt to escape detection, poachers disguised their lurchers, notably by cutting off their tails. Taplin wrote:

> This is the very race of dogs applicable to the aggregate wants of the poacher . . . no other breed of the whole species seems so peculiarly calculated for the purpose. They equal, if they do not excell, any other dog in sagacity, and are easily taught any thing that is possible for an animal of this description to acquire by instruction. Some of the best-bred lurchers are but little inferior in speed to many well-formed greyhounds; rabbits they kill to a certainty.

Taplin adds of the lurcher:

> We find him almost invariably in the possession of and in constant association with poachers of the most unprincipled and abandoned description.

Taplin believed the lurcher was a cross between

> . . . the shepherds' dog and the greyhound, which from breeding *in and in* with the latter, has so refined upon the first change, that very little of the shepherds' dog seems now to be retained in the stock; its patience, docility, and fidelity excepted. The lurcher, if thus bred, without any farther collateral crosses, is about three fourths the height and size of a full grown greyhound, and of a yellowish or sandy-red colour, rough and wiry-haired, with ears naturally erect, but dropping a little at the point, of great speed, courage, sagacity and fidelity.

Breeding, or nature, had produced in the lurcher the ideal dog for poaching. It could be used, ostensibly, as a shepherds' dog or sheepdog, but it was fast enough 'to trip up a leveret half or three quarters grown, without the owners possessing either licence or certificate.'

The lurcher was absolutely devoted to its master, who could train it to do anything he wanted. It was docile, intelligent, grateful for kindness but not resentful of injuries. The dog was so quick that it could run down any rabbit in the open or, in a warren, cut it off from its burrow. It could easily pull down a fallow deer (and it will be remembered from an earlier chapter that the poachers of Selbourne regularly took a lurcher with them in their excursions to the forest in search of deer). Once a deer was killed, even if it were night-time, the lurcher would unerringly convey its master right to the spot where the deer had fallen. If the poacher wanted hares, he merely had to set nets at the gates of the paddock, field or plantation where he was at work and place wires at the meuses. The dog would run swiftly and silently through the whole space, starting up all the hares and driving them into the snares set for them.

Anyone who had a hair or feather of game on his land regarded the lurcher with hatred and instantly suspected its owner of being a poacher. One motive the poacher had for disguising his lurcher was the desire to avoid having to pay the tax on sporting-dogs, but the principal one was 'to elude the suspicious glance of the game-preserving landlord and his emissaries.'

No dog in Britain ever drew more fire than the lurcher, not even the sheep-worrier. The gamekeeper hero of a novel by G. Christopher Davies, Peter Penniless, lies in wait for some poachers who are about to gate-net a field, having stopped the meuses. As the poachers approach, accompanied by their lurcher-dog, which has been trained to drive the hares directly towards the gates, into the nets set there and away from the hedge where there may be easy gaps through which they might escape, Peter asks his employer what he should do if the dog scents them. The employer, elder gamekeeper Quadling, replies, 'Shoot it. That's why I brought my gun. The men may be too quick for us, but I thought we might have a shot at the dog.'

Lurchers, like their masters, were trained to die bravely and to die silent. There was no greater crime than to give the game away, either by barking or informing. 'He ran mute,' writes George Jesse of a poacher's dog, 'never rent his game, and if by accident caught in a snare, made no noise, but gnawed himself out.'

It was the knowledge that their lives were forfeit when caught and not, as Jesse supposed, a bad conscience, that made lurchers hang their tail and slink away when they met a stranger. Jesse noticed this trait amongst sheep-stealers' dogs as well. A black greyhound which was assisting a sheep-stealer slunk off in this fashion when discovered by Jesse. Although both tended to use the same kind of dog, a lurcher, the connection between poachers and sheep-stealers might otherwise appear obscure. William Taplin, however, explains that both commit crimes in the dark and that the progression was from poaching to sheep-stealing. The wonderful talent of the lurcher shone out in sheep-stealing as in poaching. A Dr Anderson, quoted by Taplin, said of a certain shepherd who was hanged for sheep-stealing:

When the man intended to steal any sheep, he did not do it himself, but detached his dog to perform the business. With this view under pretence of looking at the sheep with an intention to purchase them, he went through the flock with the dog at his feet, to whom he secretly gave a signal, so as to let him know the individuals he wanted to the number of ten or twenty out of a flock of some hundreds; he then went away, and at a distance of several miles sent back the dog by himself in the night time, who picked out the individual sheep that had been pointed out to him, separated them from the flock and drove them before him by himself till overtaking his master, to whom he relinquished them.

Unfortunately for the lurcher and the poacher, the great era of conflict over the Game Laws saw the rise of not just one, but many breeds of splendid gun-dogs. 'There are three kinds commonly used in shooting,' wrote the Revd. W. B. Daniel in 1802, 'the setter, the pointer, and the spaniel.' One or other of these gun-dogs was always to be found in attendance on the gamekeeper. One game-preserver known to Daniel was the Revd Mr Corsellis. His gamekeeper had a spaniel, probably an English springer spaniel, a type that had been in use since the seventeenth century for flushing birds for mounted guns, and Daniel writes of it:

The game at that season he never regarded although in the daytime no spaniel would find it in a better style, or in greater quantity, but at night, if a strange foot had ever entered any of the coverts, 'Dash', by a significant whine, informed his master that the enemy were abroad, and many poachers have been detected and caught from this singular intelligence.

There was great competition amongst English sportsmen at the beginning of the nineteenth century to secure the ideal gun-dog. There were plenty of breeds to choose from because gun-dogs had appeared long before the gun in England. Springers had flushed game for the falconer. 'Crouchers' had driven partridges or quails into a net and setters had been developed for the same purpose.' John Dudley, Duke of Northumberland,' writes Daniel, 'was the first that broke a setting dog to the net, about the year 1555.'

Some of the gun-dogs were of English origin, some imported and others breeds developed in this country from foreign stock. Spanish pointers, brought into England during the 1650s, had been used to put up hares which were hunted by greyhounds. Clumber spaniels had been developed at Clumber Park, one of the estates owned by the Duke of Northumberland, from stock sent over by a French nobleman and later crossed with French basset hounds.

It seems that every nobleman of note in nineteenth-century England – and quite a few commoners as well – was trying to do what Daniel strove so hard to accomplish – to enrich English sport with another new and distinctive breed, preferably called after the breeder. Daniel admits, without compunction, to having hanged seventy-two of his best spaniels because they committed the unforgivable crime of hunting hare, a tendency which he blamed on a *mésalliance* between their ancestors and foxhounds. Finally he was left with six and a half brace of spaniels that he considered perfect. He was once offered £150 for them and when he refused, asked to name his own price. These paragons had been originally developed by the King of Naples. Once they had arrived in England, the strain had been much improved by the Marquis of Granby; then a Mr Hoare, from whom Daniel had obtained his spaniels, had fostered the breed. Like every other breeder, Daniel sought not merely for new dogs, but a new and more perfect way of putting them to work. Thus he had already laid down to his shooting companions that only one dog was to do the retrieving, otherwise the game would be mangled in the tussle which developed.

Nowhere was the plastic genetic material of good dogs moulded with greater success than in the setters. The year that saw the publication of one of the editions of Daniel's work, 1800, also marked the birth of Edward Laverack, a breeder who was to make the English setter notable. Laverack began his kennel with 'Old Moll' and 'Ponto', offspring of a strain which had already bred pure for thirty-five years. Five years before his death, at the Crystal Palace Exhibition of 1872, he was entering dogs which had become so associated with him that they were known as 'Laveracks'.

A new and attractive breed appeared in Scotland in the form of the Gordon setter, evolved from black and tan setters which had come into existence in the seventeenth century. The fourth Duke of Gordon, noticing a shepherds' bitch that pointed grouse, crossed the black and tan collie with a black setter and the famous black and tan setter was the result.

Ireland produced the handsome golden Irish setter, though in Daniel's day the golden was not the preferred sort. He describes them as 'bringing very high prices when of peculiar breeds. The colours of these choice sorts are deep chestnut and white, or all red, with the nose, and roof of the mouth, black.'

Guns chose setters to accompany them when they set out in pursuit of black grouse. Daniel, selecting a subject to illustrate this bird in his book *Rural Sports*, chose his own favourite setter, 'Beau', pointing a grouse.

Of all foreign breeds, no gun-dog achieved more popularity than the Spanish pointer, yet, as imported from Spain in the seventeenth century and probably re-introduced once more after the Treaty of Utrecht in 1713, he was too slow and stately to please nineteenth-century sportsmen. So breeders employed their ingenuity to develop a cross which would retain the good nose of the Spanish pointer and yet have speed and the staying-power required for two days' shooting one after another.

Soon the heavy shoulders, short muzzle and short range of the original pointer disappeared in a bewildering variety of crosses with greyhound, foxhound, bloodhound and spaniel. The new pointers were fast enough to run down a leveret, tireless hunters and good stayers which worked best when they were most heavily burdened.

Every sportsman had his own formula for a successful pointer. There was Colonel Thornton's pointer 'Dash', for example, a close cross from the foxhound. 'Dash' had a masterly way of ranging over the moors and an instinct that enabled it to walk up to a partridge without any preliminary quartering of the ground. It was regarded as the best pointer of his day and Thornton probably made a bad bargain when he sold 'Dash' to Sir Richard Symons for a hundred and sixty pounds' worth of champagne and burgundy, bought at the French Ambassador's sale, a hogshead of claret, an 'elegant gun' and – a pointer. Thornton stipulated that if 'Dash' became unable to do his work, the colonel should be allowed to buy it back, for stud, at a fee of fifty pounds.

Springer spaniels and cocker spaniels vied with one another for first place in the hearts of the great sportsmen. The springer of Philip Reinagle's day had a red, yellow, white or browny-red coat. It was 'delicately formed, with ears long, soft and pliable, coat waving and silky, eyes and nose red or black, the tail somewhat bushy and pendulous, always in motion when actively employed.'

The dog took his name from his impetuosity. 'It is the unchangeable nature of these dogs to spring, flush, or start all the game before them, and they pursue, without preference, hare, pheasant, partridge, woodcock, snipe, and quail.'

In thick undergrowth, after pheasant, most sportsmen would wish to be accompanied by a springer spaniel. So enthusiastically did springer spaniels go to work that some owners tied bells round their necks so that their whereabouts could more easily be discovered.

Smaller than the springer spaniel was the cocker spaniel, an active dog which caught the scent more easily than a springer and found it easier to force a way through low, bushy cover. Both shorter and more compact in appearance, the cocker was supposed to have a round head, short nose, long ears and curly coat. 'Colour, liver and white, red, red and white, all liver colour.'

The smallest breed of cockers was 'that peculiar breed in the possession and preservation of the Duke of Marlborough and his friends. These are invariably red and white, with very long ears, short noses, and black eyes. They are excellent and indefatigable, being in great estimation with those sportsmen who can become possessed of the breed.'

Early nineteenth-century sportsmen regarded the cocker as being the ideal dog to take out when shooting woodcock. These birds arrived in England from the Continent about the third or last week of October every year and then proceeded to work their way inland. In Taplin's day, ten brace might easily be killed in a single covert during a morning by one gun. It was only in open coverts that woodcock provided easy targets for the gun. When put up in dense woodland, they towered rapidly till they reached tree-top height. It was in shooting of this sort that the cocker proved his worth, by barking to give guns notice of the rising birds.

In spite of the popularity of land spaniels, such as the beautiful Sussex, the water spaniel was perhaps the favourite amongst all gun-dogs. William Taplin used its portrait as a frontispiece for his great book on dogs *The Sportsman's Cabinet*, which was published in 1804, and says that it was so well-known that there was no need to describe it. Taplin himself thought that the water spaniel was the result of a cross between the large 'waterdog' (the Newfoundland) and a springer spaniel. He preferred the smaller varieties of the water spaniel (which we, judging from his plates, might decide to call an American rather than an Irish water spaniel). These small varieties, Taplin tells us, were most useful for hunting willow-banks and busy, bushy, watery coverts.

Like other sportsmen, Taplin lays great stress on the importance of training for water spaniels. He began training his at the age of three or four months, accustoming them to obey the word of command every time they went for a walk. Only when the spaniel had correctly carried out its instructions did it receive a meal. It had to couch or lie close, try on for the game, come behind, and recover lost game. 'He will be more likely to remember what he is taught without blows,' writes Taplin. He emphasises the close connection which must exist between the gun and his water spaniel by urging his readers to give their dogs caresses when they had done well. A good water spaniel should have only one trainer and once its education was complete, it should be a kind of 'other self' of the sportsman.

Though most water spaniels belonged to gentlemen sportsmen and were only trained to obey the commands 'down', 'hie on', 'back' and 'hie lost', which would make them crouch down, push forward and start the game, follow on behind, or retrieve, there were a number which belonged to working wildfowlers and these dogs required a special training.

Examples of these worker-dogs were those owned by the men employed to work decoys. A decoy was a bird trap on a gigantic scale, and decoys were plentiful at the beginning of the nineteenth century in Lincolnshire, Essex, Cambridgeshire and some parts of Warwickshire.

Decoys were set up on lakes frequented by wildfowl. Channels covered with hooped nets called 'pipes' were dug out from the edge of the lake. These pipes all faced into a different compass point because wildfowl always rise and swim up wind. No matter from which direction a pipe started, however, it soon swung round and changed its course until it and all the other channels converged in a ditch which became narrower and narrower, till it terminated in a purse net.

Once the wildfowl had got so far down the pipe they would be seized by the decoyman, who would ring their necks. The birds could not see the man or the purse net, because both were concealed by reed screens worked into a kind of fence. The decoyman moved down-wind from the wildfowl and carried in his hand a piece of burning peat which he hoped would obliterate his own scent. Peepholes in the screens enabled the man to keep the wildfowl under constant watch.

The decoy did not belong to the decoyman, who was merely an employee. It was so vast and required so much investment to construct that only rich folk could afford to build decoys. All the investment would have gone for nothing but for the work of the decoy dog, which will be mentioned in a moment. Although bait such as hempseed was scattered liberally on the surface of the pond to attract wildfowl to land, and more bait was scattered in the pipes, and although decoy ducks were trained to swim confidently up the pipes to the funnel net, where they would be recognised by the decoyman and have their lives spared, all this was not enough to get the decoy working by persuading the wildfowl to come into the net.

At Aldermaston in Berkshire, where there was a decoy which covered many acres, a wire trap baited with food for the ducks had stood open for years. 'They never have *yet* gone in,' wrote the Victorian naturalist Frank Buckland, 'and it would seem that they never *will* go in.'

Though the wildfowl would sometimes obediently follow the decoy ducks into the net when the decoys were summoned by the whistle of the decoyman, they could not be relied on to do so. Taplin wrote:

Sometimes it happens that the fowl are in such a state of sleeping and dozing that they will not follow the decoy ducks. There is then no alternative but to resort to the assistance of the dog, who, having been previously and properly taught his lesson, passes backwards and forwards between the reed screens (in which there are small holes both for the decoyman to see, and larger at the bottom for the dog to pass through).

This attracts the attention of the fowl, who, not choosing to be interrupted, advance towards the busily employed animal, in a hope they may be able to drive him away. The dog all the time, by the direction of the decoyman, plays among the screens of reeds, and the wildfowl, not daring to pass him by in return, nor being able to escape upwards (on account of the net covering) rush on into the purse net. Yet, notwithstanding their general alertness upon the watch, they are sometimes so insensible to the approach of danger, that even the appearance of the dog will not attract their attention, if a red handkerchief, or something singular, is not put about him.

Taplin's explanation of why the wildfowl followed the dog up the pipe was not accepted by everyone. Some observers believed that the wildfowl were intrigued by the water spaniel's strange antics, as it danced about, now appearing in front of the reed screens, now darting behind them, occasionally jumping over a screen, but always moving farther and farther back towards the purse net, so that the birds' curiosity induced them to swim farther and farther up.

Once the ducks had been caught in the purse net, the spaniel was rewarded with a piece of cheese. Red water spaniels were preferred and near Maldon, in Essex, George Jesse noted that the decoy dogs were not water spaniels but collies, or some dog very like them.

A decoy was simple in construction and cheap to maintain. Its slanting reed screens, which were arranged in a herring-bone formation along the sides of the pipe, could be renewed from the abundant stores of reeds which were then available in the fens. Its nets of tarred hempen string and the wooden hoops covering the pipes could be cheaply replaced every few years, when this became necessary.

Apart from this outlay (and of course the value of the land, which was considerable) a decoy required no expenditure except for the wages of the decoyman. In return for the small outlay they required, decoys were extremely productive. The decoys working near Wainfleet, in Essex, recorded catches of 31,200 head of fowl towards the end of the eighteenth century. The virtual monopoly of the owners of decoys in catching wildfowl in their immediate neighbourhood had only been established after a long struggle with the local folk. In Boston, Lincolnshire, young fledgling ducks had been driven into nets by the inhabitants, who had caught as much as a hundred and fifty dozen birds at one time. This practice had only been ended by legislation passed under Anne and a statute of George II. It cannot be doubted that, to many Fenmen, the red water spaniel in the decoy was every bit as much a symbol of oppression as the Squire's pointer was to the folk of the village.

In spite of decoys, there were many parts of the Fenland, or England as a whole, where working wildfowlers continued to flourish, helped by their invaluable dogs. These animals knew quite well just how serious a matter it was for their master to return home with a good catch and that if he came back empty-handed, then he would probably give them their dinner but have to send his children supperless to bed. Doglike, they did their best to help their masters in their calling and a very close tie subsisted between the shooter and his dog.

Just such a professional wildfowler was Old Merry, of Stretham Ferry in Cambridgeshire, who flourished at the end of the eighteenth century. Merry's dog was an Old English water spaniel – a breed which seems to be represented in America in the American water spaniel but which now has no English equivalent.

Merry's dog was a constant companion for his master on his voyages, for the wildfowler spent more of his time on water than on dry land. Daniel wrote about him:

In his knowledge of the haunts of the different species of birds which visited the Fens, he was most precise and in the navigation of his punt (a small boat) along the ditches, which are in fact the only roads through the fens, his judgement and assiduity were alike conspicuous. He knew if a drought had lowered the water where he could make good his point, and frequently whilst shooting parties with other guides were wearying themselves with towing, or from the noise occasioned by being towed all the birds in the vicinity were disturbed, Old Merry was steering his punt silently to the scene of action, and in the fogs, which are so thick as to exclude objects at the smallest distance, or in the dark, he was equally collected, and knew how to proceed in the morning or return at night, in spite of all obstacles.

Merry's spaniel retrieved the birds brought down by his formidable fowling-piece:

. . . a gun upwards of six feet in the barrel, and that placed in its stock by the village carpenter, and altogether of a weight which nothing but a most powerful arm could extend and elevate . . . the charge of this demi-culverin was two pipes and a half of powder, and three of shot, and the wadding was a little dry sedge, of which he took a whisp in the punt.

The water spaniel also brought in coots and wild ducks while moulting, or fledglings 'in astonishing numbers'. On their last voyage together the dog contracted rabies. Anyone else would have shot him then and there but, very unwisely, Merry and Daniel returned with the spaniel at one end of the punt, howling dismally, and themselves at the other. Like a minority of English dog-owners, Merry believed that there was a cure for rabies, and 'he meant to secure and administer some famous never-failing remedy so soon as he got him home.' Fortunately for Merry, Daniel and all the readers who have delighted in the sporting parson's *Rural Sports*, the water spaniel knew more about the outcome of rabies than they did. Rather than harm its master, the spaniel jumped ashore the minute the punt grounded and was never heard of again.

Another dog popular with the working wildfowler was the Irish water spaniel, which for some reason William Taplin calls the 'waterdog' Taplin's illustration, which was drawn by Philip Reinagle, certainly seems to portray an Irish water spaniel, though with a curly and not a smooth muzzle and with a less pronounced tail. The most prized waterdogs had black coats and white feet. 'The perfect black,' writes Taplin, 'is affirmed to be the best and hardiest, the least susceptible of fatigue, hunger and danger, the spotted, or pied, quickest of scent and sagacity, the liver-coloured the most alert and expeditious in swimming.'

It is only fair to say that not everyone would accept my identification. Edward C. Cash, writing in *Dogs, Their History And Development* in 1927, said that waterdogs were poodles and that Taplin's illustration showed a waterdog which was related to the bearded collie, old English sheepdog and otter-hound. Taplin himself considered them to be a cross between the 'Greenland Dog', and some other British species.

Nonetheless it is noteworthy that waterdogs were already, by the eighteenth century, carrying out most of the roles which were later to be associated with the Irish water spaniel. Cash himself quotes a very interesting account by the Revd William Hamilton of a visit to Antrim, where he saw waterdogs retrieving live salmon which had escaped from the fishermen's nets.

The connection between waterdogs and fishermen is further emphasised by Taplin. 'The Water Dog is of so little general use that the breed is but little promoted, unless upon the sea coast. Hence it is that they are but seldom seen in or near the metropolis, unless among the boat men below bridge and aboard coasting vessels and colliers, where their various powers are sometimes applicably brought into action.' Apart from the localities which he has already mentioned, Taplin notes that they were to be found 'in the fenny parts of Lincolnshire and Cambridgeshire, as well as in the swampy parts of Lancashire.' They were also to be found in Scotland where they had been crossed with Newfoundlands, for strength, and were used by wildfowlers.

North of Berwick-on-Tweed, the east coast of Scotland was dotted with tiny huts built by wildfowlers. These cabins were placed high up on the cliffs and were spaced out at a distance of a quarter of a mile to a third of a mile from one another. They were built of turf taken from the cliffside and were camouflaged by the grass growing over them so that they seemed more like gentle hillocks rising from the cliff on to which they backed than buildings. The only indication that they were human habitations were the doors of the hut and three loopholes in the sides. These were four inches in diameter; two were placed to left and right and one was in the centre. Inside the fowler's shooting hut was unfurnished, save for a shelf for ammunition and provisions and a seat.

Long before dawn, the fowler would take his place in his hut, accompanied by his waterdog, and he would sit patiently waiting with his loaded gun beside him. Like Old Merry's, this piece had a barrel six feet long and it was charged with swan shot.

As dawn broke, the fowler looked out for any gannets or for the larger species of gulls, which in Scotland provided both food and useful feathers. When he sighted a bird within range he brought it down with his gun and at the sound of the shot the waterdog darted out of the door of the hut, marking the spot where the bird was falling, and dashed after it. The gannet might have fallen into one of the deep clefts of the cliff, or into the sea, sometimes at a considerable distance from land. Nonetheless the water spaniel never failed to retrieve its bird, though it often had to take an entirely different route back to the hut. A full-grown gannet has a wingspread of six feet. It also has a beak six inches long, with which it can strike hard enough to penetrate a plank of wood. The fowler's water spaniel must often have had deadly battles with any gannet which was not completely disabled.

Eventually the struggle would be over and the water spaniel would bring its quarry back to the hut, so that the shooter could now look out for his next bird. As the shot gannets piled up in the hut, the wildfowler's little son would sling them on his back and carry them back to the family home, 'at the distance of two, three or four miles, as it may be.' There the wife and the rest of the family 'are all employed in picking the feathers, and collecting the down from the bodies of the birds as fast as they arrive. This ... keeps the wife and children almost perpetually engaged, and is the principal support of the family, as it is also the staple contribution to that annually increasing infinity of feather-beds, down-pillows, and other articles of luxury and domestic refinement.'

Once plucked, the gannets, or 'Solan Geese' as they were called in Scotland, were sold in the market. Although they had such a fishy smell that the fastidious, such as Jonathan Oldbuck in Walter Scott's *The Antiquary*, insisted that they must be cooked in the open air, they were, nonetheless, a great table delicacy.

I have, perhaps controversially, tried to identify the waterdog as the Irish water spaniel, but I am unable to point to any contemporary breed in England as representative of the truffler. This was the dog which apparently combined both poodle and spaniel ancestry, which was used by truffle-hunters for finding their stock-in-trade. It is tantalising to note that the truffler lingered on as late as the reign of Edward VII, when truffling was still carried on in England, and that there was a truffle-dog kennel near Salisbury in which the king took a great deal of interest, where trufflers were bred and trained. Then, tantalisingly, the truffler seems to disappear entirely from history, like so many other fine breeds.

Originally the truffler had been a spaniel imported from Spain, but in Germany the spaniel breed was crossed with poodle blood and medium-sized, particoloured dogs were produced which were brown and white or black and white.

Though we think of the esculent roots called truffles – which usually appear on the menu not by themselves, but as an ingredient of some other delicacy such as *pâté de foie gras* – as a Continental delicacy, several species of truffles grow in this country. There is the *Tuber aestivum*, about the size of a small apple, which in fact only grows in England and which is round and warty black outside and brown-veined with white within. Its season is from July till the winter and it can be found growing in chalk or clay soils beneath beech, oak, and bird birch woods.

Another English truffle is the *Tuber brumale*, which is a winter truffle with a black and warty exterior, with an interior which is greyish-black marbled with white veins. It can be found under oak trees from October till December.

As truffles were an essential ingredient for dishes which included game or venison, English restaurants were supplied with them by a corps of truffle-hunters, aided by specially trained truffle-hounds. Nowhere, it would appear, did dogs take a greater part in hunting for truffles than in England. In Italy the truffle-hunting beast was the pig which, tethered by its hind leg, was driven among the truffles to root them out. Not merely did pigs cost more to keep, but they would invariably eat the truffles they came to unless their master could get to them first.

By contrast with the pig, the dog was not merely a better truffler by reason of its keener powers of scent, so that it could easily detect the strong-smelling truffles in their shallow hiding-places, but it was absolutely devoted to its master and would never dream of eating the tubers it hunted, because it knew they were too valuable to be eaten either by the dog or its master. Trufflers had such a high sense of duty that, although most of them had acquired a taste for the roots they hunted, they would bring to their master tiny 'red truffles' (*Melanogaster variegatus*, a kind of puff-ball) in their mouths. As a reward for diligence and honesty, trufflers would be given a small piece of cheese from their master's pocket whenever they made a find.

Hampshire was a favourite area for truffle-hunting, and here, after a shower of rain, the truffle-hunter could be seen out in the fields, carrying a small spade to unearth those truffles not laid bare by the dogs, following a pack of tiny dogs which preceded him through the parks, woods and plantations. The small dogs could force themselves through the heavy undergrowth which covered the mossy boles and decaying roots of the old beeches, oaks and limes under which truffles were to be found. Their sense of smell was remarkable. Even sportsmen who were well acquainted with the scenting powers of dogs were surprised at the truffler, which could smell one of the edible fungi twenty yards off.

In the summer of 1802 Daniel relates:

a gentleman walked with a person who is a professed truffle-hunter. His dog found in the park at Ambresbury, the seat of the Duke of Queensbury, many truffles, and as he continued his hunting, the dog, to the great surprise of his owner and the gentleman who accompanied him, suddenly leaped over the hedge which surrounded that part of the park and ran with the utmost precipitation across the field (which was a distance of at least one hundred yards) to a hedge opposite, where, under a beech tree, he found and brought to his master, as the truffle dogs are taught to do, a truffle of uncommon size, and which weighted twelve ounces and a half.

A Hampshire truffle-hunter's dog was described as follows:

She had an intelligent, clever face, with bright black eyes looking all ways at once, and sharp-pointed ears always on the alert, and never quiet for one moment. The nose was sharp pointed, and the whole face reminded me of the expression of a small quick terrier, only far more gentle and clever. I remarked on the clean-made limbs, and the long paws, which seemed made for scratching. . . . This dog was smooth coated, white, with liver-coloured spots, but the generality have rather curly hair, a remnant of the poodle.

The truffler was not the only food-hunting dog in England. We have already noticed the waterdog busy retrieving salmon which had escaped the fishers' nets in Antrim. Other 'fishing-dogs' seem to have been known in England, as Dr Kaye ('Caius') mentions them in his book on dogs. Though it is not possible to point to any contemporary dog, save perhaps the water spaniel, as a representative 'fishing-dog', it is nonetheless possible to reconstruct how the fishing-dogs set to work.

During the nineteenth century a Normandy fisherwoman was observed going to the beach with her dog. She visited the seashore regularly at low tide, accompanied by a dog and carrying a basket and a pickaxe with a very long handle.

'The dog,' says the observer, 'was white, with long hair and a bushy tail, twisted up with a double turn which he carried on one side of his back; he had a long, sharp, foxy-looking face, with bright black eyes, and his ears stood very erect and were pointed.' When the pair reached a part of the beach where there was an estuary with wide stretches of exposed sand, the fisherwoman cried, 'Go and seek, good dog, Trompette!' The dog raced off, stopped at a heap of tumbled sand and began to whine and scratch at it. The old woman seized her pickaxe, dug into the sand and unearthed a conger eel, which she hurled with great force on to the hard sand before putting it in her basket.

When asked whether there was any difficulty in training a dog to hunt eels, she replied: 'None at all, we take a young dog out with an old one once or twice, and we let them worry the eel, or perhaps eat one, and then they will hunt quite well; but some of them have finer noses than others, and of course these are the best . . . other dogs have to be taught, but my family's dogs do it at once.'

Though it is difficult to believe that the otter-hound could ever have been used for fishing, this is just what Caius suggests when he couples the fishing-dog and the otter-hound together in his book. It was certainly true that no one could expect to find any fish unless there was a pack of otter-hounds somewhere in the neighbourhood whose services could be called on when required. Unfortunately for the breed, the otter-hounds had been only too successful in the extirpating of otters. Daniel speaks of the otter-hunt as a sport of the past, while Edward Jesse, writing in 1846, remarks that it is 'an old English sport fast falling into disuse and the breed of the real otter-hound is either extinct or very nearly so.'

It was only on some of the Cumberland lakes that successful otter-hunting could be carried out. Elsewhere there were no otters to be found. In 1844 the owner of a pack of hounds advertised them for sale in the newspapers. He said he was prepared to part with them, by private treaty, because they had now cleared the rivers of three counties, including Staffordshire, of all their otters.

Though menaced with extinction, otter-hounds somehow managed to survive the nineteenth century. Some were kept with harrier packs, hence one of the names by which the hounds were called: 'Welsh harriers'. Others were kept as pets, despite their reputation for ferocity. 'There are few animals,' wrote the Revd J. G. Wood, 'with the exception of the bulldog, which fight so savagely as the otterhound, or bite so severely and with such terrible results . . . when the otterhound bites, it instantly tears its teeth away without relaxing its jaws, and immediately seizes its prey with a second gripe.'

Though supposedly savage – especially in kennels – otter-hounds were undoubtedly handsome. They were big, rough, wiry-coated dogs with whiskered muzzles.

Working-dogs with a difference were those trained to earn their masters' living by appearing in shows. Performing dogs are a very old institution in England. When William Harrison published his *Description of England*, in 1586, he recounted the talents of these four-footed artistes.

[They were] taught and exercised to dance in measure at the musical sound of an instrument as at the soft stroke of a drum, sweet accent of the cithern, and pleasant harmony of the harp, showing many tricks by the gesture of their bodies as to stand bolt upright, to lie flat upon the ground, to turn round as a ring, holding their tails in their teeth, to beg for meat, to take a man's cap from his head. . . . They were dressed in motley and short waisted jackets.

The tricks performed by Sir John Harington's dog 'Bungey' have been already mentioned. They were not performed for Harington's profit, but he may have been inspired by the success of professional dog-trainers during this period. During the last quarter of the sixteenth century a certain William Paget got into trouble with the authorities because he had declared that he would teach his dog to speak French and his servant, James Hudson, deposed that, while listening at the door of his master's room, 'he did hear Paget speak to his dog in a strange language, but what language he knoweth not.' There were no English dogs during the period covered by this book which had learned to talk, but in the eighteenth century the *philosophe* Leibnitz reported to the Royal French Academy about a dog with a vocabulary of thirty words in German. The dog was the property of a peasant who lived in Zeitz in Saxony and he had spent three years developing its ability to speak.

By the eighteenth century, performing dogs had become a regular feature of English shows. Dr Johnson attested to their popularity, the skill of their trainers, and his own dislike of women (what will a man not say, who has been crossed in love) by his famous remark: 'Sir, a woman's preaching is like a dog's walking on his hinder legs. It is not done well, but you are surprised to find it done at all.'

A picture by George Morland, *Dancing Dogs*, shows the training process being carried on. Two travelling showmen, one with a set of bagpipes, the other carrying a whip, are instructing four dogs, one of which dances with a boy. Two other dogs dance on their hind legs. They are dressed in white frocks and one wears a red jacket. Another dog, dressed in white with a pink ribbon round its waist, looks on. By the nineteenth century, dog-training had reached a pitch of perfection which elicited the admiration of the sporting writers of the time. William Taplin writes:

The dancing-dogs which were upon the stage at Sadler's Wells were curiously instructed, for, after storming a fort amidst the firing of guns, and the suffocating fumes of gun-powder, a deserter was introduced, who was shot for the offence and carried off as dead by his companions. Another feigned extreme lameness, and showed symptoms of extreme pain, when, after a variety of well-affected distortions, he gradually recovered and sported amidst his canine companions with every possible demonstration of joy.

By the nineteenth century two distinctive dog shows had developed. One was the 'Happy Family.' This show was the invention of a poor Lambeth labourer called Charles Garbett. His cat had been robbed of her kittens but she was so full of thwarted maternal instincts that she adopted an abandoned litter of young rats and reared them to adulthood. Reasoning that a 'family' made up of such supposedly mutually antipathetic creatures would be an attraction in a fair, Garbett added more animals to the show, which he eventually bequeathed to his son.

The complete show was seen in a booth at Windsor Onion Fair (the fair at which town and country folk bought their onions for the winter) by the famous Victorian naturalist, Francis T. Buckland, around 1860. It included three dogs, 'Rose', 'Tom' and 'Lumpy', all of which had natural deformities; a raven, four monkeys, two cats, four pigeons, three hawks, two ducks, four guinea pigs, two ferrets, two rabbits, thirteen black and white rats, one cock, two hens, one badger, two 'kangaroo opossums' one hare and one raccoon.

By the time of the Boer War 'Happy Families' had become synonymous with every kind of juvenile outing, particularly to the seaside. 'It is, I fear,' commented George Russell, 'a sign of growing old that Dancing Dogs and

Performing Fleas and Happy Families no longer quicken in me the eager emotions of my boyhood.'

The second and most famous of all Victorian dog shows was, of course, Punch, which should really have been called 'Toby' after the name of the talented performer whose presence was indispensable to the performance. The dog 'Toby' undoubtedly added to the rapture that all classes of Victorians experienced while watching the cautionary tale of Mr Punch. His portrait, drawn by Leech in the dog's performing costume of hat and ruff, was for many years inseparable from the cover of the journal which bore Punch's name.

The hold of the show over all classes of Victorians was, as has been already mentioned, an enormous one. The Royal children enjoyed it, though the last act, in which the Bogey Man comes to carry off Punch, was omitted in the Command Performance by the Royal Punch and Judy man because 'it was apt to harrow the feelings of the little ones and give them bad dreams.' It was not just children who could be seen watching Punch. Even Gladstone was once observed lingering on the edge of the crowd in Parliament Street one moonlit night to watch a performance, just before he walked into the House to deliver an historic speech.

It was not any old dog which could play Toby, as Alfred Story discovered in 1895 when he interviewed the Royal puppeteer, Mr Jesson, about the performances he had staged for the children of Queen Victoria and later those of Edward VII, when Prince of Wales.

It is popularly thought that a dog of breed only can be trained to take the part of Toby. This is a mistake. . . . The part is always taken by a mongrel; nothing else in the canine line will stand the training. The Toby of the present Royal Punch and Judy is eleven years old, and he has taken the part since he was a few months old. His father was twenty-three years old when he was born, and he too had been in the profession – on the stage so to speak – since he was a puppy.

This does away with another popular tradition, namely that the life of a Punch and Judy dog was six years, never more. But perhaps in the 'good old days', when there was so much tramping and rough weather to be endured, and in addition, possibly so much hard training, six years may have been the span of life allotted to Toby.

Different show proprietors wrote slightly different parts for Toby, for every show varied somewhat from another, but every part demanded skill, timing and a real sense of the theatre on the part of the dog-performer. Here, as an example of what it had to do, is the part of the play in the 'Royal Punch and Judy Show', as staged by Jesson, which contains Toby's lines.

The second scene opens with the entrance of dog Toby. Punch salutes him with: Halloa Toby! Who call'd you? How do you do Mr Toby? Hope you are well, Mr Toby.

(*To which Toby answers with a snarl or a bark*): Bow- wow- wow!

Punch: Poor Toby! (*Putting his hand out cautiously, and trying to coax the dog, who snaps at it*): Toby, you are a nasty, cross dog. Get away with you! (*Strikes at him.*)

Toby: Bow- wow- wow! (*Seizing Punch by the nose.*)

Punch: Oh dear! Oh, dear! Oh my nose! My poor nose! My beautiful nose! Get away! Get away! You nasty dog. I'll tell your master. Oh, dear! Dear! Judy! Judy!'

(*Punch shakes his nose but cannot shake off the dog, who follows him as he retreats round the stage. He continues to call* 'Judy! Judy, my dear!' *until the dog quits his hold and exits.*)

In another version of the play, it turns out that Toby is really a dog stolen from its master, Scaramouche, by Punch. Dog-stealers were certainly not an invention of the nineteenth-century dramatist, they were only too well known to dog-owners. Henry Mayhew wrote in 1862:

Dog stealing is very prevalent, particularly in the West End of the metropolis, and is rather a profitable class of felony. These thieves reside at the Seven Dials, in the neighbourhood of Belgravia, Chelsea, Knightsbridge, and low neighbourhoods, some of them men of mature years. . . . Sometimes they belong to the felon class, sometimes not. They are often connected with bird-fanciers, keepers of fighting-dogs, and persons who get up rat matches.

Dog-stealers had two main methods of setting to work. One was to lure away a dog which had been noted down as being likely to fetch a ransom by leading past the house where it lived a bitch in heat. Women owners were robbed for preference, as having more tender hearts than men. 'They steal fancy dogs ladies are fond of,' Mayhew wrote, 'spaniels, poodles, and terriers, sporting-dogs, such as setters and retrievers, and also Newfoundland dogs.' Dog-thieves also used 'a piece of liver prepared by a certain process and soaked in some ingredient which dogs are uncommonly fond of.' (What was it?)

When the dog had been lured within reach, it was snatched and imprisoned in a bag which the thieves carried with them. Once it was safe in their possession, they waited for a reward to be offered by the owner, which was usually £1 to £5. Once this was offered, or an advertisement for the dog appeared in *The Times* or some other newspaper, or by handbills circulated in the district, a confederate of the thief appeared to negotiate for the return of the dog. So as to raise the reward, the owner would be told that the dog would be killed if he did not give what was asked. Some dogs were stolen three or four times.

The sums mulcted from the wealthy were out of all proportion to the rewards mentioned by Mayhew. One dog-stealer extracted £977 4s 6d. from several victims. The Duke of Cambridge paid £30 to get his dog back. Elizabeth Browning wept for three days and three nights before paying £50 for the return of her famous spaniel 'Flush'.

There was one kind of dog-stealer more to be dreaded by owners than the dog kidnapper and that was the anatomist. The nephew of the great surgeon Sir Astley Cooper, Bransby Blake Cooper, noted that:

During this time Astley, who was always eager to add to our anatomical and physiological knowledge, made a variety of experiments on living animals. I recollect one day walking out with him, when a dog followed us, and accompanied us home, little foreseeing the fate that awaited him. He was confined for a few days, till we had ascertained that no owner came to claim him, and then brought up to be the subject of various operations. The first of these was the tying one of the femoral arteries. When poor 'Chance', for so we appropriately named the dog, was sufficiently recovered from this, one of the humeral arteries was subjected to a similar process. After the lapse of a few weeks, the ill-fated animal was killed, the vessels injected, and preparations were made from each of the limbs.

Sir Astley Cooper was obviously no dog-lover and this quality makes him all the better a witness when he describes how a murder was detected by a dog, as in the supposedly fabulous case of the dog of Macaire.

Among Cooper's neighbours were Thomson Bonar, a prosperous Broad Street merchant, and his wife. One morning Sir Astley, who was on very friendly terms with the Thomson Bonars, was horrified to be told by their servant, Nicholson, that they had both been murdered in the night. Nicholson had come from Chislehurst specially to give Cooper this news. He rode back with Cooper to Chislehurst and then unaccountably disappeared. Sir Astley, whose suspicions had been aroused by his strange conduct, ordered a police search to be made for the servant. Nicholson was found by the police and taken to the Counter Prison in Giltspur Street, where Sir Astley Cooper called to see him.

Whilst speaking to him, a little black and dun terrier dog placed its fore paws on his knees and began to lick his breeches, which were made of some dark-coloured velveteen. Observing this, the Governor [of the prison] ordered him to remove them. On afterwards holding them up to the light, the front part of each thigh was evidently stained, and a little moisture soon proved it to be blood.

The Governor remarked that my dog was a sagacious little fellow, but I could not own him, for I had never before seen him, and all the inquiries which were made subsequently could not discover a master for him. It was the more extraordinary because a public notice was posted at the gate of the prison, forbidding the entrance of dogs. In the evening I sent to the prison, to beg to have the dog, as

I had heard he had not been owned, when, remarkable to say, he had disappeared, as strangely as he had entered, and was never afterwards found.

Nicholson, after trying to commit suicide, confessed that he was the murderer. The servant had undergone what we would now call a 'fugue' in which he found himself climbing the stairs towards his master and mistress' bedroom. 'Afterwards stopping on the way, and addressing himself by name, saying: "Nicholson, what are you going to do?" and a reply, which he strenuously maintained he heard made to him by a voice at his side, "To murder your master and mistress."'

It is now necessary to come back from the digression concerning dog-stealers, a digression suggested by that stolen dog, Toby, and to return to the last of our dog artistes. This was the military mascot (mascots of the Senior Service have already been dealt with). A mascot was very much a performing dog. Though originally introduced into the regiment as a pet of officer or man, it eventually became adopted by the corps as a whole. It usually wore a smart uniform and had to march in step when the regiment paraded ceremonially for inspection. Though dogs had originally been brought to the field to provide companionship, they soon proved their worth in another way by stimulating the morale of the men by the courage they displayed in the face of the enemy.

Some became nationally famous, such as 'Dick', a fox terrier which took part in the Battle of Rorke's Drift on 22nd January 1879. The South Wales Borderers had been annihilated by overwhelming numbers of Zulus at the Battle of Isandlhwana, all but a few fortunate fugitives, and a single company ('B' Company, 2nd Battalion, 24th Regiment) which had been posted in some farm buildings at a place called Rorke's Drift. The company was now attacked by more than ten times their number of Zulus, who fought the defenders of the farm hand to hand for more than twelve hours between twilight and dawn the following day. Bullets and assegais smashed the windows of the farm, which finally caught alight and blazed fiercely. All through the siege 'Dick's 'owner, Surgeon Reynolds, continued to tend the wounded, although his charges had to be evacuated elsewhere in the farm when the roof over their heads caught fire. 'Dick' remained by its master's side through all the excitement, only leaving it once, when a Zulu who had somehow penetrated the defences darted at Surgeon Reynolds to kill him. Instantly 'Dick' darted at the Zulu, and drove him out of the hospital by biting him on the shins. The defence of Rorke's Drift brought the award of more medals to the garrison than had been earned in any single previous action. 'Dick' was not decorated, though it had saved its master's life and with it the lives of the forty wounded in the hospital. Medals for dogs were unheard of, until a year later came the news of Maiwand.

During the Afghan campaign of 1880 there marched, along with the

Berkshire Regiment, a dog called 'Bobby'. The Berkshires' mascot was a small, rough-haired white mongrel terrier which had been born in Malta. The Brigade of which the 66th Regiment (the Berkshires) formed part was surrounded by overwhelming numbers of Afghan foot and cavalry and made a gallant but unavailing resistance. Standing back to back, the survivors sold their lives as dearly as they could, rationing their cartridges so that every shot took effect. Eventually there were only eleven of them left, together with 'Bobby' which stood in front of the devoted band, barking defiance at the enemy, as one by one the men of its regiment fell.

Although they were not dog-lovers, the Afghans were obviously impressed by the little mongrel's bravery and instead of being killed, it was led off as a prisoner to the camp of one of the Afghan generals, Ayoub Khan. Later, when Kandahar was relieved, 'Bobby' was able to rejoin the remnant of regiment. News had now reached the expeditionary force, no doubt through prisoners and deserters from the Afghans, of 'Bobby's' part in the battle.

When the regiment returned to England, 'Bobby' was ordered to Osborne, where the dog was shown to Queen Victoria who listened in rapt attention to the account of its services in Afghanistan. She was particularly moved by the account of the wounds that 'Bobby' had received in the battle, and of its escape, and asked if she could see its wound scar. 'Bobby's' uniform, a smart red regimental coat with a crown and chevrons in pearls, was accordingly removed, and the Queen could see the healed scar which had seared its coat so that no hair grew there.

When the Queen's curiosity was satisfied, a unique ceremony took place. Victoria presented 'Bobby' with the Afghan Campaign Medal, tying it to the mascot's collar with the campaign ribbon of red and green, tied into an ample bow. After this 'Bobby' was photographed for the Queen, sitting on a table, and thereafter she never failed to enquire after the mascot's health.

The new spirit of kindliness towards dogs and other creatures during the nineteenth century made it possible, for the first time, to pass legislation limiting man's cruelty towards them. An outstanding instance of this cruelty was bull-baiting. By the nineteenth century it was no longer the pastime of royalty, the nobility, or any but a handful of the most misguided of the gentry, but it was all the more difficult to abolish in that it was the sport of the toughest and most hard-bitten of the workers of the industrial revolution.

Bull-baiting was an institution amongst the poor, who sometimes benefited directly from the pastime. At Wokingham, in Berkshire, a baiting had been set up by the will of George Staverton of Staines, in Middlesex, which had been drawn up on 15th May 1661. Staverton had left the whole rent of his house (after two lives) to buy a bull and be baited every year in Wokingham, in the market place, on St Thomas's Day. The proceeds of the gift money collected from the spectators were to be laid out in shoes and stockings to be distributed to the children of the poor, while the poor were also to be given meat from the bull.

It was in vain that the gentry protested at the crowds gathered to watch this 'hellish sport' at 'a town no more than twelve miles from the seat of Majesty at his court at Windsor, and thirty only from the metropolis of this great and enlightened kingdom'. It was equally useless for the incumbent of the parish, the Revd Mr Bremner, to preach on the day before the baiting and say 'what a prodigy must he be in a Christian land, who could thus disgrace his nature by such gigantic infamy, at which the blood of a heathen, of a very Hottentot might curdle! Two useful animals, the bull who propagates our food, and the faithful dog who protects our property, to be thus tormented, and for what purpose?'

Bulldog breeders paid no heed to sermons of this sort. They were concerned with obtaining the rewards connected with the pastime. 'Prizes in gold, silver, or collars,' wrote William Taplin, 'are usually advertised at the most celebrated places of sport, for the best dogs who run at, and pin the bull, thereby inducing the owners to bring them the greater distance.' Large sums were placed on the often very cruel bets laid on the bulldogs by their owners. Sheridan remarked during a debate on a bill to prohibit bull-baiting and bull-running, which had been introduced into the House of Commons in 1802:

Cruelty to the bull was not the only cruelty exercised on these occasions. What sort of moral lesson, for instance, was it to the children of the farmer, who brings his aged bull-bitch, many years the faithful sentinel of his house and farm-yard, surrounded by her pups to prove at the bull-ring the staunchness of her breed? He brings her forward, sets her at the infuriated animal, she seizes him by the nose and pins him to the ground. But what is the reward from her owner, amidst the applauses of the mob to his favourite animal? He calls for a hedging bill, and to prove her breed, hews her to pieces without quitting her grip, while he sells her puppies at five guineas apiece.

Publicists who sought to get bull-baiting abolished mounted a two-fold attack against the pastime. On the one hand they tried to convince the establishment that bull-baiting had a very degrading effect on its fans. Mr Bremner gave his opinion in the sermon already quoted:

The heroes of a bull bait can produce, I should think, but few, if any disciples brought up under their tuition who have done service to their country, either as warriors, or as citizens, but abundant are the testimonies which have been registered at the gallows of her devoted victims, trained up to these pursuits of bull-baiting'.

Nowhere was the passion for baiting and bulldogs stronger than among the nailers of South Staffordshire, while to the inhabitants of West Bromwich, 'of all the canine species, none were so highly prized as bull-dogs.'

It was to these advocates of the pastime that publicists addressed their second attack against it, which took the form of an appeal to the kindliness and manliness of their hearts, which after all the fires of the Industrial Revolution had not quite dried up.

If you want to know for certain what are the moral effects of such practices the incumbent of West Bromwich, the Revd Charles Townshend wrote:

on the minds of men addicted to them, only look round a moment amongst your own acquaintance of this sort. What kind of husbands and fathers do they make? Are their wives as cheerful and happy as they have the means of making them? Are their children as well clothed, as well fed, and as well taught, as they might be? . . . At the conclusion of a bull-baiting, where do the principal parties concerned in it most commonly resort? Do they go home to their families, or straight away to the alehouse, where drinking, gambling, and swearing are the order of the day?

Then, let me ask, who but a bull-baiter ever turned his own infant out of the cradle to put his crippled dog in its place? Who else robbed his sucking child of the mother's breast, that a whelp of a favourite breed might be nourished with the food to which it was considered to have the best title of the two?

It took two bills to stamp out bull-baiting in England as the first bill did not mention the word 'bull' and so was impossible to enforce. In 1835, however, a Quaker called Pease introduced a bill which actually named the bull and it passed both Houses. Dog-fighting was also banned, along with the 'hellish pastime', but because it was much more difficult for the authorities to detect dog-fighting it continued and still continues today in a clandestine way.

The dog that was to be most used in dog-fighting was the bull terrier, a cross between a large terrier bitch and a bulldog. It was faster than the bulldog but just as fierce. Deprived of its bulls, the old English bulldog soon became a breeder's monstrosity, in the same class as fancy mice or Shubunkin goldfish. 'Most of the old bull baiters have become extinct,' wrote G. R. Jesse in 1866, 'and their breed of dog also.' By contrast, the bull terrier always remained a working-dog, not just a triumph of inbreeding. It was kept by all classes, not only by dog-fighters, and was a ladies' dog as well. Agnes Weston, the philanthropist who opened 'Royal Sailors' Homes' to provide accommodation for bluejackets, wished fervently that she had brought her bull terrier with her when, on opening a new home in a derelict building, she found a large grey rat eating her breakfast. Apart from the three baiting breeds, mastiff, bulldog and bull terrier the only relic of bull-baiting we still have today is the custom of pinning rosettes on winning dogs at dog shows. These rosettes, made from coloured ribbons and stuck on to the dogs with pitch, had once adorned the favourite mastiffs in the bull-ring. The dog was considered to have fought particularly well if, during the combat, the rosette became transferred from it to the bull.

The public conscience might have made the first step towards abating cruelty towards dogs by abolishing bull-baiting, but it still remained very callous in other respects. Dogs were certainly not looked on as a blessing by Britain's legislators, many of whom were now industrialists and not country gentlemen with a sporting background. On 8th February 1831, before the switch away from the old kind of Member of Parliament took place, an M.P. had unsuccessfully tried to limit the dog population of Britain by law. He introduced a bill 'to prevent the spreading of canine madness.' Another attempt was made the following year, once more without success, because the House of Commons was too concerned about the Great Reform Bill of 1832 to bother about rabies.

Yet if no national action against dogs was taken it was all too easy for local massacres to take place whenever there was a real, or imagined, rabies scare. In 1835 the streets of St George's parish, Hanover Square, were cleared of dogs, some of them probably not true strays but merely animals that had stepped out of their homes for a walk. At about the same date the Hyde Park keepers shot seven dogs on one day 'on suspicion' of their being mad. Hydrophobia continued to be a background nightmare for Victorians – particularly children – right to the end of the century. Gwen Raverat, who had been born in 1885, was afraid of cycling along the Backs in Cambridge, for fear of mad dogs. Whenever there was a scare her father, George Darwin, would have the family dogs muzzled. Eventually muzzling and quarantine brought their reward and rabies was eliminated from the British Isles entirely.

Another area in which kindness to dogs was notable for its absence was that of the dog-fight. Successful fighting-dogs enjoyed the same prestige as champion pugilists. When 'Old Sal', a bull-bitch whose pregnancy had been unduly delayed, finally safely produced a litter, the bells of the parish church were rung for joy. In Wednesbury, nursing mothers did not disdain to suckle orphaned pups and (according to legend) breeders encouraged their dog' pups to bite their human acquaintances, so as to enter them early for the sport.

The aristocracy of England certainly did not lag behind the nailers and colliers of South Staffordshire when it came to enthusiasm for dog-fights. Lord Camelford possessed a dog named 'Belcher', which had fought 104 battles without a single defeat. When two other champion dogs, 'Boney' and 'Gas' fought one another at the Westminster Pit on January 18th 1825, the pit was packed out by 300 fanciers. The stakes, wrote the *Sporting Magazine*, were forty sovereigns, 'and everything was arranged to the satisfaction of the amateurs. The pit was lighted with an elegant chandelier and a profusion of wax-lights.'

The most unpleasant feature of dog-fighting was that it encouraged the mutilation of all puppies, not merely those bred up for the pit. Because a fighting-dog could be pinned by the ear by its opponent, fanciers cut off the ears of puppies. Dogs habitually mutilated in this way included: black and tan terriers, (Manchester and toys) bull terriers, White English terriers, Irish terriers, Yorkshire terriers and Great Danes. Prosecutions by the Society for the Prevention of Cruelty to Animals (later a Royal Society) were useless to check the practice, as the penalties awarded against those found guilty were minimal. It was not till very far on in the century that the animal painter Sir Edwin Landseer began to influence public opinion by ostentatiously refusing commissions to paint portraits of any mutilated dog. Edward, Prince of Wales, let it be known that he disapproved of this practice because it inflicted unnecessary suffering. Yet it was only when the Kennel Club passed a rule that no cropped dog could win a prize at one of their shows after 31st March 1895 that the practice finally ended.

One kind of dog-fighting was regarded with a good deal of tolerance and that was the combat between terrier and rat. The rats destined for the pit were caught by the professional ratcatcher. There were many of these offi- cials, from the Royal Ratcatcher with his imposing uniform with a pattern of field-mice destroying sheaves embroidered upon it, to the humble, free- lance catcher described by Charles White in 1840: 'The genuine rat catcher is an experienced hand in his way. He employs the best terrier dogs, from the wire-haired Scotch breed to the smooth milk-white species.' White goes on to describe how the catcher, wearing his official uniform – a broad blue belt ornamented with pictures of rats – would station his terriers on one side of some newly made corn stacks, while he sent his ferrets in at the other. 'They generally make very short work of it, although they are often very severely bitten.' Any rats that were caught live would be popped into an iron cage which the catcher carried and sold to the impresarios who arranged rat and terrier fights.

Rat-fighting had an enormous following in Victorian England, especially amongst the young. 'There's the young gentlemen from the Abbey School comes here in shoals,' the proprietor of the Westminster Pit told George Borrow. 'Leaving books and letters, and masters too. To tell you the truth, I rather wish they would mind their letters, for a more precious set of young blackguards I never seed. It was only the other day I was thinking of calling in a constable for my own protection, for I thought my pit would have been torn down by them.'

Enthusiasm for rat-fighting was carried up to university, where C. S. Calverley, at Cambridge, recalled how as an undergraduate he:

> Dropped at Callaby's the terrier
> Down upon the prisoned rat.

It is not difficult to enter into the enthusiasm of the rat-fighting enthusiasts when we read of some of the champions of the game. 'The endurance
and gallantry of these little creatures are so great,' wrote J. Wood, 'that they
will permit several rats, each nearly as large as themselves, to fix upon their
lips without flinching in the least, or giving any indications of suffering.'

'Tiny', a bull terrier, weighed only five and a half pounds yet could kill
fifty rats in 28 minutes and 5 seconds. It was estimated to have killed more
than 5,000 rats during its lifetime, a weight of a ton and a half rats. According to Wood:

He used to go about his work in the most systematic and business-like style,
picking out all the largest and most powerful rats first, so as to take the most difficult part of the task when he was fresh. When fatigued with his exertions, he
would lie down and permit his master to wash his mouth, and refresh him by
fanning him, and then would set to work with renewed vigour.

Once bull-baiting was abolished, the next great target of the dog-loving
interest emerged as the abolition of the use of dogs for transport. Draught-
dogs were a very old institution in England. Robert, the son of William the
Conqueror, had been forced to use dogs as transport on the First Crusade
because the horses and mules had died. Much later, during the sixteenth
century, Dr John Kaye had mentioned 'the marvellous patience' of the
tinker's cur which trotted along beside its master, loaded down with a pack
saddle containing his tools, tin and solder. In the following century dogs
drew carts containing choice wines such as the famous Bristol Milk
through the streets of Bristol, because the ground was so honeycombed
with the wine merchants' cellars that heavy carts and horses might have
broken through the pavement.

By the nineteenth century there were more transport-dogs than there
had been at any previous time. George Jesse writes:

Many of the butchers' carts, in London were drawn by teams of dogs, often five
in number. The carts had high wheels, and in the double shafts in front two large
dogs were harnessed; three smaller ones ran underneath. They went at a high
speed, and only appeared in the morning and evening in the streets.

Newfoundlands, large bulldogs, great butchers' curs, and others, formed the
teams. They generally barked whilst running, and the noise and excitement
created in a race between rivals may well be imagined.

Letters were also carried in dog-carts. The teams, which went from
Steyning to Storrington, used to lie down on Storrington Green for a rest in

the middle of the day. Fish, which had to be transported rapidly, was carried from Southampton to London in small carts drawn by two or four dogs, usually Newfoundlands. Four of them could pull three to four hundredweights of fish. Unfortunately the driver added to the weight which the dogs had to draw by sitting on the cart.

According to one authority, long teams of dogs pulled the carts of the travelling shows which visited country fairs. It is difficult to believe this assertion. The cost of feeding a team large enough to pull a show van would have been very great, while nothing is said about draughtdogs in that classic of show life, 'Lord' George Sanger's *Seventy Years a Showman*.

Draught-dogs often had their feet badly cut by the flints on the road. Great play was made with this fact, with the slowing down of traffic, which was already very slow by Victorian times, by dog-drawn vehicles, and also the disturbance caused by the barking of the dogs to 'citizens resident in the Metropolis'.

Not all draught-dogs were transport ones. During the early nineteenth century a number of sporting dog-owners drove themselves to town in light carriages drawn by dogs. In 1820 there is mention, in *The Sportsman's Repository* of a man who 'exhibited a carriage drawn by six dogs. These were the largest and most powerful which we have ever witnessed.' The same magazine also mentions 'a Monsieur Chabert ... [who] ... has arrived in the Metropolis from Bath, with his great Siberian Wolf Dog, which he now offers to the public for the sum of two hundred pounds. He has had a gig purposely constructed, in which, he says, this dog can draw him thirty miles a day.'

In 1824 the Society for the Prevention of Cruelty to Animals was founded. From the moment of its institution, members campaigned against cruelty to dogs, including their use as transport animals. In 1835 the Society succeeded in getting an act passed preventing cruelty to animals and the days of dog transport were numbered.

On the basis of this act Robert Batson, a Society member, brought a prosecution in January 1836 against an owner of transport-dogs. The Lambeth Police Court magistrate inspected the three dogs which had drawn the prisoner's cart, and found that they were half starved and covered with sores. He sentenced the owner to fourteen days imprisonment. Two of the dogs were found good homes, the third had to be destroyed.

Further prosecutions did not secure nearly such heavy sentences, only light fines, in spite of the evidence given as to bad treatment of the dogs. One was made to pull a load of five hundred pounds at a speed of twelve miles an hour. Some were whipped till they died, others hired out, for a penny a day, to children who were supposed to feed them while they worked, but omitted to do so.

Public feeling was won over to condemning dog transport by the quite erroneous assertion that it caused hydrophobia. In 1838 witnesses gave evidence before the Committee appointed to enquire into the provisions of the Metropolitan Police Officer's Bill that over-working of dogs 'in trucks' exposed them to rabies and caused the 'somewhat more frequent occurrence of the disease in recent years.'

In 1839 the Metropolitan Police Act carried a clause declaring that, after 1st January 1840, 'every person who within the Metropolitan Police district [within a radius of fifteen miles from Charing Cross,] shall use any dog for the purpose of drawing any cart or barrow, shall be liable to a penalty of not more than 40s. for the first offence, and not more than £5 for the second or any following office offences.'

In spite of appeals by costermongers that their trade would be 'knocked up', if they could not keep dogs, which, in any case, they had always treated well, the law went into effect. It was not just the costers who were menaced by the proposed change in the law: some disabled people had been able to get about in carts pulled by dogs. Captain M. E. Haworth recounts how

... before the legislature forbade the use of dogs as animals of draught that there dwelt upon the Great North Road, sometimes in one place, sometimes in another, an old pauper who was born without legs, and being of a sporting turn of mind, had contrived to get built for himself a small simple carriage, or wagon, very light, having nothing but a board for the body, but fitted with springs, lamps, and all necessary appliances.

To this cart he harnessed four foxhounds, though to perform his quickest time he preferred three abreast. He carried nothing, and lived upon the alms of the passengers by the coaches. His team were cleverly harnessed and well matched in size and pace. His speed was terrific, and as he shot by, a coach going ten or twelve miles an hour, he would give a slight cheer of encouragement to his team, but this was done in no spirit of insolence or defiance, merely to urge the hounds to their paces. ... For many years Old Lal continued his amateur competition with some of the fastest and best-appointed coaches on the road, his favourite ground being upon the North Road, between the Peacock at Islington and the Sugar Loaf at Dunstable.

Lal's harness was always kept in tip-top condition, polished with oil and rotten stone supplied to him by his great friend Daniel Sleigh, 'a double ground horsekeeper' at the Sugar Loaf at Dunstable. 'The glossy coats of Lal's team on a bright December morning,' writes Haworth, 'to say nothing of their condition, would have humbled the pride of some of the crack kennel huntsmen of the shires.'

The team usually did an eight-mile stage and back each day. They slept beside the wagon and Lal would uncouple two of them to go foraging from the hog tubs. Occasionally, as a treat, he would buy them food. Lal died, as he had lived, on the road, thrown from the carriage when his team bolted, perhaps at the sight of a fox. After their master's death Daniel Sleigh looked after them.

Opposition to the proposed ban centred round the friends of humble people like Lal. What would happen to the dogs which could no longer be employed, asked these critics. Yet opposition to working-dogs was particularly strong in London, where a correspondent of *The Times* pointed out the nuisance incurred by 'the suburbs being now overrun with large fierce dogs belonging to the bakers and others which are let loose in the public roads, to the great annoyance and terror of passengers.'

There were now several members of the R.S.P.C.A. in Parliament and they began to press for an extension of the law to the whole of Britain. A bill to this effect was introduced in July 1840 but it failed because of the objections by members that it would inflict hardship on poor people who could not afford to keep donkeys or horses. This bill was accordingly withdrawn and a subsequent one failed to pass the Lords, but in February 1843 yet another bill to the same effect was brought in.

An M.P. named Barclay urged that it would be

> ... an uncalled for, an unnecessary violation of the rights of a large class of humble traders by whom dogs were used. The parties using them for purposes of draught were generally knife-grinders and hawkers of various small wares through the country and in towns; the aid of dogs was found very useful to bakers, butchers, and other traders. The prohibition of this aid from dogs was not justified on the plea that so employing them was cruel.

Yet the promoters of the bill had little difficulty in proving that draught-dogs were cruelly treated. Lord Wicklow described how dogs drawing heavily laden carts went from Brighton to Portsmouth in one day and back the next, a distance of about sixty miles. Supporters of the bill used an even more telling argument, that numbers of accidents took place because horses became frightened at the sight of the dog-carts. In spite of all the arguments for it the bill did not pass, yet the indefatigable R.S.P.C.A. finally managed to get a clause added to another bill in June 1854 'for the more effectual prevention of cruelty to animals'.

The Lords objected to this clause, on the grounds that it would confiscate the property of large numbers of the poorest folk and mean that they would hang the 20,000 dogs they owned. Yet, as the Bishop of Oxford pointed out to his fellow peers, nobody liked dog-teams except those who owned them. In Sussex and Hampshire, where they were most in use, they were most unpopular and some town councils such as that of Portsmouth had already made laws to stop them. The dogs were driven forty or fifty miles upon a hard road till they were able to go no farther and then they would be killed and new animals put in the traces. A dog-team could be tracked for twenty miles or more by the bloody pawmarks that they left on the road. Oxford's eloquence was not wasted and the bill became law on 1st January 1855.

The abolition of dog transport must have brought about a sickening drop in the dog population of England and the imposition of the dog tax of 1864 had an even worse effect. Blind people, who had been led about by their spaniels, felt they had cause for complaint. So did truffle-hunters and shepherds, who were dependent on their dogs. Dreadful massacres took place all over the country. In Cambridge the streets were so littered with bodies that the magistrates had to dispose of them. The High Constable arranged to have 400 dead dogs buried. In Birmingham more than a thousand were destroyed and there was another great slaughter at Liverpool.

Just before the dog tax induced thousands of owners to turn their pets into the streets, a step had been taken to care for homeless dogs for the first time. While out for a walk one evening in 1860, two friends, Mrs Tealby and Mrs Major, came across a starving dog which they took home to Islington and bedded down in the scullery. With the aid of Mrs Tealby's brother, the Revd Edward Bates, they tried to found a private refuge for dogs. When this proved too ambitious a venture, they tried appealing to public charity in the newspapers.

In spite of scathing comment from *The Times* that the organisers of such a home had obviously taken leave of their senses, there was a large enough response to let Mrs Tealby and her associates, helped by a Miss Morgan of Brixton Hill, set up a Temporary Home for Lost Dogs. Though the home could only handle a fraction of the homeless dogs which roamed the streets, it did at least enlighten the public to the extent of the problem.

Just as important as the setting up of the first dog's home in securing better treatment for all types of breeds was the work of the publicists who now began to educate the public as a whole about every aspect of dog-keeping. Daniel (who is not solely concerned with dogs) and Taplin had been sporting writers for a limited public which could afford expensive books. The later generation of nineteenth-century publicists, men such as Frank Buckland, tried to reach a very wide public in magazines like *Nature* and promote in them a love of animals as a whole. Needless to say, if you love animals as a whole you are very likely to love dogs in particular. This was certainly the case with Buckland, and the readers of his articles and his best-selling books, such as *The Curiosities of Natural History*, must have thrilled to hear of his efforts to tame a ferocious Turkish wolfhound called 'Arslan', just one of the pets of the Buckland household.

The nineteenth century was an era of exhibitions and much of the publicity that attended dogs gathered round the new institution of dog shows. The first of these had been held in Newcastle in 1859; it was an endeavour by a sporting gun-maker called W. R. Pape to publicise his wares by giving shotguns as prizes for the best entries, in a show which was limited to pointers and setters. Pape was particularly fortunate in his judges, who included J. H. Walsh, famous under his pen-name of 'Stonehenge' as a writer on dogs.

The Newcastle show attracted so much attention that it was followed by a foxhound show at Redcar and eventually by the first really large show, held in 1863 at the Ashburnham Hall, Cremorne, Chelsea. In the same year, field trials for dogs were suggested in *The Field* and held at Mr S. Whitbread's estate at Southill, near Bedford, in 1865. Thereafter so many shows were held that the committee members who arranged them got into the habit of meeting one another regularly. They were receptive to the suggestion, made by a Warwickshire country gentleman called S. E. Shirley, that they form a club which should continuously promote the aims that they had upheld, sporadically, by holding shows. The result of this suggestion was the Kennel Club, founded in 1877 under the patronage of Edward, Prince of Wales.

This august body immediately became the Jockey Club of the dog. On a previous page it has already been noticed how it was able to put an end to ear-cropping and tail-lopping. The club undertook the first important publication of pedigrees of dogs, other than foxhounds, in its Stud Books. It enforced registration of all dogs entered at Club shows, under a distinctive name. One of the great drawbacks to the general acceptance of dogs had been some of their owners. Victorians had written of 'doggy men who always seem to congregate in doorways of clubs.' The Kennel Club purged dog-owners as a whole of the aura of raffishness with which they were associated in the minds of some of the public. Not the least important club rule was that which rigorously barred as a member anyone who had ever defaulted on a bet.

The air of respectability and the royal patronage that dog-breeding had now acquired was soon to be deepened by the founding of another aristocratic and imperial institution, Crufts Dog Show. An enterprising dog biscuit manufacturer named James Spratt had started a 'dog cake' manufactory in Holborn which soon took up so much of his time that he enlisted a young assistant – Charles Cruft – to do the book-keeping and market the biscuits. As a dedicated bagman covering the length and breadth of England and the Continent, Cruft soon discovered that he could sell his biscuits better if he attached to them, in customers' minds, the idea of enlarging and improving pedigree stock. So he now added to his other activities as Sales Manager that of Show Arranger.

After much successful experience of shows on the Continent, at which the idea of dog management was stressed, Cruft held the first English show in the Royal Aquarium, Westminster, in 1886. No visitor would experience any difficulty in finding the show premises, for the Royal Aquarium, in spite of its name, was a very well-known London music hall – quite notorious in fact. The first show, which was for terriers only, brought a large turn-out – 600 entries in all.

Helped by preferential treatment from the railways, which advertised special arrangements for sending dogs to show by train and even employed an efficient dog-van designed by Cruft, entries continued to grow. For the 1880 show Cruft needed a larger hall and he chose the Central Hall, Holborn. There were now more than 1,500 entries and the value of the prizes totalled more than £1,200.

One of the 220 classes was, alas, for 'stuffed dogs'. These abominations had been gathering force since the Great Exhibition of 1851, in which M. Ploucquet's exhibits of hounds and their quarry had attracted more attention from the crowd than any other specimens of taxidermy. There was no harm in thus preserving for posterity some really notable dog. 'Bobby' of the Berkshires, which had been run down by a runaway cab-horse, was preserved in this way in the regimental museum. 'Wimbledon Jack', which had collected a lot of money for charities in a box strapped to his back, was long represented at Wimbledon Station by his stuffed skin in a glass case. Many ordinary people with ordinary dogs, however, seem to have longed to have them immortalised in this way. Even some Victorians, however, felt askance at the sight of a stuffed dog. In *The autobiography of Mark Rutherford*, the crass and insensitive husband first demonstrates his inability to love his wife as she deserves by telling her to take down her shelves laden with poetry books as he wants the space for a glass case with a stuffed dog.

An entirely unobjectionable means of keeping up the remembrance of past pets, the dogs' cemetery, had quietly grown up during Victoria's reign. The Queen had had quite a lot to do with the trend, burying her favourite dachshunds under tombstones with inscriptions at Windsor. Princess Alexandra's dogs were buried in a little cemetery in Marlborough House Garden. They include 'The favourite Japanese dog of Her Royal Highness the Princess of Wales. Died July 10, 1884. Aged 2 years.' These were private cemeteries; the first public dogs' cemetery for dogs, which was opened towards the end of the century, was not in England but in Paris.

It is now necessary to return from the digression suggested by Class 220 at Crufts, Show of 1890, 'Stuffed dogs, or dogs made of wood, china, etc.' In the following year there were 2,000 entries, including many exhibits from royalty. Queen Victoria won First Prize and Cup in the open class for collie dogs with 'Darnley II'. She also entered three Pomeranians, 'Gena', 'Fluffy' and 'Nino'. Queen Victoria was always fond of German dogs. Soon after her marriage she was presented with several dachshunds by friends of Prince Albert. Victoria's dachs may have been the first kept in Britain since Roman times, when dog remains found at Corbridge Roman Station on the Wall indicate that these animals were known here. Victoria was also largely responsible for the re-entry into England of the Pomeranian, another dog well known to Roman Britain. After her Coronation Ceremony in 1838, she had hurried home from the Abbey, removed her robes of state and given her Pomeranians a bath. Two years before she had exhibited her trio at Crufts, she had visited Florence and made acquaintance with the local breed, a fancy toy variety.

In 1892 Queen Victoria once more exhibited Pomeranians at Crufts. Her relative, the Czar, sent in Russian wolfhounds, as did the Grand Duke Nicholas of Russia and Prince Constantine of Oldenbourg.

Charles Cruft was a superb showman who had omitted nothing which could draw either exhibitors or visitors to his shows. Competitors knew that every care would be taken of their exhibits. They were fed and attended to free of charge and there were eight vets in attendance (in 1901 three of them professors of veterinary medicine). By 1890, Cruft had begun to print detailed descriptions of the breeds, written by specialists in each, and attach engravings and photographs to show what individual dogs looked like. No breeder, however important, could resist the attraction of seeing his creations publicised in this way. For the ordinary breeder the greatest attraction was the enormous prizes offered, together with the even more rewarding possibilities of selling a dog directly from the show. In 1901, for example, the comparatively new chow chows exhibited by Captain D. H. Barker sold for £500 each. White Scotch terriers were such a novelty that a stud fee was £10, which was a sum worth having in 1901.

The years between 1886, when the first Crufts Show was held, and the death of Queen Victoria on 22nd January 1901, mark a change in the outlook of dog-owners and breeders which was perhaps greater than any that had occurred before in the whole history of the dog. Hitherto the principal value of a dog to a breeder had been the amount of money he might win in bets. Now, almost overnight, the price for really desirable dogs became such that no breeder could really ignore it. Breeding and management had been carried on by rule-of-thumb methods. Now they became fully scientific, with the vet not the groom as an adviser. The advent of the enormous prize for a winning dog had brought tensions and jealousies which had never existed when dog-breeding was merely an amusement. Although a few lucky dogs might in the past have been immortalised by the pencils of a Stubbs or a Reinagle, the advent of the photograph meant that famous dogs became stars in their own right. We have already noticed this tendency illustrated by the Queen's desire that 'Bobby' of the Berkshires should be photographed for her. Other famous dogs which were 'presented' to Victoria and photographed were 'Master M'Grath', bred by Lord Lorgan and Albert Smith's two St Bernards. The advent of the illustrated interview, in which celebrities – whether they were actresses, judges, or naval officers – were invariably photographed with their dogs, also helped to build up the personal cult of the dog.

Yet perhaps the most important effect of Crufts had been to emphasise the fashion in dog breeds. There were, obviously other reasons besides fashion which caused a shift in emphasis in dog-ownership, such as a movement into smaller houses or flats.

In 1895, the most popular breeds were: the collie, followed by the smooth-coated fox terrier, St Bernard, pug, Pomeranian, Newfoundland, retriever, Great Dane, wire-haired fox terrier, Irish terrier, Dalmatian, bloodhound, bulldog, Dandie Dinmont, setter, pointer, toy spaniel and Japanese spaniel.

By the end of the century fox terriers were the favourites, followed by Irish, Scots and wire terriers, dachshunds, bassets and Skye terriers. Larger dogs such as St Bernards, Newfoundlands, Great Danes, mastiffs, deerhounds and Borzois had lost much of their popularity.

The popularity polls of annual shows at Crufts merely reflect a trend which had already begun early in Victoria's reign. It was essentially an era of change and experiment, in which worker-dogs were made over into pets, attempts were made to revive old breeds on the verge of extinction, existing breeds were developed into toys and more and more exotic breeds. Not all these changes can be discussed in detail, but this chapter might well conclude with a reference to one or two of them.

Sheepdogs, which were to develop into a number of fashionable breeds, were represented in early nineteenth-century times by the Old English sheepdog, the shepherd's dog and the Scotch sheepdog, usually called a collie (which in the nineteenth century was always spelt 'colley'). Allied to the sheepdogs were the drover's dog (a cross between a sheepdog and a mastiff), which helped convoy the sheep from farm to market, and the cur dog which was half sheepdog and half terrier.

Of these the cur was the farthest down the social scale of dogs. It was a farm watch-dog, or the guard-dog which a labourer set over his coat and lunch of bread and cheese while he worked in the field. Dog-lovers felt that the cur was ugly; Taplin says it 'is of a black, brindled, or of a dingy – grizzled brown, having generally a white neck, some white about the belly, face, and legs, sharp nose, ears half pricked, and the points pendulous, coat mostly long, rough, and matted, particularly about the haunches, giving him a ragged appearance.'

Yet everyone is agreed that the cur was a very useful dog. It could drive cattle or sheep, separating them into a line if they became entangled and making sure that they kept up a steady pace. It was so faithful to its owner, whether a farmer or a labourer, that it would obey no one but him and though starving would stand guard faithfully night and day over a dairy full of milk and cream without ever dreaming of touching a drop.

It was the sheepdogs which were most admired in this group of dogs and most developed into pets. By 1895, as Crufts records show, they had become the favourite pet. The sheepdog enjoyed a mysterious prestige in nineteenth-century times because it had been identified by Louis Leclerc, Comte de Buffon (1707–88) as the original ancestor of all European dogs. If by the turn of the nineteenth century no dog-lover was any longer prepared to accept Buffon's contention in its entirety, they were still disposed to have a great admiration and affection for sheepdogs. William Taplin pays it the compliment of a plate in his book which he rightly calls 'a most admirable representation, taken from the life, and the landscape from nature.' 'What immense flocks,' he adds, 'are seen to cover the downy hills of Hampshire and Wiltshire as far as the eye can reach . . . by a signal from the shepherd, this faithful, sagacious animal replete with energy, vigilance and activity, will make his circle, so as to surround a flock of hundreds, and bring them within any compass that may be desired.'

It was difficult to tell whether it was the cleverness of the dog, or its fidelity, that attracted most attention. Sheepdogs had covered the bodies of their masters when they had been engulfed in snowstorms and kept them alive by the warmth of their own bodies. They had taken home messages or gloves or handkerchiefs as appeals for help from injured shepherds and guided back the rescue party expertly.

Respect for the sheepdog reached its peak when Sir Edwin Landseer painted a picture of *The Old Shepherd's Chief Mourner*, with a collie crouching beside the coffin which contains its dead master. Not even the dog's greatest admirers however, could have predicted what an effect it was going to have on English history during the early part of the nineteenth century. An Old English sheepdog called 'Cap' was owned by a shepherd called Roger who lived near Matlock in Derbyshire. The shepherd lived all alone with his dog in a cottage in a wood. One day the village boys stoned 'Cap' and one of its legs was so badly hurt that it could not put it down on the ground. Mournfully Roger went to feed the sheep by himself and to get a bit of rope to hang 'Cap'.

While he was feeding the sheep a young girl and a clergyman rode past and stopped by the shepherd, whom they both knew. When they asked where 'Cap' was, Roger told them what had happened and they rode over to his cottage, borrowing the key from a neighbour to get in. 'Cap' recognised them and crawled out from beneath the table. While the girl held its head, the clergyman examined the dog's leg. He explained to his young companion that the injury was not a break in the bone, merely a bad bruise that hot fomentations would cure. Then under his direction the little girl tore up some old flannel for bandages, lit the fire with the shepherd's tinder-box and boiled some water. She then applied the bandages, wrung out in hot water, to the injured leg. They left the cottage and on the way home met the shepherd, now carrying a piece of rope. They persuaded Roger not to hang his dog, promising to call the following day and renew the fomentations with fresh flannel. Two days later they met Roger and his flock on the hillside and an excited and grateful 'Cap' bounded up to them. Florence Nightingale had nursed her first patient back to health.

Queen Victoria shared her subjects' fondness for exotic dogs. She possessed 'Looty', a dog which had gazed on two empresses, Victoria herself and Tzu Hsi, last Dowager Empress of China. 'Looty' had belonged to the Chinese Empress's aunt who had thrown herself down a well when the allied forces occupied the Summer Palace at Peking in 1860. Admiral Lord

John Hay and Lieutenant Dunne found the five Pekingese which had belonged to the Princess, a dog and four bitches, and brought them back to England. There Dunne presented 'Looty' (so called because he was loot from the Summer Palace) to the Queen.

The rather sedentary life of Victoria, who had not taken much interest in hunting since the days when she accompanied Albert and his dog 'Solomon' stag-shooting at Balmoral, accounts for the popularity during the latter part of her reign, of lap-dogs at court. Dogs such as the Maltese dogs and Skye terriers were darlings of ladies at the time. Victorian women regarded a toy dog as very good value as a watch-dog for, wrote one nineteenth-century naturalist, J. G. Wood:

Although from their diminutive size, these little dogs are anything but formidable, they are terrible foes to the midnight thief, who cares little for the brute strength of a big yard-dog. Safely fortified behind a door, or under a sofa, the King Charles sets up such a clamorous yelling at the advent of a strange step, that it will disconcert the carefully arranged plans of professional burglars with much more effect than the deep bay and the fierce struggles of the mastiff or the bloodhound.

Victoria's preference for small dogs explains why she did not keep the last of the English dogs we shall encounter in this book – the St Bernard, though she did ask Albert Smith (1816–60) to bring his two St. Bernards to court for her to see. The St Bernard was the third favourite dog at Crufts in 1895. Victorians genuinely admired St Bernards for their heroic qualities but, as had been the case with the Dandie Dinmonts, the great Swiss dog was also popular because of its literary associations. In their case the literary public had been introduced to them, not through a novel, but through travel accounts such as William Brockedon's famous *Passes of the Alps*.

On the crest of the Great St Bernard Pass, leading from Switzerland to Italy, stands the hospice of the Augustinian monastery of St Bernard, 8,200 feet above sea level. Here, before the Great St Bernard tunnel was cut, the hospice of the monastery stood open for weary travellers across the pass, of whom as many as 500 might be fed by the monks in one day. Brockedon relates:

The perilous journey by this route during the winter is more frequently undertaken than is generally imagined; many are prompted by the necessity or urgency of their affairs, at this season, to traverse the mountain; they are generally pedlars and smugglers, who travel in defiance of storms and avalanches. In these high regions the snow forms and falls in small particles which congeal so soon and so hard, that they do not attach, and form flakes in descending, and instead of consolidating beneath the pressure of the feet of the traveller, the snow rises around him like powder, and he sinks to his middle: whirlwinds, called *tourmentes*, raise the snow in dust; unable then to discover the path, he falls over some precipice. The avalanches too have numerous victims; those of spring are occasioned by the submelting of the snow, which undermines their support. The winter avalanches are produced by the accumulations of snow on the steep sides of the mountains, which, having little cohesion, at length become heavy enough to exceed the supporting power, when enormous masses slide off into the valleys beneath, with a suddenness and violence which the prior at the covent compared to the discharge of a cannon ball.

Lying as it did in such a dangerous situation, it was small wonder that the hospice offered two remarkable sights to the traveller. One was the morgue, in which the bodies of travellers who had perished in the snow and whom no one had claimed were placed to mummify in the dry air, while the other was the St Bernard dogs which were trained to find lost travellers and dig them out before they could freeze to death.

Under every circumstance in which it is possible to render assistance, the worthy *religieux* of St Bernard set out upon their fearful duty, unawed by the storm, and obeying a higher power; they seek the exhausted or overwhelmed traveller, generally accompanied by their dogs, whose sagacity will often detect the victim, though buried in the snow. The dogs also, as if conscious of a high duty, will roam alone through the day and night in these desolate regions, and if they discover an exhausted traveller will lie on him to impart warmth, and bark or howl for assistance.

Brockedon figures two of the dogs in his illustrations. They are described by another Victorian traveller as being 'of large size, particularly high upon the legs, and generally of a milk white or a tabby colour.' One dog, 'Barry', had saved more than forty travellers. It set out alone to look for them; if it found one whose rescue was beyond its powers, it would return to the convent for help. The monks credited the dogs with the power of knowing when avalanches were about to fall. They had even turned away rescue parties from their usual route when an avalanche was about to overwhelm them.

Just how and when the St Bernard emerged is something of a mystery. It was apparently unknown during the eighteenth century, when the difficult task of finding travellers lost in an avalanche of snow was accomplished by probing for them with a long pole. Brockedon's appears to be the first full account of the dogs and when he wrote only a few had arrived in England. In 1815 a St Bernard called 'Lion' was brought to England and painted by Landseer. Albert Smith, the most talented and most unjustly neglected of all unread Victorian novelists, used to own a pair of these dogs which sat on the platform with him when he lectured. A portrait of one of them, specially drawn for J. G. Wood's *Illustrated Natural History*, appears as an illustration to this book.

As her Pomeranians share her death-bed with Victoria, we must leave the history of the British Dog. Why close the story on 22nd January 1901? One reason is that, after that date, the story of the dog becomes not so much a chronicle as a catalogue. Innumerable new breeds, sometimes more than one a year, are brought in to swell those which already exist. As the number of breeds increases, the importance of the dog diminishes somewhat. While Victoria is still queen, the dog is still king of the affections of many Britons. So far, although there are many who do not know how to treat dogs and ought not to be allowed to own them, no one has questioned their right to exist or suggested that we would be better off without them. Dogs and men are still a 'Happy Family' and so it is appropriate at this time for Toby to make his bow, and retire behind the curtain.

Select Bibliography

Apsley Lady Viola, *Bridleways Through History* (London, Hutchinson, 1936).

Ash, Edward C., *Dogs: Their History and Development* two volumes, (London, Ernest Benn, 1927).

Beaufort, The Duke of, and Mowbray Morris, *Hunting* (London, Badminton Library, 1888).

Beavan, Arthur H., *Animals I have Known* (London, T. Fisher Unwin).

Berners, Juliana, *The Book of St Albans* ('The schoolmaster's printer', St Albans, 1486).

Blake Cooper, Bransby, *The Life of Sir Astley Cooper, Bart*, two volumes (London, Parker, 1843).

Bradley, H. and C. T. Onions, *Shakespeare's England*, volumes I and II (Clarendon Press, 1966).

Brockedon, William, *Illustrations of the Passes of the Alps, By Which Italy Communicates with France, Switzerland, and Germany* (London, Printed for the Author, 1828).

Burleigh, R., Juliet Clutton-Brock, J. Felder and G. de G. Sieveking, *A Further Consideration of Neolithic Dogs with Special Reference to a Skeleton from Grimes' Graves.* Journal of Archaeological Science, vol. 4, p. 353–76, 1977.

Caius (Kaye), John, *De Canibus Britannicis* (London, 1570).

Carleton, John William, *The Sporting Sketch Book*, (London, How & Parsons, 1842).

Christopher Davies, G., *Peter Penniless*.

Croxton Smith, A., *British Dogs* (London, Collins, 1946).

Dalziell, Hugh, *British Dogs* (London, The Bazaar).

Daniel, Revd W. B., *Rural Sports* two volumes (London, Thomas Davison, 1801–1802). (Also other editions.)

Davis, S. J. M., and F. R. Valla, 'Evidence For The Domestication of the Dog 12,000 years Ago In The Natufian of Israel'. *Nature* 7.12.78, 608–10.

Degerbøl, Magnus, 'On a find of a preboreal domestic dog from Starr Carr, Yorkshire'. Proceedings of the Prehistoric Society, XXVII, p. 35, 1961.

Gardner, Phyllis, *The Irish Wolfhound*. (Dundalk, Ireland, *The Dundalgan Press*, 1931).

Harcourt, R. A., 'The Dog In Prehistoric and Early Historic Britain', Journal Archaeological Science, vol. i, 151–75, 1974.

Harrison, William, 'Description of England' in *The Chronicles of England, Scotland, and Ireland*, two volumes (London, 1577).

Haworth, Captain M. E., *Road Scrapings* (London, 1882).

Hayhow, David, 'Canis At Maiden Castle. A Detailed Re study.' Dissertation. Institute of Archaeology, London University, 1976.

Henderson, Isabel, *The Picts* (London, Thames and Hudson, 1967).

Hilzheimer, Max, 'Dogs in Antiquity'. *Antiquity*, vol. VI, 411, 1932, 'Pedigree of the Keeshond'. *Antiquity*, vol VII, 96, 1943.

Jesse, Edward, *Anecdotes of Dogs* (London, 1846).

Jesse, George R., *Researches Into the History of the British Dog*, two volumes (London, Robert Hardwicke, 1866).

Lennox, Lord William Pitt, *Fashion Then and Now*, two volumes (London, Chapman & Hall, 1878).

Lockhart, J. G., *Narrative of the Life of Sir Walter Scott* (London, Everyman, 1922).

Longrigg, Roger, *The History of Foxhunting* (London, Macmillan, 1975).

Mayhew, Henry, ed. Peter Quennell *London's Underworld* (London, Spring Books, 1966).

Miller, Mrs Hugh, *Cats and Dogs* (London, Nelson, 1868).

Paget, Guy, *Sporting Pictures of England* (London, Collins, 1945).

Ross, Anne, *Everyday Life of the Pagan Celts* (London, Carousel, 1972). *Pagan Celtic Britain* (London, Cardinal, 1967).

Stables, Gordon, *From Greenland's Icy Mountains* (London, S.P.C.K.)

Story, Alfred T., *The Strand Magazine*, Vol. X, p. 461 (London, George Newnes, 1895).

Stubbes, Philip, *Anatomie of Abuses* (London 1583).

Taplin, William (attributed to by Edward C. Ash), *The Sportsman's Cabinet*, two volumes (London, J. Cundee 1803).

Vesey-Fitzgerald, Brian, (ed.), *The Book of the Dog* (London, Nicholson & Watson, 1948).

Walsingham, Lord, and Sir Ralph Payne-Gallwey Bart., *Shooting – Moor and Marsh* (London, The Badminton Library, Longmans, 1886). *Shooting – Field and Covert* (London, Longmans, 1920).

White, Charles ('Martingale'), *Sporting Scenes and Country Characters* (London, Longmans, 1840).

Wilson, Elizabeth, *Four Centuries of Dog Collars* (London, Philip Wilson, 1979).

Wood, Revd J. G., *The Illustrated Natural History. Mammalia* (London, Routledge).

York, Edward, Duke of, *The Master of Game* (London, Chatto & Windus, 1909).

Youatt, William, (ed E. J. Lewis), *The Dog* (Philadelphia, Lea and Blanchard, 1848).

Index

Index